# HORSE&HOUND

# *The* HORSE *and* PONY CARE *Bible*

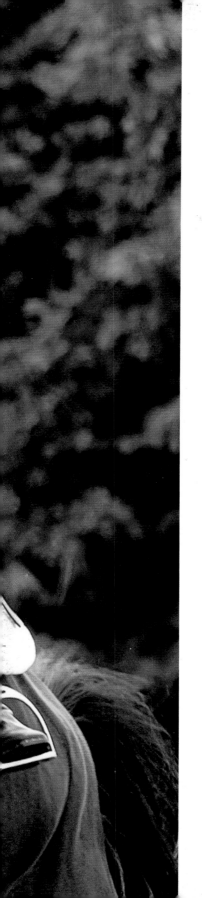

**HORSE & HOUND**

# The HORSE and PONY CARE Bible

CAROLYN HENDERSON &
KAREN COUMBE

EBURY
PRESS

1 3 5 7 9 10 8 6 4 2

Published in 2007 by Ebury Press, an imprint of Ebury Publishing

A Random House Group Company

Text © Carolyn Henderson & Karen Coumbe 2007

Material © IPC Media Limited 2007

The Random House Group Limited Reg. No. 954009

Addresses for companies within the Random House Group can be found at
www.rbooks.co.uk

A CIP catalogue record for this book is available from the British Library

The Random House Group Limited makes every effort to ensure that the papers used in our books
are made from trees that have been legally sourced from well-managed and credibly certified forests.
Our paper procurement policy can be found on
www.randomhouse.co.uk

To buy books by your favourite authors and register for offers visit
www.rbooks.co.uk

Printed and bound in Singapore by Tien Wah Press

ISBN 9780091917678

# CONTENTS

# INTRODUCTION

EVERYONE WHO GETS hooked on riding dreams of owning a horse or pony. Whether you are an adult who is finally achieving a long-term ambition by learning to ride, someone who rode as a child and recently picked up the reins again, or a parent whose child puts 'A pony' at the top of every Christmas and birthday wish list, this book can help you turn your dream into a reality.

Realistically, there are some riders for whom horse ownership will prove to be impossible, perhaps because of financial or time constraints. But if this applies to you, the pleasure you get from your riding and your ability in the saddle will increase enormously if you learn about horse care: so again, this book will help. Successful riding means much more than sitting correctly, pressing the right buttons and winning rosettes; it means establishing a partnership with an animal who has a mind of his own. By understanding how to keep a horse happy, healthy and fit, you will also gain insights into improving your communication with him, both in the saddle and on the ground. It is no coincidence that the top riders in all disciplines regard their horses' physical and mental welfare as the top priority, because they know they are essential ingredients for success.

Equally important, good communication makes it far more likely that you or your child will stay safe around horses. Riding is a risk sport and accidents can also happen on the ground. The smallest pony is heavier and stronger than any adult and all equines, even the oldest and quietest,

*Learning about horse care will increase the pleasure you get from riding.*

*Successful riding means forming a partnership with an animal who has a mind of his own.*

are creatures of instinct. Fortunately, they have incredibly willing and generous temperaments when handled and trained correctly, but being aware of how and why horses behave in certain ways will help you avoid misunderstandings and minimize the risk of accidents.

Even experienced owners should find food for thought in this book. It is easy to become blasé or stuck in a rut and, as everyone who rides and keeps horses finds out, you never stop learning about them. There is also hot debate about the best methods of handling and keeping horses and many owners are confused about the pros and cons of traditional methods compared with so-called 'natural horsemanship'. In fact, the best traditional horsemen – a term that also encompasses women – have always based their methods on being able to get inside a horse's head and 'think like a horse'. The difference between their philosophies and those of some modern trainers who have achieved celebrity status is often not as great as is imagined and they, too, rely a great deal on applying horse psychology. However, whilst some trainers have grown up with horses and often take for granted what they do without marketing or labelling their skills, others take a different attitude. There is nothing wrong with either approach and problems only arise if individuals are regarded as gurus with almost magical abilities.

So, throughout this book, you will find the tried and tested mixed with the latest ideas – or, more accurately, the latest ways of expressing ideas that work. You will also find that suggestions are backed up by science, as this is a really exciting time for research into all things equine. Vets, scientists and zoologists now know more about everything from how to feed and keep horses to why things can go wrong and what to do about it. For instance, they have identified why keeping horses in certain ways can be stressful and can lead to repetitive behaviour patterns (called stereotypic behaviour) and how best to avoid or manage this problem.

Most owners have to fit in looking after and riding their horses with work and family commitments. Whilst a horse's welfare and well-being must never be compromised, this book also suggests how to organize your time and priorities. For instance, 50 years ago professional grooms would strip and clean tack thoroughly every day; nowadays, even professional yards rarely have the time or the staff to do this and shortcuts can be made without compromising safety or the comfort of horse and rider. This book will show you how to set and maintain good standards in all aspects of horse care, but in a realistic way.

No book can be a substitute for experience, but hopefully this one will help you work out how to care for a horse in the best way possible and how to build a network of specialists to underpin your work and his welfare. Looking after a horse and being responsible for his welfare can seem an overwhelming responsibility, but whilst the buck inevitably stops with the owner, it's important to learn when you need to call on specialist advice. For instance, you need to know when your horse is showing signs of illness or injury so that you can call in your vet – who, in turn, may involve another health professional such as a chartered physiotherapist, or a farrier who can carry out remedial shoeing.

You will also find that, whilst you can read this book from cover to cover, it may sometimes seem that your horse has different ideas. It's all very well maintaining that horses are meant to live outdoors 24/7 and it's certainly true that all horses need time in the field to graze, relax and be with other equines. But what if your horse makes it quite clear that he wants to come

*Keeping a horse happy, healthy and fit through a varied exercise and work regime will build up your relationship with him.*

in to his stable at night? It's also a fact of life that, in the real world, the theoretically perfect isn't always possible: perhaps you or your livery yard lack enough well-managed land to make a permanent outdoor lifestyle possible. Because of this, you'll also find suggestions for alternative solutions if you can't do it by the book.

Looking after horses means establishing the baselines for best practice, but treating every animal as an individual. It means being open minded, but not woolly minded: common sense is important. It's fascinating, sometimes frustrating, but always incredibly rewarding. If you haven't taken on the responsibility before, you'll find it enriches your life whether you become an owner or help someone who is – and if you're already a horse owner, there's always something new to think about.

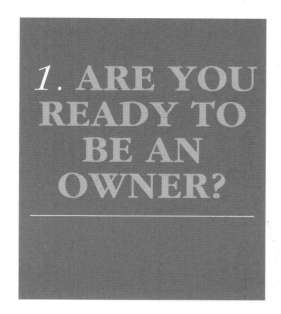

# 1. ARE YOU READY TO BE AN OWNER?

Flicking through the advertisement pages of magazines such as *Horse and Hound* or looking on Internet sales sites will show the would-be horse owner hundreds of tempting prospects. But before you turn window shopping into serious searching, make sure that you are ready for the huge responsibilities horse ownership brings. The same applies if you are a parent weakening before the pleas of a child who longs for a pony, because apart from being responsible for the financial outlay and upkeep, you will find yourself with a heavy practical involvement; as explained later in this chapter, this can mean everything from transporting your child to the livery yard to checking levels of supervision and helping with those tasks a child can't manage alone.

Looking after a horse or pony takes time, money and dedication. If you have plenty of one commodity and not enough of another, there are often ways to compensate – for instance, some owners don't have the time to do all the work themselves but can pay others to help out – but no matter how good your back-up, your horse will ultimately depend on you. Riders who are used to turning up at a riding school, enjoying a lesson or hack and handing back the horse at the end of it often wish they had the freedom to ride when they want to, on a horse who is their sole partner rather than one ridden by lots of others. But when you are responsible for that horse and his tack and equipment, an hour's hack translates into three hours or more daily commitment.

Whilst most owners become fond of their animals, horses are not pets. They are working animals who need to be fed, exercised, groomed and managed correctly. Dog owners will point

*If you start with basic grooming equipment, you can then add extras to create a well-stocked grooming kit such as this one.*

out that the same applies to these animals, but the work and time involved in looking after the dog who shares your home is only a fraction of that needed to look after a horse. Even if you are lucky enough to be able to keep your horse at home, extra responsibilities and costs such as maintaining grazing will eat into your time and money.

## COUNTING THE COST

THERE ARE times when it seems as if owning a horse is the equivalent to throwing banknotes to the wind. Hopefully, the pleasure and satisfaction you get will compensate and you may find that your spending priorities change drastically – holidays may become a chance to spend time with your horse rather than lie on a beach, and paying for a set of shoes for him every six weeks will seem eminently sensible compared to forking out the equivalent for high fashion footwear for yourself. Nevertheless, it's still dangerous to underestimate the costs.

*Every horse or pony needs regular attention from a farrier – one of the costs to budget for when you are thinking of buying or loaning.*

### INITIAL COSTS

Buying a horse is only the beginning, but you need a ballpark figure with which to start your list of expenses. Studying the For Sale adverts will show a huge range of prices asked, as the value of an animal depends on so many things, including conformation, type or breed, age and competition success or potential to succeed. Note that safe all-rounders who are sound, capable of having a go at most things up to Riding Club level and good to hack out – the sort of animal a first-time buyer will be looking for – are always in demand, and this is likely to be reflected in their price. However, a genuinely suitable horse at the upper end of your price range is likely to prove a better purchase than one who seems cheap but comes with various ifs and buts.

You may be able to buy your horse or pony's tack and equipment with him, especially when purchasing an outgrown pony. Provided the items are in good condition and fit well, this is a good option, but see Chapter 4 for more advice. If you have to kit him out, factor in the cost of tack, rugs, grooming kit and tack-cleaning equipment and any extras you may need, such as protective boots.

### RUNNING COSTS

After your initial outlay, there will be normal running costs for day to day care. If you are going to keep your horse on DIY livery, these will include rental of stable and grazing, feed, bedding and farriery. You will also need to pay for insurance and preventative healthcare (worming, vaccinations and dental care). Regular lessons, which are essential to ensure that you and your horse progress and that any small problems can be sorted out before they become big ones are another part of your budget.

And there's more...The list of what you need for your horse never seems to stop growing. As well as incidentals such as the cost of equipment which needs to be replaced or repaired, there are extras such as paying someone to clip your horse (or buying your own clippers); lungeing equipment and extra rugs. If you intend to compete, you will also need to think about the cost of buying and running a horsebox or trailer and suitable towing vehicle, or hiring a professional transporter. Even if you insure your horse for veterinary fees, which is strongly advised, you will pay a certain amount towards the cost of every incident. Hopefully, accidents and illnesses will be minor and infrequent, but you need to be prepared.

**GOOD FOUNDATIONS**

It may be tempting to buy a horse early in your riding career, but first you need to build a firm base of skills in riding, handling and practical care. It is also important to gain experience in riding and dealing with a variety of animals, as this improves your knowledge and confidence and will help you decide what sort of horse you want to look for. The more you can do under skilled supervision, the better you will cope when decisions are down to you. No matter how confident you feel in a riding school situation, becoming an owner always has its challenging moments to start with!

Both riding and handling skills require an understanding of equine psychology, as explained in the next section. And whilst there is much talk about the necessity for a horse to have a good

RIGHT *Routine veterinary costs include vaccination against equine influenza and tetanus.*

OPPOSITE *Read a horse's body language – this horse's pricked ears and general demeanour show that he is alert and interested, but calm.*

temperament, you also need to be able to analyse your own character strengths and weaknesses and make sure that whenever you are around horses, you behave appropriately, even if you've had a bad day at work or your family has been driving you bananas.

Making progress with schooling and competition is covered in Chapter 12, but right from the start it's important to develop patience and consistency. It's no good hurrying to tack up your horse and not treating him with your usual care and consideration because you're trying to beat the clock, then getting cross with him because he seems tense. Nor is it fair to accept a form of behaviour one day, then tell your horse off the next when he behaves in exactly the same way, but you are not in quite such a good mood. When you are around horses, you need to be able to react quickly but calmly, which means being aware all the time of what you are doing and how the horse is reacting. It isn't fair to get annoyed when he treads on your toe – horses don't do that sort of thing deliberately and, in most cases, it happens because you are in the wrong place at the wrong time. Similarly, a horse who consistently goes into canter on the wrong leg isn't misbehaving; he is either unbalanced or stiff, or the aids you have given him are not correct or clear enough.

Developing riding and handling skills and confidence is a matter of time and experience. Although owning a horse will hopefully enable you to progress quickly, you need to be competent

in a school situation and out hacking before you think seriously about starting your search. A good instructor who knows your history, strengths, weaknesses and temperament will usually be able to advise you when you're ready, but make sure you can tick all the boxes on the skills checklist at the end of this chapter. You'll find out about all these topics as you read though this book.

Before you actually start looking for a horse, try to ride as many different types as possible so that you get an idea of what you enjoy. A good riding school will help and riding holidays which incorporate long rides over varied terrain can also be a good way of gaining experience: although you will still be under supervision, you will have to think for yourself and establish a partnership with an unknown horse.

## UNDERSTANDING HORSES

Horses, like people, are individuals. Whilst breeds and types may tend to share common characteristics – for instance, a Thoroughbred (TB) will tend to be quicker in his reactions than a horse with a high percentage of draught blood – their environment and experience will also have an effect. However, 6,000 years of domestication has not changed the fact that all horses are creatures of instinct and an understanding and appreciation of horse psychology will make you a better rider as well as a better owner.

LEFT *Heavy horses like this one, or horses with a high percentage of heavy horse blood, are usually less quick to react than Thoroughbreds or those with a lot of Thoroughbred blood.*

RIGHT *The Flehmen reaction allows a horse to identify or assess a particular smell.*

No matter how quiet an individual horse or pony seems to be, he is still a prey animal, just as you and your dog are hunters. This means that if something frightens a horse, his instinctive reaction is to run away: something behaviourists call the 'fright and flight' reaction. Although horses will occasionally kick and bite, they usually do so in defence rather than as overt acts of aggression; the horse who swings his head round and tries to bite you when you do up his girth is reacting to discomfort, or to the memory of previous discomfort caused by inconsiderate handling.

The horse is also a herd animal, who needs the company of his own kind. It is unfair to expect a horse or pony to live alone, though some are said to adapt well to living with other species for companions, such as goats. (However, as goats are also happiest living with at least one other of their kind, it may be that each makes the most of a not quite satisfactory partnership!) Although a horse who has been educated correctly should acquire the confidence to be ridden and hacked out alone, there are some who are always happier and more reliable when hacked out in company, and equines always find security in numbers.

The appearance of any equine, whether horse, donkey or zebra, gives clues to how he sees and hears. Because his eyes are set at the sides of his head rather than in the front, as ours are, he has a wider overall field of vision. But he also has blind spots directly under his nose and behind him, which means that when you ask him to jump, he needs the freedom of his head and neck when coming into a fence.

Horses have much more acute senses of hearing and smell than we do. Their ears are mobile and shaped to channel sound and, like dogs, they can hear frequencies that we can't. This also means that horses are much happier with people who are quiet than those who talk loudly or shout. If you speak softly and soothingly to a nervous horse, it will help to calm him.

Horses also have a highly developed sense of smell; when a horse raises his top lip and displays what is known as the Flehmen reaction it might look as if he is laughing, but he is actually partially

*Horses will naturally 'groom' each other using their teeth, and the base of the withers is a favourite spot. Most horses will enjoy being scratched here with your fingers.*

closing his nostrils and using the vomeronasal organ at the top of the nasal passages to identify or assess a particular smell. Some horses find certain smells frightening or stimulating – many hate the smell of pigs, and women handlers of breeding stallions are often advised not to wear perfume around them, as stallions sometimes find it arousing!

Touch is a vital sense for your horse's survival as well as his satisfaction. He uses his muzzle, mouth and nose to investigate everything from strange objects to plants in the pasture – which, of course, he can't see because they are directly under his nose when he is grazing. Horses also groom each other with their teeth on the withers, neck and back, so scratching a nervous horse on the withers when riding can be a reward and/or may encourage him to relax and lower his head.

## BODY LANGUAGE

If you watch a group of horses in a field regularly, it's soon possible to work out the hierarchy. One will be the boss and if he wants to drink first or graze in a particular place, others will defer to him. If the group is made up of adult mares and geldings, then for 'he' you can often read 'she', as mares tend to be dominant. This is another reflection of life in the wild, because whilst a herd will be led by a stallion, the dominant mare holds just as much authority.

Good horsemen have always known how to read equine body language and influence it with their own, but modern-day trainers such as Monty Roberts, Pat Parelli and others have helped make this skill more accessible. Everyone knows that a horse who flattens his ears, snakes his head and bares his teeth is not exactly making friendly overtures, but there are other more subtle signals that can give clues to how he is feeling. The following head to toe guide will help you read the signals a horse is giving, but it's important to look at the whole picture rather than just individual aspects.

*Ears:* pricked up and forwards show that the horse is alert and focusing on something interesting or alarming. If one or other ear is relaxed and slightly out to the side, the horse is relaxed or listening to something. A horse who flicks back one ear in a relaxed fashion when being ridden is usually paying attention to his rider.

*Eyes:* bright, alert eyes mean an alert horse. Tired, dull eyes point to a tired or ill horse. Whilst a frightened horse may show the white of his eye, don't confuse this with the horse who naturally shows a permanent white ring (sclera) round his eyeball. Similarly, a big eye is attractive but a small, piggy one doesn't necessarily mean a piggy temperament.

*Nostrils:* relaxed nostrils mean a relaxed horse. Flared nostrils mean interest, alarm or excitement, though if the horse is galloping they are a sign of his greater effort to breathe.

*Legs:* a resting horse will often drop his hip and rest the hind leg on that side. However, shifting frequently from one hind leg or foreleg to the one on the other side often indicates discomfort or pain, which could be sited in the foot, limb or body. A horse or pony who shifts his weight markedly to his hind legs may be showing signs of pain from laminitis (see Chapter 10.) A sound horse who holds his hind leg in the air may be threatening to kick.

*Tail:* a tail which is clamped down may mean a horse is nervous, cold or ill. One who holds his tail higher than normal is often feeling exuberant.

The horse who 'grows' and makes himself appear as large as possible is either alarmed by something or adopting a dominant posture towards another. Dropping the head, licking and chewing are usually signs of submission.`

## TALKING 'HORSE'

Understanding how horses get their message across helps you to do the same. For instance, if you want to encourage a horse to come up to you, turn so you are half facing away from him, let your shoulders droop and don't look him in the eye. If you want him to back up, square your shoulders, look him in the eye, step towards him and exude confidence. But use common sense at the same time: marching up to a loose horse may influence him to the extent that he whips round and gallops off, kicking out as he does so.

Using these principles in a small, enclosed area, usually a round pen, can bring about the situation the influential trainer Monty Roberts labelled 'join-up', where the horse decides that the most comfortable place to be is with the person who is in the pen with him and will walk closely behind as the handler turns, stops and starts. But though it is a useful exercise in the hands of such a skilled trainer, it is a means to an end, not an end in itself.

The same applies to methods used by other trainers, such as Pat Parelli. His system uses progressive exercises or 'games' on the ground, but the fact that a horse reacts as the handler wants him to does not mean that he is automatically safer to ride or that you have suddenly achieved some sort of mystic communion with him.

## TESTING THE WATER

IT'S IMPORTANT to have some practical experience of what's involved in looking after a horse before you commit yourself – for the horse's sake as well as your own – and there are several ways to test the water. Many riding schools run courses designed to give adults and children a taste of ownership, covering everything from grooming to the theory of feeding, shoeing and preventative health care. In the UK, choosing a school that is approved by the British Horse Society and/or is a member of the Association of British Riding Schools guarantees that everything from the competence of the instructors to the suitability of the horses has been inspected and approved. Official bodies in many other countries offer broadly similar accreditation. The International League for the Protection of Horses, a UK-based charity which helps equines worldwide, runs courses for would-be owners and The Open College of Equine Studies, also based in the UK, offers correspondence courses incorporating practical modules ranging from courses for those who simply want to learn more to ones leading to recognized qualifications. To find out more, see the Appendix of Useful Addresses.

Helping friends who own horses is another option, as long as you can be sure they are knowledgeable enough to do things correctly. Once you have the necessary practical skills and confidence, you could also consider entering into a share arrangement with someone who owns a suitable horse or pony but needs practical and perhaps financial help with looking after and riding him. This will usually involve a trial period followed by a long-term commitment and is discussed in more detail in Chapter 3. Sharing the right horse with the right person can be the answer if you can't commit to full-time ownership but want some of its pleasures and advantages.

*Good children's ponies, like this versatile skewbald,*
*are worth their weight in gold.*

# EXPERT QUOTE

*'In general, parents should be cautious about buying a pony before a child is about 10 years old. It's important that children have experience of riding lots of different ponies under the supervision of a good teacher, as they will reap the benefits throughout their riding life.'*

JULIAN MARCZAK, CHAIRMAN OF THE ASSOCIATION OF BRITISH RIDING SCHOOLS

**PARENTS AND PONIES**

IF YOUR CHILD longs for a pony and you don't know the fetlocks from the withers, it can seem like a daunting prospect. On the one hand, you want to offer encouragement, and the idea of having a pony in the family may seem attractive, particularly if you share their enthusiasm. On the other hand, it may seem like stepping into a foreign country, complete with its own language.

The good news is that you will never again wonder what to do with your spare time, because you probably won't have much. The bad news is that, if there are other children who are not so enthusiastic about ponies and riding, you have to organize family life with absolute precision to make sure that no one feels hard done by or left out – and that includes the adults, the family dog and so on.

No matter how knowledgeable your child seems, or claims to be, it is essential to get expert advice. Even the most capable child needs adult supervision...and, of course, you will have to pay the bills.

Your child must be competent at riding and handling ponies before ownership can be considered. This means at least two years of lessons at an approved riding school where horse care and management form part of the syllabus – see if your child can tick the boxes of our checklist and if not, set the challenge that you can only start thinking about pony ownership when this has been achieved! Make the most of 'own a pony' weeks, which many riding schools hold in the holidays, and find out about joining your local branch of the Pony Club. Children don't have to own ponies to become members and some riding schools have good relationships with their local branches and will provide mounts for instructional rallies.

Riding schools and Pony Club branches provide a wonderful support network for parents entering into pony ownership and you should get lots of help and encouragement from instructors and other parents. Pony Club branches in particular are a great source of suitable ponies, as there are often families with outgrown ponies looking for good homes for them. The best ones often have a waiting list of would-be buyers!

Knowledgeable horsy families often have ponies who are passed down from one sibling to the next, which means children start riding their own ponies at a very early age. This isn't always a good thing, as the more ponies a child rides, the more their riding ability and confidence progress.

# SKILLS CHECKLIST

Before you think about buying a horse or pony, make sure you've got what it takes.

## RIDING

Be confident at walk, trot and canter in a school and in the open. Be able to influence your horse rather than being a passenger.

Be able to adapt your riding to individual horses or ponies so that you can get the most out of both forward-going and less responsive animals.

Hack confidently on the roads and on bridlepaths and tracks in small and large groups. (You may eventually want to hack out alone on your own horse, but most riding schools will not be able to permit this for insurance reasons.)

Know the Highway Code and how it relates to horses and riders. Consider training for and taking the BHS Riding and Road Safety test. (Although riding on roads is less prevalent in many countries than it is in the UK, any rider who needs to use busy roads should be fully conversant with national guidelines regarding mounted road use.)

Ride competently round a small course of show jumps and be able to jump small cross-country fences.

## HANDLING

Understand how horses have evolved and why their instincts and physical characteristics affect the way they behave and react.

Be able to catch and turn out a horse in the field when he is with a group of others.

Understand how horses communicate with each other through body language – and how to read these signals and use your body language to influence horses.

Understand the need for fair, consistent behaviour at all times.

Know how to tack up and untack and how to make sure tack and equipment such as protective boots are adjusted correctly. Be able to carry out regular cleaning and safety checks.

Know how to fit and adjust rugs.

## ROUTINE CARE AND MANAGEMENT

Understand the principles of feeding and how to assess a horse's condition.

Understand why grooming is more than a matter of appearances and be able to groom a horse who is stabled part of the time. Appreciate why the grooming regime for a horse or pony who lives out all the time is different from one who is stabled.

Recognize when feet and shoes are in good (and poor) condition and understand the importance of correct farriery.

Understand why it is important for every horse to have an environment that is as free from dust and mould spores as possible. Know the pros and cons of different types of bedding and be able to muck out a stable.

Know about safety on the yard.

Know why good pasture management is essential and be aware of the basic principles.

Know the difference between suitable and unsafe fencing and know the hazards to watch out for and deal with in fields, particularly ragwort and other poisonous plants.

## HEALTH CARE

Know the signs of a healthy horse and how to recognize when there might be a problem. Be able to check a horse's temperature, pulse and respiration rate.

Understand the principles of preventative health care: worming (including pasture management) vaccination and dental care.

Know how to spot signs that a horse needs immediate veterinary attention. Be aware of emergency situations such as colic and some wounds.

Be able to identify lameness.

Have knowledge of basic first aid and know what should be in an equine first aid kit.

# 2. FINDING THE RIGHT HOME

**B**EFORE YOU think about buying a horse or taking one on loan, you need to sort out suitable accommodation. Providing the right home means finding or establishing a set-up where he will be happy and healthy and you will be able to get maximum satisfaction from looking after and riding him. Whilst his needs must come first, it's important that you take into account your lifestyle, when you are able to ride and what you want to do with your horse. An adult rider who works long hours and has to ride outside daylight hours in winter will need a yard that has facilities to match, such as a floodlit school. On the other hand, someone who can be flexible about working hours and/or family commitments and mainly wants to hack may be prepared to go without the luxury of a school in return for excellent off-road riding.

Even if you have your own grazing and can provide stabling or a field shelter at home, you need to consider whether this is actually the best option. Keeping a horse at home is wonderful but, for a start, you need a suitable companion for him – as discussed in the first chapter, horses are herd animals and it's unfair to keep one on his own. It is also far better for a novice owner to have the back-up of an experienced yard manager; just knowing that there is someone trustworthy you can ask for advice provides a valuable comfort zone.

Whilst keeping a horse at home offers many advantages and benefits, it can also have its lonely moments, so if part of the enjoyment you get from riding is the social side, you need to ask whether you will still be able get this when you're home alone. Horses at home can also be a tie and you need to make sure you have adequate back-up, either from other family members, friends or paid helpers.

*Find a home for your horse where he will be safe and you can enjoy looking after him.*

## HOME COMFORTS

IF YOUR HORSE could describe his ideal home, it would probably comprise four main priorities: adequate, safe grazing; shelter; one or more amenable companions and a certain amount of routine. Most people now agree that daily turnout in a safe field is essential for a horse's mental and physical well-being and top competitors in all disciplines insist that their horses are given this opportunity to unwind and just 'be horses'. Racehorse trainers have traditionally kept their charges stabled whenever they are not working, but this attitude is no longer universal and some adopt the philosophy that periods of daily turnout add to their charges' well-being and performance. Some owners opt for a 24/7 outdoor lifestyle and many animals do well on it; however, not everyone has enough land to be able to do this and it cannot be taken for granted that every horse will thrive on being kept this way.

The ideal compromise is often to keep your horse on a combined system, whereby he is turned out during the day and stabled at night. When summer temperatures soar, you may want to reverse this, turning him out at night and bringing him in during the hottest periods and when insects are at their most prevalent. As you get to know your horse, and if your yard allows routines to be adapted, you will find out what suits. Basic principles are often guidelines that may have to be adapted to your horse's needs; for instance, if he is overweight or susceptible to laminitis (see Chapter 10) you will need to adapt his routine accordingly.

## LIVERY OPTIONS

FOR MOST PEOPLE, the best way to start horse ownership is to find a good livery yard. This traditional term derives from the delivery of food and care and means that you rent accommodation for your horse and either do all the work involved in looking after him yourself, or pay for someone to carry out part or all of it.

There are four main types of livery, each with its pros and cons.

*GRASS LIVERY – RENTAL OF GRAZING ONLY.* This is not suitable for all horses and ponies and, in all cases, a back-up stable must be available in case of injury or illness.

*DIY LIVERY – RENTAL OF STABLE AND GRAZING; YOU DO ALL THE WORK.* This is cost-effective in terms of outlay and can give immense satisfaction, but places heavy demands on time and travelling. Also, as with keeping your horse at home, it means that you are sometimes tied down. It's essential to have an emergency back-up system, perhaps with one or more other owners at the yard, or the yard manager.

*PART-DIY.* You do most of the work and pay for the yard manager or staff to help out, perhaps by bringing in or turning out your horse and, when appropriate, feeding and adjusting rugs. This works well for many owners.

*WORKING LIVERY.* Your horse or pony is kept at livery in a riding school and earns all or part of his keep by being used to instruct pupils and/or staff. This can sometimes work with children's ponies, but is often unsatisfactory. The school may want to use your horse when you want to ride him and you will probably get to the stage where you don't want him ridden by lots of different people – or will feel that although you wanted to school him, you have to hack instead because he's already worked on a lesson.

**FULL LIVERY.** The yard looks after everything from feeding to tack cleaning and, when necessary, exercise. All you have to do is turn up and ride whenever you want to. This is expensive and doesn't give you the same chance to get to know your horse as the other arrangements, but it may be the only option for those with demanding work or family commitments who can afford it.

## FINDING A YARD

LIVERY YARDS range from large, purpose built set-ups to a few stables rented out on a DIY basis. Wherever you live and work, you can find somewhere to keep your horse, even in urban areas. However, if your only option is to keep a horse on a yard where he can never be turned out, you have to ask yourself whether this is fair to him: in the majority of cases, the answer will be no. There are many working horses in cities, such as those used by the army and police forces, but their work regimes are different from those of the average horse kept mainly for pleasure.

*It's important to find a livery yard where you and your horse will be happy and where high standards are maintained.*

At present, the position in the UK is that livery yards do not have to be licensed, though that may change. The British Horse Society operates its own approval scheme, under which yard proprietors have to be insured against public liability and open to unannounced annual inspections. This should guarantee a certain level of standards, but a yard that isn't approved will not necessarily be inferior. Some BHS and ABRS approved schools also take liveries; this can work well, but you may find that you are unable to use facilities such as arenas whenever you want to because they are in use for lessons.

People who visit lots of yards, such as vets from local equine veterinary practices and qualified freelance instructors, will probably not be able to give official recommendations but may point you in the direction of possibilities. You then need to do your own research on the phone, followed by visits. The most popular yards often have waiting lists and it's worth waiting for a space to become available rather than settling for a yard you have doubts about.

You could, of course, keep a horse at a stopgap yard and move when your first choice has a vacancy – but you risk being stuck somewhere you're not really happy with and putting your horse through the upheaval of moving home twice. You should also be prepared to pay a retainer as soon as a vacancy arises, because you can't expect a yard proprietor to lose money on an empty stable that another owner would take immediately. Find your yard, then find your horse!

## LOOKING ROUND

When you find a likely prospect or two, make an appointment to visit. This will enable you not only to see the yard and the people running it, but to work out how long it will take you to get there. If you intend to see to your horse before going to work at peak traffic times, you might need to check that this will be feasible. Similarly, if hacking out is going to be an important part of your riding, see what traffic levels are like at times when you are likely to be riding, and at weekends.

Some yards are kept smart and pristine whilst others are more workmanlike. The most important thing is that the environment is safe for horses and people, so first impressions are important. You don't want to see field gates hanging off hinges, dirty or unsafe water supplies in the field, broken fencing, children running around out of control or mucking out forks left where someone is going to tread on them. There is always going to be more mud in winter than in summer, but you still don't want to see acres of it.

Is there a list of yard regulations where everyone can see it? Are there fire precautions and instructions for what to do in an emergency? Are numbers for local equine vets displayed? If you intend to keep your tack at the yard, is the tackroom secure? Tack thefts are so common that you need to take every precaution against them (see Chapter 4). Similarly, if you hope to buy a trailer or horsebox and keep it at the yard, is there a safe parking area that is as secure as possible, and is there a rental charge for the parking space?

When you visit, are you made to feel welcome or simply ignored? If there are clients around and they have time to talk, it's a good idea to ask how long they have been there and generally get a feel for whether they are happy or have a list of grumbles. Be diplomatic and ask the yard owner if it's all right to do this, as walking on to a yard and immediately conducting an inquisition won't exactly give a good impression!

# QUESTIONS TO ASK

Be prepared to ask lots of questions about a yard – and be equally prepared for the proprietor to give you an even more thorough grilling. It's a good sign, as it means the proprietor wants to make sure that you and your eventual horse will fit in to the set-up. It only takes one inconsiderate client to disrupt a happy yard. Some of the questions below can be asked on first phone inquiry, whilst others can be raised when you visit.

● Does the yard owner have specialist equestrian knowledge? You need to be tactful in the way you ask this, but it's important for a first-time owner to know that a yard is run from a solid base of knowledge and experience. Farmers have been encouraged to diversify into horses and some now offer liveries, usually on a DIY basis. Many such yards are excellent, especially for experienced owners, but you need to be careful. For instance, is the fencing suitable for horses? Was the grazing laid down for dairy cattle, which can cause problems, as explained later in this chapter? Similarly, if the farmer offers hay or includes a supply in the cost, is it suitable for horses? Unfortunately, some people believe it is acceptable practice to feed dusty and/or mouldy forage to sheep or cattle and may carry this through to horses. Silage is fed to cattle, but is not recommended for horses – see Chapter 5 for more information.

● What are the basic costs? If you are looking for part livery, what help is available and what are the extra charges?

● Does someone live on the premises and what are the security arrangements? If a horse gets colic overnight, you need someone to be aware of it and call the vet and if thieves target the yard, you don't want your horse, tack or transport to be vulnerable.

● Does the yard have public liability insurance and/or approval by the BHS, ABRS or equivalent national body?

● How many clients are there and what are their interests? Some adult riders won't want to be on a yard where there are lots of children; on the other hand, if you're looking for a home for your child's first pony, you won't want your child to be the only one there.

People with particular interests often gravitate to particular yards because of the facilities. Yards aimed at serious competitors are often more expensive and whilst the yard staff and clients may be perfectly pleasant and welcoming to a first-time owner, you're likely to feel a bit like a fish out of water. A yard which caters for owners with varied interests will probably be more suitable, as you'll find people to hack out with and will hopefully be encouraged to try a wide range of activities with your horse.

● Could you turn out your horse all year round? Some yards have to restrict winter grazing, but you don't want your horse standing in for long periods.

● Does the yard supply feed and bedding and if so, is there a choice? Yards which buy in bulk can often pass on savings to clients, but you may not want to be restricted to, say, only being able to use straw bedding – or, because of the implications for respiratory health, having to stable your horse next to others bedded on straw.

● Is there a worming programme? (See Chapter 9.)

● Is the yard 'open all hours', or are there restrictions on the times owners can visit?

● What period of notice must you give to leave, and the owner give to ask you to go?

● There should be a written contract between you and the yard owner specifying who does what, costs and yard regulations. Expect to be asked to give permission for the yard owner to call a vet to your horse if you are not able to be contacted in an emergency and to be able to give permission for the horse to be euthanased if, in the vet's opinion, this is essential on humane grounds. You may also be required to insure your horse for veterinary fees and third party liability, which most owners regard as an essential part of horse ownership (see Chapter 3).

A conscientious yard owner will want to know not only what sort of horse you are hoping to buy – and may even know of a likely prospect or two – but will need to find out your level of experience. Be honest: people who talk the talk but can't walk the walk soon get found out. Explaining that you're looking for a good yard because you know that there will be times when you need back-up and advice will earn you more respect than pretending to know more than you actually do.

**HOME TRUTHS**

WHETHER YOU KEEP your horse on a livery yard or at home, you need to be able to know what comprises an ideal environment. Few of us achieve perfection, but you should never compromise his safety or welfare. This means understanding about fields, fencing, stables and, if appropriate, field shelters and their maintenance. For those hoping eventually to keep horses at home, there is a section at the end of this chapter on the practical issues involved.

### FIELD OPTIONS

Many owners think of their horses' fields as nothing more than convenient turnout and grazing areas where grass grows as if by magic. But you need to consider both quantity and quality: is there enough grazing for the number of animals it is expected to sustain and is it of the correct quality? The usual yardstick is that each horse needs a minimum of 0.4 hectare (1 acre) of grazing, though researchers say that the stocking ratio of a field should ideally be lower so that horses have a wider area to cover and aren't forced into unwanted proximity with others. However, don't feel that you are automatically undermining your horse's psychological health if he and one or two companions don't have a vast area to roam around at will!

Grass itself is a crop, which sounds obvious but is something many people forget. This means that if you are laying down grass specifically for horses, you should get specialist advice on the seed mix to use. It should comprise a mixture of varieties that will be palatable, hard-wearing and not too rich in nutrients (though good doers and animals susceptible to laminitis will need specially tailored grazing regimes even on grass grown from ideal seed mixtures). Be careful if you keep your horse on grazing originally laid down for cattle, perhaps on a farm that has diversified into offering horse liveries. The varieties sown will have been chosen to boost milk and meat production and can definitely be too much of a good thing for horses.

Horses are browsers as well as grazers. If you watch horses grazing in a field that has a wide variety of plant species, you can see them using their lips to search out the tastiest morsels. In an effort to provide their horses with choice and variety, some people like to plant 'herb strips' – but these aren't always successful. Horses, like people, have individual tastes and whilst many like plants such as dandelions, you don't want these to take over your grassland. It's also important to remember that horses may like plants that are not necessarily good for them, such as white clover; this is often regarded as a risk factor for laminitis and other problems in susceptible horses.

## GRASS MAINTENANCE

The better grazing is looked after, the more it will provide a good environment for your horse. Horses are the world's pickiest eaters – they like short grass rather than long and, unlike cows, will designate parts of the field as toilet areas where they drop their dung and then won't fancy eating the grass. Whilst you might feel that this is perfectly understandable, it means that the grass must be kept in optimum condition.

Grass needs a combination of warmth and moisture to grow. The usual advice is that peak growth and nutrients are achieved in spring, summer and early autumn – but whilst that generalization may still hold, climate changes can alter the pattern. A particularly hot, dry summer can turn a green field into a dried up brown one and autumn and early winter weather patterns which mimic those of spring mean that grass may grow accordingly.

This means more than ever that those new to pasture management (and even those who are not so new) need advice from experts who understand not only how best to maintain grazing but also horses' specific needs. In Britain, many areas of grassland are naturally acidic, on or below pH 5.5, whilst the optimum pH is 6–6.5: different departures from the optimum may occur in other places. A soil pH that is too low or too high means the availability of minerals and trace elements will be reduced. Soil analysis, which includes measuring pH, should be carried out every two or three years so that deficiencies can be

rectified. Advice can be sought from a local contractor who understands the nature of your land. In Britain, advice is also available from ADAS (formerly the Agricultural Development Advisory Service, but now known only by its acronym).

In an ideal world, enough grazing should be available on permanent pasture to supply food and turnout all year round, without the need to fertilize. In practice, many owners need to fertilize their grass, though hopefully not every year. Again, get expert advice on the correct use of slow-release fertilizers which do not produce a sudden flush of rich grass.

### DROPPINGS DUTY

One of the most important routine jobs for any horse owner is to pick up droppings from the field regularly, ideally every day. The main reason is that this helps to minimize the horse's worm burden. All animals – even humans – have internal parasites, but if they are not kept at minimum level your horse's life is at risk. Worms cause weight loss, lethargy, colic and ultimately may be the main cause of death (see Chapter 9 for information on control).

It is vital that yards remove droppings regularly or insist that owners carry out this work. Big yards often have paddock cleaners that suck up droppings, whilst those of us who are not so fortunate have to rely on a wheelbarrow and a pair of rubber gloves! Chain harrowing to spread droppings is not effective. If it is done on a hot, sunny day, the ultraviolet rays may kill off some of the worm eggs – but this is still a poor second best to removing droppings. If droppings are spread in the wrong weather conditions, it will make the problem worse.

The use of herbicides is another contentious area, with some people believing that blanket spraying is unnecessary and ill-advised. Unless you have a weed problem that has spread through a wide area, spot spraying may be enough. Some plants need to be kept under control because they choke the grass, but others are poisonous and must be removed. In particular, ragwort is a killer (see below).

Herbicides can be selective or systemic. Selective products attack broad-leaved plants such as docks and thistles but will not damage grass, whilst systemic ones will kill anything. They must be used responsibly and with expert advice; in Britain, an ADAS equine consultant or a BASIS (British Agrochemical Supply Industry) specialist will help. Considerations include not only the best products to use, but when, how and in what weather conditions spraying should be carried out.

### POISONOUS PLANTS

Whether you keep your horse on your own land or on rented grazing, it is your responsibility to make regular checks for poisonous plants and get rid of them. There are many species that are poisonous to horses; some are dangerous or even fatal in small doses whilst others need to be ingested in large amounts over a long period to cause problems. Of those listed, some are common throughout the UK whilst others grow in restricted areas. Most are not confined to the UK, and other countries may have their own indigenous species (such as loco weed in the USA) which are also poisonous to horses.

You also need to check that grass clippings, garden plants and other items of garden waste are not being tipped over the field fence. These can cause all sorts of problems; for instance, grass clippings ferment and many garden plants are poisonous to horses. The following list shows some of the plants to watch out for and their effects.

**BRACKEN:** horses who have been eating bracken for several weeks develop a vitamin B1 deficiency. Signs include muscle tremors and twitches and a staggering gait. Treatment is usually successful if the problem is spotted in the early stages.

**BUTTERCUP:** if ingested in large quantities, may cause inflammation and blistering of the mouth area and colic.

**CLOVER:** may be linked to laminitis, photosensitivity and possibly grass sickness.

**LABURNUM:** all parts of this ornamental tree are poisonous and ingestion may result in diarrhoea, colic, muscle spasms, seizures and even death.

**OAK:** both oak leaves and acorns contain tannic acid. Horses who eat either or both may suffer gastric problems or, in the worst scenario, death through kidney failure.

**PRIVET:** a common garden hedge plant that can produce signs ranging from colic and a staggering gait to death.

**RAGWORT:** one of the biggest and most widespread problems in the UK. See next section.

**ST JOHN'S WORT:** linked to photosensitization and other problems.

**YEW:** highly poisonous – a single mouthful can kill. This evergreen tree is often found in churchyards and there have been cases of horses grazing in fields alongside them eating clippings tipped over fences and dying as a result. Yew is also prevalent in wooded areas on chalk upland: beware of horses with a seeming death wish trying to snatch mouthfuls whilst out hacking.

### REMEMBER

Poisonous plants can be found in hay and haylage as well as growing in fields and hedgerows. When dried and baled, they may be impossible to spot by visual inspection – and will also be more palatable. It is therefore vital to buy all forage from a reputable source.

Horses are more likely to take them in whilst grazing if the field is in poor condition with little grass, underlying the need for good pasture management.

*It's vital to recognize and protect your horse from poisonous plants such as bracken (FAR LEFT), acorn (MIDDLE LEFT), yew (LEFT) and ragwort (OVERLEAF).*

*Watch out for ragwort in both the flowering stages* (ABOVE LEFT) *and rosette* (ABOVE RIGHT), *as shown here.*

## THE SCOURGE OF RAGWORT

It has been estimated that every week, at least ten horses in the UK die from ragwort poisoning. It causes cumulative liver damage that is eventually fatal; there is no cure or antidote and although the liver can function until 75 per cent of it has been destroyed, once that barrier has been crossed there is no hope and euthanasia is essential to prevent the horse dying a painful death. Ragwort is also a danger to other animals and to people: blood tests taken from volunteers who pulled up ragwort without wearing gloves showed the presence of toxins in their systems. Despite the fact that it is covered by the Weeds Act 1959, it is so common that it has been labelled a threat to biodiversity.

One of the best ways to prevent it growing in fields is good pasture management coupled with vigilance. Maintaining a thick, healthy sward means it is more difficult for ragwort to take hold and walking paddocks daily to check for this and other hazards means you can take action as soon as plants are found. As with other poisonous plants, it is a real danger in hay and haylage.

Ragwort can be dug up and pulled by hand (using gloves), or sprayed with selective herbicide: cutting is not effective. It has a long tap root and the easiest way to dig it up is to use a special ragwort fork. *Plants should always be removed from the field and burnt*, as they become more palatable when wilted. Ragwort is biennial and forms rosettes in the first year and flowers in the second. Rosettes can easily be missed, as they lie flat to the ground. Because it is biennial, a destruction programme will take at least two years – and if the pasture has been infested for some time, it could take even longer. Seeds can remain dormant in the soil for up to 20 years.

There is still controversy over whether ragwort can be controlled by introducing Cinnabar moth caterpillars, which feed on it. The majority view is that this is not feasible and some experts believe that the Cinnabar itself is being poisoned.

*'I would not normally advocate the eradication of any species, but this one has nothing to offer. I don't accept that eradicating ragwort would eradicate the Cinnabar moth, which feeds on it. Ragwort is burgeoning and the Cinnabar is declining. In fact, I believe it is being poisoned. The moth was common throughout the years that ragwort was rare and now that ragwort is widespread, Cinnabar moths are difficult to find. If we care about the moth, we have to find out why its population is declining in the face of an ad lib supply of "feed".'*

DR DEREK KNOTTENBELT, LEADING VET AND CAMPAIGNER AGAINST RAGWORT

### ON THE LEVEL

Horses usually prefer shorter rather than longer grass and, if they have a choice, will often graze down short areas to bare ground and leave longer ones. It makes it easier to keep a field in good condition – especially if you have limited grazing – if the grass is topped (cut) to a height of about 7.5 cm (3 in). This also helps to maintain a thicker sward that will stand up better to wear and tear, as topping the grass encourages it to tiller out (encourages more leaves to grow on each stem.)

The best way to stop land becoming 'horse sick' is to rest fields, or parts of fields in rotation. Yards and studs with lots of grazing often use sheep and cattle to help keep land in good condition; this can work on smaller ones, too, if you can take horses off the field for a few weeks and find a farmer prepared to bring stock to graze it. Sheep are a better bet for wet or naturally soft land, as their feet pat down the land without damaging it. If your existing fencing is not suitable for sheep, the farmer should supply temporary electric fencing to retain them. Don't be tempted to add sheep netting to your existing fencing – this is unsuitable for horses and potentially dangerous.

Judicious harrowing and rolling also helps keep fields in good condition. On large areas, this will need to be done with a tractor and agricultural equipment, but small fields can be cared for using small harrows and rollers towed by a four-wheel drive vehicle. Harrowing land in the spring, as soon as it is dry enough, will pull out dead grass and make room for new growth.

### FENCING FACTS

Safe fencing is vital, both for your horse's safety and that of people using nearby roads. If your horse escapes from his field because the fencing is inadequate or poorly maintained and a road

*Stud fencing* (ABOVE) *enables you to keep horses in the field safely whilst ensuring that other animals, such as dogs, are kept out. Post and rail fencing* (RIGHT) *is a traditional favourite that is still many owners' first choice.*

accident results, you could be held to be responsible and liable. In fact, there have been judgements where owners have faced claims for punitive damages even when it is believed horses have been deliberately let out – so as well as checking fencing, check your third party liability cover (see Insurance in Chapter 3).

There are many different types of fencing suitable for horses, ranging from post and rail to special plastic – and there is even a new type said to keep out midges! Thick hedging has always been recommended as a first choice, as it provides shelter as well as a barrier, but modern farming practices mean that traditionally maintained hedging is, sadly, not often seen. However, it is possible to combine hedging with other forms of fencing, such as post and rail or electric fencing.

The main considerations are that a fence will keep your horse in the field whilst also keeping him safe. Barbed wire is totally unacceptable and whilst plain, high-tensile steel wire does not have sharp edges, it can cause terrible injuries to people and horses if broken: because it is tensioned so tightly, it curls up and springs back in a metal whiplash when released. As mentioned earlier, squared wire fencing designed for use with sheep can also be dangerous, as it

Hedging and trees give natural shelter in a field as well as forming a barrier. Unless hedging is thick and well maintained, it will need to be reinforced by other fencing, such as post and rail or electric.

*High-tech fencing made from special plastic is relatively expensive to buy, but safe and low on maintenance.*

may be possible for a horse or pony to put his feet through one of the squares and get caught. Stud fencing designed especially for horses does not carry this risk, as the squares are smaller.

Permanent electric fencing is a feasible solution in some circumstances, especially where cost is a major consideration (although not, perhaps, as a main boundary between field and road). Temporary electric fencing is useful for splitting fields into smaller sections.

If you are choosing fencing for your own land, take into account the maintenance factor as well as the initial price. Top-quality post and rail fencing should last for many years and the wood will have been treated to make it very light on maintenance, but cheaper fencing may need treating with preservative at regular intervals.

**STABLES AND SHELTERS**

**PROS AND CONS OF STABLES**

One school of thought says that a stable is equivalent to a prison, but a more generally accepted view is that, as long as a horse gets plenty of daily turnout, it is acceptable to stable him for short periods or overnight in suitably designed accommodation. However, if he has respiratory problems or shows signs of stereotypic behaviour – behaviour patterns that indicate he is stressed at being confined – then a properly managed, permanent outdoor lifestyle will mean that he is happier and healthier. Nevertheless, even if you want to keep your horse out 24/7, access to a stable is always essential, as there may be times when, because of injury or illness, your vet recommends that he is stabled.

Stables can be individual buildings, or units in a large covered area. Whatever type your horse is housed in, he must have plenty of room, good ventilation and be able to see and, ideally, touch a compatible neighbour. Large yards, rehabilitation centres and veterinary hospitals have isolation boxes so that infections can be contained, but horses usually need company: if, in normal circumstances, a horse is contained in a stable from which he can't see another horse, this really is tantamount to putting him in a prison. Although stable units under a single roof – sometimes called American barns – make stable work more comfortable in bad weather, individual stables are generally accepted to be healthier because you do not have a large number of horses sharing the same airspace. However, well-designed barn-type stables with good ventilation are healthier than badly designed individual units.

*The American barn system of stabling means that horses are under one roof – which is more convenient for those looking after them, but means that careful attention must be paid to ensuring adequate ventilation.*

Traditional barns with open fronts and partially open sides can make good housing for compatible horses. Logistically, they have to be used with a semi deep litter system of bedding, but the good ventilation usually compensates for the disadvantages of this unless horses are particularly susceptible to respiratory problems. Stereotypic behaviour, especially weaving, is sometimes reduced by keeping a horse this way, as he is not confined in a small area.

## SIZE MATTERS

Although there are recommended minimum dimensions for stables, there is no such thing as a stable that is too big. Not only does it give the horse more freedom to move around, it is usually easier and cheaper to keep a large box clean: you will have to put down more bedding to start with, but the horse is less likely to kick droppings about. The absolute minimum sizes quoted are based on floor space and are usually:

> Pony up to 148 cm (14.2 hh) – 3.05 m (10 ft) square
> Horse up to 162 cm (16 hh) – 3.65 m (12 ft) sq
> Horse over 162 cm (16 hh) – 4.26 m (14 ft) sq

Internal headroom should be at least 3.65 m (12 ft) as this gives better ventilation. Big horses should ideally have more. Door openings should be a minimum of 1.22 m (4 ft) wide, even for small ponies, as otherwise there is a risk that they could bang their hips going in or out. Doors must always open outwards so that if a horse lies down or rolls and gets cast (stuck) his door can still be opened. Horses and ponies should be able to look over their doors without having to raise their heads – so small ponies need scaled-down doors.

## A BREATH OF FRESH AIR

The horse's respiratory system can soon be compromised by a combination of poor ventilation and dust and spores from bedding and forage. This can lead to a condition known as recurrent airway obstruction (RAO); research shows that a high percentage of horses who are stabled all or part of the time have a degree of airway inflammation, which can eventually worsen into full-blown RAO. So whilst you don't want your horse to be subjected to draughts, you do want the design of his stable to ensure frequent changes of air.

If you are building your own stables, the manufacturer should be aware of this and include suitable inlets. A window at the back as well as the front of the stable is well worth the small extra expense, as it gives your horse a different view as well as good airflow. If you are renting a stable, then to a certain extent you are stuck with what's already there – but improving ventilation doesn't have to involve major work or expense.

Drainage is also important, so if you're building stables, get advice on how to make sure they drain easily and efficiently. Most modern stables have concrete floors and a very slight slope from front to back will allow liquid not absorbed by bedding to run through openings at the back into a suitable drainage outlet.

*A well-made field shelter provides protection from wind and rain in cold weather and from flies in the summer.*

## FIELD SHELTERS

Although most horses are happier outside, they must have shelter all year round – from heat and flies in the summer as well as the obvious wind and rain. Trees and hedges provide natural shelter, but if these are lacking, a purpose-built one will be necessary. Conventional designs are like open-fronted stables, but although some horses use them quite happily, others prefer to stand outside and use one of the shelter walls as a windbreak. For this reason, windbreaks made from solid 2 m (6 ft 6 in) sections, laid out like the spokes of a wheel, are often effective and appreciated.

### OPEN DOOR POLICY

Traditional stable doors have top and bottom halves. No matter how cold it is, or how hard it rains, don't shut the top one, because you will be doing more harm to your horse's health than if you leave it open. If you are worried that he will get cold or that the rain will blow in, compensate with a good rug.

If possible, site a shelter on the highest part of the field so that water drains away rather than into it, and with its back to the prevailing wind. It must be large enough for the number of occupants to use it without being crowded, and the opening must be wide enough to prevent a dominant horse either keeping another outside or trapping him inside. One reason for horses standing outside rather than inside a shelter is that they simply don't feel safe because of bossy field companions.

## A HOME AT HOME

ALL THE CONSIDERATIONS mentioned in this chapter apply to keeping a horse at home as well as at livery, with one important extra consideration. If you are building new accommodation for your horse, or adapting existing buildings, you will probably need to get planning permission – which in some cases, can be easier said than done. In Britain, it is certainly the case that some authorities are friendlier in their attitude towards horses than others, but 'horsiculture' – scruffy buildings in scruffy fields, often in urban or semi-urban surroundings – has done nothing to endear horse owners to planners. There have even been instances relating to perceived change of use cases where owners have been told to apply for planning permission to erect show jumps in their field so they can school their horses, even though these are not permanent structures.

*You will probably need planning permission to build stables or adapt existing buildings.*

Although the following points apply to regulations in the UK, planning laws are notoriously complex in many countries, and it is easy to fall foul of them. For instance, in the UK it has been a traditional rule of thumb that if buildings are erected within the curtilage of a dwelling house and the horses are kept for pleasure rather than business use, planning permission is not needed. However, it is not safe to assume this, or anything else! Don't build stables or put in an arena thinking that no one will notice: they will, and if retrospective planning permission is refused you can be forced to remove buildings and facilities.

In many cases, planning permission will only be granted for wooden stables. This is a legacy of home owners erecting brick 'stables' which were then converted to granny flats. Good-quality wooden stables should last for many years if properly maintained and for most people, they are the only cost-effective option.

Although most people will have a budget to stick to, try to think ahead. Three stables are better than two even if you only intend to keep one horse and a companion; you never know how your plans will change and you can never have too much storage space.

Things to bear in mind when planning your new set-up include:

● You will probably need planning permission for permanent field shelters. However, mobile shelters that can be moved with a four-wheel drive vehicle are said to be exempt.
● There must be reasonable access for large lorries with heavy loads and they must be able to get close enough to the actual site to deliver readily.
● The base your stables are built on is as important as the buildings themselves. Laying a large area of concrete is usually a professional job.
● When comparing stable manufacturers' prices, check what is included and what counts as an extra. For instance, some companies install full kicking boards as standard whilst others fit half-height ones and charge extra for them to be extended. Fixtures and fittings such as tying-up rings will not be included.
● Think ahead to possible future needs rather than sticking to present ones.

# 3.
# ACQUIRING
# A HORSE

O NCE YOU'VE decided that you are ready to commit to your own horse or pony, the first question is whether you are going to buy, loan or share. Buying a horse in partnership is a recipe for disaster: it works for some racing and competition horse syndicates, but not amongst private individuals. Loaning or sharing may seem attractive from the financial point of view in that you don't have the outlay of a purchase price, but this should not be your only consideration. For instance, how would you feel if you became fond of a horse and the owner decided to end the agreement? Equally, whilst there are many successful share arrangements, they only work if a lot of thought goes into them and both parties are equally reliable and conscientious.

## SHARE AND LOAN AGREEMENTS

A WRITTEN AGREEMENT is advisable when sharing a horse, so that there are no misunderstandings, and is essential when loaning. You or the horse's owner may even want to have an agreement drawn up by a solicitor, but if so, choose one with specialist equestrian knowledge. Some essential points to consider in a loan agreement are:

*It takes time to build a partnership as great as that between endurance rider Linda Hams and Perfeq Hidden Challenge.*

- How long is the arrangement for and how much notice should be given on either side to terminate it? The usual system is to agree an initial period and extend it if it is successful so that it is renewable annually. Specify the notice that should be given on either side to terminate the agreement but expect the owner to insist on being able to terminate it without notice if he or she is unhappy at the way the horse is kept.
- What are the owner's access rights? Most people will want to visit by appointment – and also without notice.
- Where is the horse to be kept? Responsible owners will want to inspect or at least be consulted on suitable accommodation. Some animals will be offered for loan on condition that they stay at their current yard.
- Are there any restrictions on how the horse is kept and what he can be used for? For instance, does he need a particular sort of bedding or an expensive form of shoeing? Can you use him for all activities or are certain ones prohibited?
- Who pays for what? As well as the day to day running costs, which are usually down to the borrower, there are issues such as insurance premiums and repair and replacement of tack and rugs.
- Is it purely a loan agreement, or a loan with a view to you buying the horse? If the latter, agree a purchase price now to avoid possible misunderstandings or unpleasantness later.

## LOANING FROM A CHARITY

One of the most satisfying ways of taking a horse or pony on loan is through a registered charity. The best-known in the UK are probably the International League for the Protection of Horses (ILPH) and the Blue Cross. The animals they take in and, where possible, re-home arrive at the centres for a variety of reasons. Many are the victims of ignorance or cruelty and arrive with physical and/or mental problems, from which they undergo an often lengthy period of rehabilitation. Others are left to the charities in their owners' wills – but they, too, are thoroughly assessed before entering the loan schemes.

These charities need to ensure that the horses in their care find suitable, preferably long-term homes, whether they are loaned as pleasure/competition animals or companions. The emphasis is on caring, not on sentiment, and the horses' welfare comes first. They are never sold and potential borrowers must expect to undergo a friendly but thorough assessment of their knowledge and ability and to pay a loaning fee to cover administration. Accommodation must be approved and inspectors make unannounced visits to check the horse's welfare.

*Taking a horse on loan from a registered charity, such as this one being rehabilitated by the ILPH, can be incredibly rewarding.*

## WHERE TO BUY

THERE ARE THREE WAYS to buy a horse – from a professional seller (dealer), from a private seller or at auction. There is also one important piece of advice to keep in mind: *caveat emptor*, or 'buyer beware'. Buying a horse is fraught with pitfalls, not least because you are buying a creature with a mind of his own.

Buying from a reputable dealer is often the safest avenue for a first-time buyer, not least because, in Britain, you have the greatest protection under the Sale of Goods Act 1979 if things go wrong. As dealers by definition make a living out of buying and selling horses, you are unlikely to find a bargain, but you should find a suitable horse at a fair price. Although there is no legal definition of a dealer, it is generally accepted that anyone who sells horses regularly with the intention of making a profit is selling professionally.

Good dealers rely on their reputation and are upfront about their businesses. Amateurs who dabble in buying and selling and masquerade as private sellers are not, and Trading Standards officers have brought successful prosecutions against such individuals. Dealers worth their salt know how to assess horses and riders and will want you to be so happy with your horse that you enthuse about them to your friends. Another advantage is that if you don't get on with your purchase, many

will exchange him for another within a certain period. However, if you have any doubts, don't buy: it isn't fair on the horse and it will involve you in unnecessary expense and frustration.

Buying from a private seller also has its advantages and potential pitfalls. If you're lucky, you'll find a nice horse who is for sale for a genuine reason and the owner will be as concerned about the home he goes to as the price he achieves. If you're unwary, or unlucky, you'll be offered someone else's problem. Buying privately does not offer the same protection under the Sale of Goods Act and you may also find that private sellers are not as knowledgeable about market prices. This *may* work in your favour, but in all probability private sellers are more likely to exaggerate the ability and perceived value of their horses.

Buying at auction is not usually an option for the inexperienced UK buyer, though it is standard practice in Continental Europe. It is the accepted way of selling racehorses and there are prestigious sales for high-value performance horses – but as you're unlikely to be paying £30,000 or more for a potential star, the latter are wonderful to visit but not really a practical proposition! There are many other sales and markets, but the lack of trial facilities and the need to understand and translate warranties and catalogue descriptions puts them in the province of experienced buyers only.

Whatever approach you take, never consider buying a horse without seeing him – preferably twice – trying him and arranging a pre-purchase veterinary examination. The growth of internet sites, many with video footage, has tempted some buyers to 'click and buy', often with disastrous results. Cases where horses have turned out to be the wrong age, unsound and unsuitable have resulted in unscrupulous sellers being prosecuted, but this does not necessarily compensate buyers either financially or emotionally.

## LEGAL IMPLICATIONS OF PURCHASE

IN LAW, horses are regarded as goods and chattels and the sale of a horse will be treated in the same way as the sale of a washing machine or car. No allowance is made for the fact that horses are living beings with minds of their own. Although all purchases are covered by the Sale of Goods Act, this gives very limited protection to a purchase made by one private individual from another. Whilst everyone hopes that nothing will go wrong when you buy a horse, litigation has become part of modern life – so you may want to take the various pros and cons into account.

If you buy a horse from someone who sells horses as a business, your protection is much greater, as there is an implied term that the horse has to be of merchantable quality and fit for the purpose. This does not apply to private sales. Good dealers are open about the fact that they are in the business of buying and selling horses. However, even limited selling may be regarded as a business – so whilst people who sell three or four horses a year may maintain and even believe that they are private sellers, a court may decide differently. Many publications and websites now state that they consider anyone who sells more than three or four horses a year to be a business seller.

Similarly, a riding school which regularly sells horses and ponies, or a breeder who breeds animals specifically for sale, is likely to be regarded as a business seller. Someone who takes a horse to sell on the owner's behalf is acting as an agent and should be open about the fact: adverts will often include a phrase such as 'sold on behalf of a client'. A sale conducted through an agent will usually be regarded as a business sale.

One of the main considerations about an agency sale is whether negotiations are entered into between the buyer and the agent, or whether the agent simply introduces the buyer to the seller. In the first case, legal recourse might be against both agent and owner/seller, but in the second, it may be purely against the owner/seller.

You do not necessarily need to be suspicious of the fact that a horse is being sold through an agent. Some people do not have the time or the facilities to sell a horse and may feel that a professional seller who is used to assessing horses and dealing with potential buyers may do a better job in getting the right home and the right price.

Buying horses has become much more litigious in recent years. Whilst it is possible that there will be misunderstandings as you establish a relationship with a new horse, a responsible seller – whether professional or private – will try to help. If you do your homework properly, the chances of things going wrong are minimized, but if you feel that the seller has misrepresented the horse, act quickly. If a phone call doesn't sort things out, get advice from your local Trading Standards office or a solicitor with specialist equestrian knowledge.

## PERFECT PARTNERS

YOU SHOULD APPROACH finding a horse with as much care as finding a partner – because in both cases, you have to live with each other. Before you even start looking, try to work out a blueprint of your ideal horse in terms of height, age, type and experience. Whilst you need to be flexible – because the perfect horse simply doesn't exist and you will always have to compromise on some things – you need to keep these guidelines in mind so you don't find yourself riveted by adverts for big four-year-old top-class dressage prospects when what you're really looking for is a modest-sized all-rounder who's been there, done it and got the T-shirt.

### HEIGHT AND TYPE

Over the past 20 years, bigger horses have become more fashionable: horses of 170 cm (16.3 hh) plus are commonplace, especially in the dressage world. But bigger doesn't necessarily mean better, especially for a first horse. Very few adults need a horse taller than 168 cm (16.2 hh) and most first-time buyers will be best suited by one between 153 and 162 cm (15–16 hh). Riders of modest physique should also consider one of the larger Mountain and Moorland breeds, such as a Connemara or Welsh Section D; native ponies are sound, relatively cheap to keep and highly versatile.

The animal's weight-carrying ability and conformation are often more important than his actual height. A smaller horse who is deep through the girth, broad enough through the chest and with correctly made limbs will carry a longer-legged and/or heavier rider than a taller animal with a shallow body, narrower chest and less correct limbs. For instance, a good 155 cm (15.1 hh) heavyweight cob should carry a rider of 89 kg (14 st).

## AGE

It used to be said that the perfect age for an all-round riding horse was between 5 and 8 years old, as these parameters should ensure that he had enough basic experience but still had many working years left. Although many people will still look on this as the ideal range, it would be a mistake to limit yourself in this way. Older horses and ponies have lots to offer the first-time owner and there are many who, thanks to advances in veterinary science and nutrition, continue to show younger animals the way in their teens and twenties.

Young horses and novice riders are not usually a good combination, though one school of thought says that a sensible young horse with a correct basic education can make a good partner for a first-time owner who is a reasonably competent rider and has plenty of back-up. The reasoning behind this argument is that the horse will not have developed bad habits or behavioural problems – but against that, things can go wrong very quickly and a willing 4-year-old can soon become a bewildered and unhappy one. In general, the best age range for a first horse usually proves to be between 7 and 13. Ponies usually have longer working lives than horses and it isn't unusual for a pony to be going strong in his twenties, having helped to teach several generations of children to ride.

Once an 'ordinary' horse gets past the age of 10, his value may start to drop. Those who are well schooled and perhaps have good competition records will hold their value, as they are much in demand as schoolmasters. When you're starting out, particularly in competition, there is a great deal to be said for having a horse who knows more about the job than you do.

The other factor to consider is that buying a horse in his teens brings with it the responsibility of safeguarding his welfare in his later years. If you buy a nice all-round 12-year-old and decide in three years time that you need a horse who can progress to a higher level of work or competition, you have to accept that his market value may have dropped and it may be more difficult to find him a new home. Inevitably, too, there comes a time when a horse reaches the end of his working life and if it is inappropriate or impossible to retire him, his owner has to make the final decision to have him put down (see Euthanasia in Chapter 10).

Native ponies such as this Connemara can make great mounts for many adult riders, being versatile and hardy.

This show cob performs equally well side-saddle and astride.

## GENDER

The horse world is full of wonderful sayings; one of them is that 'you ask a mare, tell a gelding and discuss it with a stallion!' It's worth bearing that in mind when considering whether you want a gelding or a mare, or would be happy to consider either. Stallions are not an option for novice owners – or, come to that, for many others.

Although all horses are individuals, geldings are usually less complicated to keep because they are not affected by the drive to reproduce. Whilst there are many wonderful mares, some are not as easy to ride and handle when they are in season – they may, for instance, be less attentive and/or find the pressure of the rider's legs uncomfortable. It isn't a fault, just a fact of life. However, some riders enjoy working with mares.

## EXPERT VIEWS

*'You have to remember that whilst a gelding is a castrated male, a mare – like a stallion – has had nothing taken away. A good mare can be brilliant, but the majority of riders want geldings'.*

LYNN RUSSELL, SHOW PRODUCER AND DEALER.

*'There's a lot of narrow-mindedness in the horse world when it comes to mares generally. If you see a horse and like it, don't be put off just because it's a mare'.*

LUCINDA FREDERICKS, WINNER OF BURGHLEY AND BADMINTON HORSE TRIALS ON THE MARE HEADLEY BRITANNIA.

## TEMPERAMENT AND MANNERS

When professional riders talk about the need for a horse to have a good temperament, they mean that he must be trainable – he must want to work and will thrive on the demands of competition. Whilst they enjoy the bonus of a horse who has a pleasant disposition, they won't necessarily mind if he doesn't enjoy attention, is grumpy in the stable, or even bites or kicks. But for most everyday riders, looking after a horse is part of the pleasure of owning him and it is therefore important that he is safe to handle. Safety is vital in the case of a child's pony or a horse kept in an environment where children are around.

Horses, like people, have different characters and personalities. Some of this may be shaped by nature; for instance, Thoroughbreds tend to be highly reactive because they are bred for speed.

*Many riders are prejudiced against mares – but it's better to be open-minded and assess each one as an individual. Event rider Lucinda Fredericks and the brilliant mare Headley Britannia are real adverts for girl power.*

Certainly 'nurture' also has a lot to do with it: a horse who has been poorly educated or unfairly treated may have become grumpy because he is confused and defensive. You may also find that a horse's temperament changes as he becomes more settled in a new home. One who has been kept on a large yard and given little individual attention may blossom when in a one to one relationship; on the other hand, a horse who doesn't really want a lot of fussing and stroking and has switched off through being forced to tolerate it will often relax and be much happier when given his 'own space' and allowed to indicate when he would like attention.

However, it's important to be honest about your own personality and whether or not you can adapt to a horse's, or whether you need a certain type. If you're going to be upset because a horse isn't the touchy feely type, don't buy him.

Horses and ponies for first-time buyers should be as problem-free as possible, though – despite what is said in some adverts – no horse is 'bombproof'. However, they should be safe to hack in traffic and to ride in open spaces, both alone and in company, and good to handle, shoe, catch, load and travel. Only you can decide what you can put up with and what is unacceptable, and different buyers may have different criteria: for instance, some owners may not mind if a horse is difficult to clip. There will also be instances when you have to rely on a seller's assurances and keep your fingers crossed.

## STEREOTYPIC BEHAVIOUR

Another issue you may have to consider is whether you are prepared to take on a horse who shows stereotypic behaviour, the modern and much fairer term for what used to be called stable vices. These are patterns of repetitive behaviour that are generally agreed to be related to stress, especially that caused by being stabled for long periods – though there may also be a genetic element. There are three declarable forms, which must be stated under most auction conditions of sale – weaving, crib-biting and wind-sucking. Owners selling directly rather than at auction should declare any form of stereotypic behaviour and buyers should ask for a written guarantee that the horse has never demonstrated them.

All vary in degree from mild to severe. A weaver may move his head from side to side over the stable door or, at the worst end of the scale, move his whole body and transfer weight from one front leg to another, putting strain on his joints. Crib-biters seize hold of a solid surface, usually a door or fence post, and bite down on it. This is often accompanied by wind-sucking, when the horse takes in gulps of air; occasionally, a horse will wind-suck without crib-biting. The last two forms of behaviour may predispose a horse to certain types of colic.

There are ways of reducing or even eliminating stereotypic behaviour through good management, but if a horse has been known to demonstrate it, it must be declared when he is sold (see above) and unless he is an absolute superstar, it will reduce his value. This means that if you can put up with it, you may get a cheaper horse. On the other hand, it will usually make him more difficult to sell if you eventually decide that it would be best for both of you to move on to a new partner. There may also be some livery yards unwilling to accommodate such horses; crib-biters can cause a lot of damage to stables and fencing and some people think that horses copy such behaviour. (It has been shown that a horse will only copy stereotypic behaviour if he is already predisposed towards it – but

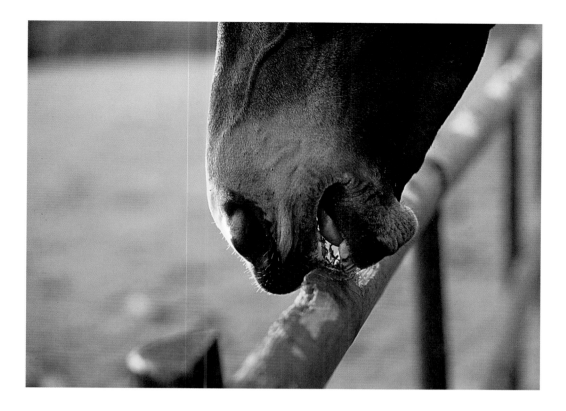

*Crib-biting, where the horse bites on a convenient surface such as a fence rail, is a form of stereotypic behaviour that some buyers would find unacceptable.*

that won't make you popular if your horse's neighbour suddenly decides that weaving or crib-biting looks like a good way to pass the time!)

Another habit that can cause problems, but which is not regarded as notifiable to a buyer, is box-walking. As the name suggests, this is when a horse walks round and round his stable; apart from increasing wear on his shoes and potentially putting extra strain on his joints, it may mean it is harder to keep weight on him. A lesser consideration is that bedding will be permanently dirty.

The basic answer to most stereotypic problems is to keep the horse living out all the time, though not everyone can manage this. Horses do not weave in the field, though some may crib-bite on fence posts and rails.

## FINDING PONIES

Safe ponies for children are worth their weight in gold and many are sold or loaned through word of mouth when their riders outgrow them. Local Pony Club branches are a great network and your child's riding teacher may know of possibilities. Riding schools sometimes sell ponies into private homes; sometimes this works, but sometimes ponies who are brilliant when they lead busy lives are less reliable when their working regimes are reduced.

Unless you are buying a competition pony for an experienced child, which is a totally different ballgame, considerations such as looks and in some cases, age, are not high priorities. What matters is that the pony should be safe for a child to handle under supervision and should give confidence to his rider.

Children grow at an alarming rate and it may seem tempting to buy a pony bigger than your child needs so that he or she will 'grow into' him. Unfortunately, this may result in the child being unable to ride him effectively or even safely. It's far better to buy a pony who is of suitable size now and accept that, in a year or two, you may have to find him a home with a new family and look for the next model up – unless, of course, there is a younger sibling in the background longing to take over.

## QUESTION TIME

Asking the right questions, and giving realistic answers to anything you are asked, can help ensure that you do not waste your or the seller's time. Essentials to consider include:

● Does the horse belong to the seller, or is he being sold on an owner's behalf?

● Does he have a passport? It is now illegal in the UK to sell a horse without one.

● If breeding is mentioned, is the horse registered with the relevant breed society? This can make a big difference to value and in some cases, competition prospects. For instance, mountain and moorland ponies have to be registered with their relevant breed societies to compete in showing classes at anything above local level.

● Is the horse's age verified by documentation, such as breeding papers? Ageing by dentition is traditionally not as reliable after the horse has reached 8 years old and vets say it may also be unreliable with younger animals. Whilst still a useful guide, documentation is better.

● Has the seller measured him, using a proper measuring stick with the animal standing on level ground, or relied on guesswork when quoting a height? If it's guesswork, some people are better at guessing than others and you may find that what is described as a 153 cm (15 hh) horse is actually a 148 cm (14.2 hh) pony.

If height is an essential consideration for competition – when just a millimetre can mean a horse or pony is ineligible for a class – has the animal got a height certificate? Ridden animals between 4 and 6 years old need annual height certificates and a life height certificate will be given at 7 years. However, there has been such controversy over animals said to be over height, even though in possession of life height certificates, that some disciplines carry out re-measurements in some circumstances.

● Make sure that the seller reiterates important points even if they are stated in the advert, and if necessary ask for elaboration. For instance, if the horse is described as good in traffic or good to hack, check whether he will hack alone as well as with other horses and if he is at all worried by large vehicles or busy roads.

If the advert states that a horse is 'good in all respects' you still need to go through every area that is important to you.

● Is the horse shod and is he good to shoe? Some owners prefer to keep their horses barefoot, but this doesn't work for everyone. If the horse is barefoot, could it be because he is difficult with the farrier, which could be a big problem if you intend to have him shod?

● Has he ever demonstrated stereotypic behaviour? Most sellers will declare this, but if someone tells you that a horse might weave for the first few days in a new home but will

## SPEAKING THE SALES LINGO

Once you have an idea of the sort of horse or pony that should suit you, you can start reading the adverts seriously. Magazines such as *Horse and Hound*, websites, local publications and notice boards in saddlery shops, feed merchants and show centres should throw up some possibilities. Whilst you may be lucky and find the ideal animal on your doorstep, don't limit yourself too strictly. Although travelling is expensive in terms of time and fuel costs, asking the right questions and making sure that you see photographs and hopefully a video or CD of a horse in action should ensure you don't waste your time.

Every horse will be described in glowing terms, ranging from 'attractive' or 'good looking' to 'stunning'. This is where it's essential to see at least a good photograph, as it will enable you to differentiate between optimism and reality – and many advertisers include pictures with their

then stop, you are unlikely to have any legal comeback if your purchase weaves on day one and is still doing it six weeks later. (Having said that, some horses *do* weave or box-walk for a few days in a new home and then stop when they settle down. If you find yourself in this situation, inform the seller immediately and negotiate whether to return the horse immediately or wait for an agreed time to see whether he settles.)

- If you are buying a horse with a competition record at affiliated level, make sure you know his registered name. You can then check this with the relevant governing body. If he has competed at unaffiliated level, you are relying on a seller's honesty – though genuine sellers will show you photographs, dressage sheets, videos, etc. If you are considering buying a horse or pony who has competed locally, you may find that the seller will be able to supply references from Riding Club or Pony Club branch officials.

- How long has the seller owned the horse? This is more relevant to private sales, as many dealers bring in horses from other countries and produce them for a relatively short time before offering them for sale. However, if someone has only owned a horse for a few months, there has to be a good reason why he is being sold on so quickly.

- Why is he for sale? Most genuine sellers won't mind you asking and there are lots of genuine reasons. A pony may be outgrown, or new work or family commitments may mean an owner no longer has enough time. Very few people will say, 'He's a nappy little so and so and I'm fed up with him', or 'I'm frightened of riding him' – but if this is the case, the truth will come to light if you ask the right questions and/or watch the owner ride the horse.

- Has the horse had any veterinary problems whilst in his present ownership? In theory, certain types of medication should have been noted on the horse's passport, but you can't always rely on this. Ask all sellers if the horse is open to a pre-purchase veterinary examination and ask private sellers if they would give you permission to ask their vet about the horse's medical history. Anyone who turns down these requests probably has something to hide.

- Tell the seller exactly what you want to do with a new horse. Be realistic: don't say you want to compete at affiliated level if you know you won't want to do anything other than local shows. Be honest about your experience in riding and handling horses – which will become evident when you go to look at likely candidates – and explain the sort of environment in which your horse will live. Ask if the seller thinks this horse will suit your requirements and if you could give him a suitable home.

adverts. Having said that, there are definitely cases where handsome is as handsome does. If you're buying a first horse, you will want to make sure that his conformation doesn't mean that he is less likely to stay sound or be a comfortable ride, but it probably won't matter that he wouldn't make a county level show horse.

You need to read between the lines as well as what is actually stated. For instance, if a horse is described as 'good to hack in light traffic' it may mean that he has never seen anything else – or it could mean that he goes ballistic when anything other than the occasional car goes past. And if he's good to catch, clip and box, is he a nightmare to shoe, or has the owner not thought to include that quality?

## ABBREVIATIONS

When you're studying the adverts, you'll see many abbreviations.
Some of the commonest are:

| | |
|---|---|
| AA – Anglo-Arab | PB – part-bred, e.g. part-bred Arab |
| AHC – annual height certificate | PC – Pony Club |
| BD, BE, BSJA winnings – British Dressage, British Eventing, British Show Jumping Association winnings | RC – Riding Club |
| | SJ – show jumping |
| | SS – side-saddle |
| CB – Cleveland Bay | TB – Thoroughbred |
| HT – hunter trials | TBx – Thoroughbred cross |
| HW/HWT – heavyweight | TC – team chase |
| LHC – life height certificate | WB – Warmblood |
| LW/LWT – lightweight | WH – working hunter |
| MW/MWT – middleweight | WHP – working hunter pony |
| MM – mountain and moorland | XC – cross-country |

**TRYING HORSES**

NOW COMES the exciting bit – assessing and trying potential purchases. Don't be surprised if the prospect suddenly seems nerve racking, but try to give yourself confidence by reminding yourself that you've ridden different horses and have asked the right questions before arranging to look at animals for sale. Don't be tempted to try horses you know are out of your price range and/or beyond your capability: joy riding isn't fair to the horse or his owner and you could end up overhorsed and on the ground.

A novice buyer should take an adviser; this should be someone knowledgeable and with wide experience of assessing horses, such as an instructor who knows you and your capability. Unless you have a generous, experienced friend, expect to pay for your adviser's time. To keep costs down, you may want to make a first visit alone and bring in your helper for a second look if you think the horse is the one for you – but don't get pushed into making an immediate decision by a seller who tells you that someone else is coming that day. That may or may not be true, but it's better to lose a particular horse to another buyer than be pushed into making an unwise purchase.

Your adviser may suggest that you take someone with you to take photographs or a video of the horse. It's courteous to ask if the seller would be happy with this. If you're not taking an adviser on your first visit, do take a friend or partner for moral support and to listen to what's said – as long as he or she doesn't try to sound knowledgeable when this isn't the case. Adult buyers looking for a mount for themselves should leave their children at home: you can't expect someone else to keep an eye on them whilst you're looking at and trying a horse, and stables are not safe environments for unsupervised children.

Make sure you fix a definite time to see the horse and get the full address of the stables. When directions turn out to be vague, you can waste a lot of time. Get the phone number of the yard and/or the owner's mobile phone number and give them your contact numbers. This means that if you do get lost or held up, you can ring ahead and if there is a problem with the horse or someone gets there before you and offers to buy him, the seller can let you know. For safety's sake, take a fluorescent, reflective tabard so that if you like the horse enough to ride him on the roads you know you will be seen by drivers.

## ASSESSMENT FROM THE GROUND

Most people will present a horse in his stable, unless he lives out all the time. If he's in the field, you can see what he's like to catch – but, if possible, you need to see him in his usual stable to see how he reacts. First impressions are valuable but not always cut and dried; a relaxed horse can look unprepossessing but change dramatically when more alert. What you don't want to see if you're looking at a first purchase is a horse who seems nervous or grumpy when you approach.

If the owner doesn't have the horse's passport ready, ask if you can see it. Your vet will check identifying marks as part of the vetting procedure, but you need to check if there are any glaring discrepancies that mean the passport does not belong to this particular horse. It should also enable you to check the horse's age; breeding details (if the passport is issued by a breed society) previous owners and medical history from the date the passport was issued.

It is important to check whether the horse is freeze-marked. This is a system of security marking and a horse so marked will have a unique set of letters and numbers, either in the saddle area or on the shoulder. On dark-coloured horses, white hairs will have grown through on the marked areas, making them easy to read. This obviously doesn't work on greys and with horses of this colour the hair follicles are 'killed off' so the marks show as bare skin. These horses are marked on the shoulder so that there is no saddle pressure on bare skin and the area needs to be kept clipped in winter to keep the mark clear – so check that a grey with a thick coat doesn't have a concealed freeze mark.

A horse who is freeze-marked with the letter L in a circle has been subject to a loss of use claim and the seller should have told you about this beforehand. It does not necessarily mean that the horse will not be suitable for your purpose, but a seller who has 'forgotten' to tell you about it is not being straight – would you really want to buy a horse from that person?

*Check whether a horse is freeze-marked, a form of security marking that can also show you whether he has been the subject of an insurance loss of use claim.*

Microchipping is another security measure, but there is no visible outward sign. If you are told that a horse is microchipped, your vet will need to check the reading with a special scanner, though this should be done as a routine part of the pre-purchase examination.

When you walk into the stable, the seller will probably put on the horse's headcollar. You can then spend a minute or two letting him get used to your presence and see if anything strikes you immediately about his attitude and conformation. Be polite – don't just march up to him and ask him to pick up a front leg; run your hand down his shoulder to the fetlock so that you warn him what you are going to do. Be equally careful and considerate when picking up his hind feet. As you assess his manners and how easy he is to handle, notice whether his feet are in good condition or crumbling around the nail holes.

Being able to assess a horse's make or shape, often called 'having an eye for a horse' only comes with experience and even then, some people are better than others. Leave the finer points to your adviser and the vet who carries out the pre-purchase veterinary examination, but think about the following:

- Does the horse look as if all his component parts go together, or as if he's been put together from two different kits? For instance, does his back end match his front end, or does it look weaker? Do his legs match his body, or does he have a stocky body on spindly legs?
- Do his feet look as though they are in proportion to his limbs? You don't want to see soup-plates on a finely built horse or pony feet on a heavy cob. It takes an experienced eye to spot the difference between really bad feet and feet that are simply in need of a good farrier, but do have a look.
- Do his front feet make a matching pair and the hind feet another, or is one foot bigger than its partner? Normal front feet have rounded toes and normal hind feet are more oval at the toe.
- From the front, is his chest wide enough or do both front legs 'come out of the same hole?' Does he stand with his toes turned in or out?
- From behind, do his hocks turn inwards like a cow's? Cow hocks are weak hocks.
- Is there any obvious swelling down the back of his legs, perhaps from an old tendon injury?
- When he stands square, are his fetlocks very close together? This makes him likely to brush (knock one leg against the other).
- When he is on level ground, is he slightly higher at the withers than the hindquarters (or at least at the same height)? An adult horse who has finished growing and is still higher behind and therefore 'built downhill' will naturally tend to go on his forehand.

### LUMPS AND BUMPS

Whilst it is wonderful to have a horse with clean limbs – no lumps, bumps or blemishes – a horse who has led an active working life may have acquired the occasional one. Many are only of significance if you want to show the horse, but your vet will advise you. The most common blemishes are:

*SPLINTS:* bony growths between the splint and cannon bones, more commonly found on the front legs and usually caused by wear and tear or a blow. Once formed, they rarely cause problems unless they are high up and interfere with a joint.

*CURBS:* swellings below the point of the hock. They are unsightly, but rarely linked to unsoundness unless the hind leg is weak.

*CAPPED HOCKS OR ELBOWS:* swellings that are usually caused by the horse scraping the area on a hard floor or kicking the wall of a stable or horsebox. Again, they are unsightly but not an unsoundness.

*BOG SPAVINS:* fillings of the natural depressions of the hocks. Blemishes, but not usually an unsoundness. (They are not to be confused with bone spavins, which are an unsoundness and usually show only on X-ray.)

*THOROUGHPINS:* swellings above the hock joint. Not usually a soundness problem if the hock conformation is good.

*WINDGALLS:* soft, painless swellings near the fetlock. Cosmetic blemishes that don't usually cause problems.

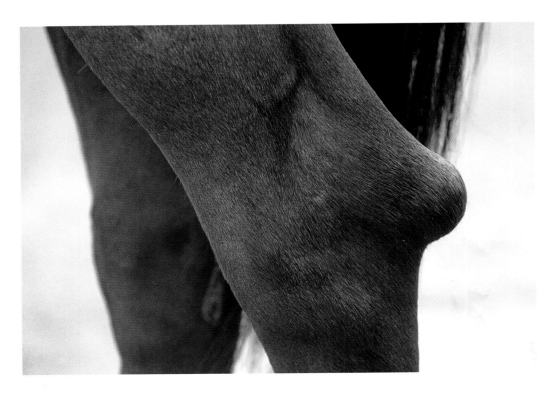

*A badly capped hock; this is usually a blemish rather than an unsoundness and many examples will not be as marked.*

## MOVEMENT

It's always lovely to see a horse who is a straight, free mover, but there are plenty of good horses whose movement deviates slightly from the ideal, even in top-level competition. The commonest faults are dishing, brushing and forging. Dishing is when the horse throws out one or both front feet; brushing is when he knocks one leg against its partner and a horse who forges hits the back of a front shoe with the toe of a hind shoe.

If the problem is marked, it may lead to soundness problems, but mild deviations could be acceptable; for instance, the horse who turns a toe out isn't usually a risk, but if he swings a front leg out from the shoulder, the resulting strain is much greater. Again, your vet will advise you. A problem in an unbalanced or weak horse may improve as he strengthens up and learns to carry himself, but poor movement caused by conformation faults will always remain.

Movement also affects whether or not the horse is a comfortable ride. One with a straight shoulder and up and down action will have a trot like a sewing machine, whilst a horse with a sloping shoulder and pasterns will be smoother and more comfortable. To assess a horse's movement, you need to see him led towards, past and away from you in a straight line, on a loose lead rope, first in walk and then in trot.

*'I love to see a horse who comes out of his stable looking as if he's going somewhere, as if he's looking forward to his work.'*

PIPPA FUNNELL, WINNER OF EVENTING'S ROLEX GRAND SLAM

### MOVING DESCRIPTIONS

Adverts will sometimes describe horses as having 'uphill', 'extravagant' or 'big' movement, particularly if they are being sold as dressage or show animals. Another favourite phrase in the dressage world is 'off the floor paces'. Whilst such horses may look spectacular, they aren't always easy to ride; a big mover demands a balanced, supple rider who can absorb the movement without restricting it or losing balance.

### IN THE SADDLE

If you like what you see on the ground, the next stage is to ask the seller to ride the horse to (hopefully) demonstrate how obedient and well-schooled he is. If you've already decided that this horse is not for you, don't take things any further, as it isn't fair to the horse or the seller. It's essential that you see a horse ridden before trying him yourself, as if he does have any nasty habits that the seller has forgotten to tell you about, you don't want to find out the hard way. It also gives you the chance to see whether he looks to be lazy, responsive or forward-going. Again, if you realize that the horse is too forward-going for you and you know that you would not be happy riding him, say so rather than getting into a situation that could upset everyone, including the horse.

Watch whilst the horse is being tacked up. Does he accept the bridle easily, or throw up his head? When the saddle is put on and the girth fastened, does he remain calm, or does he lay back his ears and threaten to kick or bite? Threatening behaviour may mean he has been inconsiderately handled, but it could also mean that he is uncomfortable because of a badly fitting saddle.

Notice what sort of tack is being used and how it is adjusted (see Chapter 4). A horse suitable for a first-time owner should go nicely in some kind of simple snaffle. If the horse is presented in a potentially more severe bit, or a noseband which fastens both above and below the bit is done up very tightly, beware.

Professional sellers are used to showing off horses and should demonstrate all three gaits on both reins without being asked. It's worth asking if the horse has already been ridden that day, but you have to take the answer on trust. Private sellers may be less confident about riding in front of prospective purchasers, but be wary of anyone who makes excuses not to give a reasonable demonstration. If you want to jump, ask to see the horse in action over fences – a small course is ideal, but not everyone has that facility. Some yards may even have a cross-country course, but although this is useful in building up your impression, remember that the horse will be used to the fences and confident in jumping them. By default, any stops or run-outs should sound a warning bell!

## All mod cons

Whilst great facilities such as an outdoor or indoor school and a course of smart show jumps make it easier to try a horse, don't be put off if things are more basic. A horse who will go nicely on the flat in the corner of a field should work even better in competition surroundings – and homemade jumps are just as good as designer ones so long as they are safe in design and construction.

When you ride the horse, give yourself time to adjust to him and for him to adjust to you. Make sure your stirrup leathers are the correct length – does he stand whilst you adjust them and check the girth, or fidget? Start in walk and ask for changes of direction and transitions to and from halt, only going forward to trot and eventually canter when you feel comfortable.

Novice buyers often feel they should ask the horse to perform to the same level as that demonstrated by the seller, but don't feel pressurized. The seller knows the horse and is probably more experienced than you; just because he can jump a 1 m (3 ft 3 in) course, it doesn't mean you have to. By all means ask questions of the horse, but stay within your safety zone. Ask yourself: if I got to know this horse better, would I feel confident to try different or more challenging things? If the answer is 'yes', that's a good sign.

If you want a horse to hack out on, it's essential to try him on the roads – but only do this if you felt confident and happy in the school or schooling area. Don't expect to be allowed to ride off into the sunset on your own: for a start, you may not know the area and in any case, would you let a complete stranger go off on your horse? The seller should be able to accompany you or arrange for someone else to do so and hopefully you will be able to see how the horse reacts to traffic and other hazards. If you get the chance to have a short canter on suitable going, so much the better.

Assuming that you are escorted by another rider, make sure that you ride the horse behind, in front and, if or when it is safe to do so, alongside your escort. At least one and preferably both of you should wear fluorescent, reflective clothing such as a tabard so that you are more visible to other road users. As mentioned earlier, it's a good idea to take one with you when you go to try a horse and don't feel embarrassed about wearing it if the other rider doesn't bother – you're the one with the brains! As you ride, try to assess the following:

- Is the horse happy to change places, or does he hang back when in front?
- Does he seem relaxed in the company of another horse?
- Does he spook at anything?
- Is it obvious when you've turned for home? Some horses will immediately become more forward-going, which isn't a problem unless they start jogging or pulling.
- When the yard is in sight, make sure that you are in front and warn your escort that you are going to ask the horse to walk past the entrance. He might seem a little puzzled, but should respond without napping when you ask him to go forward.

## PROCEEDING TO PURCHASE

No matter how much you like a horse, it isn't a good idea to commit to buying him after one visit. A lot of sellers will try to persuade you to do so, but explain that you want to be sure that this is the one for you so that you have the best chance of establishing a long-term partnership. You can't expect to 'reserve' a horse without paying a deposit, but it's better to take that chance than be rushed into buying a horse you're not sure about. Genuine sellers will appreciate that, and also the fact that a novice buyer will want to get expert advice. If, on the way home, you find yourself becoming less and less enthusiastic about the horse, he isn't the one for you and it's courteous to let the seller know immediately.

But if you liked the horse, enjoyed riding him and felt that you would be happy to see him looking over your stable door every morning, arrange to return as soon as possible – preferably the next day. Your adviser will want to run through the same trial process, see you ride the horse and probably also sit on him briefly to assess the horse's responsiveness, stage of schooling and suitability for you. Second time round, you should be more confident, so you might be able to ask a little bit more of the horse. You should also ask the seller to let you tack him up and untack him.

In most cases, a second visit will be enough to tell you whether or not you want to buy a horse. Some sellers will want to be just as sure that their horse is going to the right person and may encourage you to return and spend more time handling and riding him; if so, take advantage of the offer. For professional sellers, however, time is money; they may also have other potential buyers who are prepared to make a quicker decision.

### TRIALS AND TRIBULATIONS

You may be offered the chance to have a horse or pony on trial for a short period to see if you suit each other – though don't expect it or be annoyed if the seller refuses. Put yourself in the seller's position: would you let a novice rider take your horse away to some environment where you weren't around to supervise the handling or riding? Trial periods are much more commonly offered for children's first ponies but, again, a stranger is unlikely to trust you with a well-schooled competition pony. If the horse or pony is local to you, you may be able to negotiate a trial period of a week or a fortnight during which the animal stays at his current yard and the owner is able to keep an eye on you.

If a trial period is negotiated during which the horse is moved to your yard, it's sensible to draw up a written agreement covering duration, price agreed, how the horse is to be kept and what happens if he is stolen, injured or – in a worst case scenario – has to be put down. Some owners will already have their horses insured against these eventualities, but if not, you need to arrange cover yourself (see later in this chapter.)

Once you have decided to buy a horse, expect to be asked to pay a deposit. This will usually be refundable only if the horse 'fails' a pre-purchase vetting and there should be a written agreement stating this. In theory, horses do not pass or fail vettings but are found suitable or unsuitable for a particular purpose; however, vets themselves still use these terms and they are generally accepted. Professional sellers may have their own terms and conditions of sale and these must be read carefully; for instance, some dealers will offer to take back a horse who proves unsuitable within a certain time and exchange/part exchange him for one of equal or higher value. This does not mean that you will get your money back – and for some reason, it often seems that exchange horses are always worth more than the original purchases!

You also need to arrange a vetting and to think about insurance. Not having a horse vetted is a false economy, even if you are buying a child's pony worth only a few hundred pounds. Only a vet will be able to tell you if, for instance, an animal has a sight defect, which would jeopardize your or your child's safety and certainly lead to heartbreak. When a private seller has owned a horse for a year or more, you may want to ask permission to speak to their vet about his medical history.

If you are buying locally, your instructor or horse-owning friends will suggest a suitable equine vet. If you are travelling further afield, your own vet or the vet you intend to use when you have found a horse may be able to suggest someone in that area, and dealers will know of vets in their area and may recommend names to you, but it's up to you who you use. In general, most vets are reluctant to examine horses for purchase that belong to their own clients, as there may be a conflict of interest. If they do agree to advise you, their examination should include disclosure of any pre-existing knowledge about the horse.

## THE VETTING PROCESS

There are various standard vetting procedures, those used in the UK being mainly the two-stage and five-stage versions. The five-stage is more thorough and complete and includes a period of strenuous exercise and a re-examination after rest; as such, it is recommended for all horses in full work. The two-stage is really only appropriate for unbroken horses who cannot undergo the strenuous exercise and for some children's ponies – for instance, those who will only be asked to walk and trot on a lead rein.

The examining vet considers the horse's suitability for a particular purpose, so it is important to brief him or her accurately on what you intend to do. This is because there may be considerations that would preclude a horse from one job, but would not be considered to prejudice his use for another.

Ideally, you should be there when the horse is vetted. The vet will explain any findings and their implications at the end of the procedure, unless something is discovered that means it is not worth going on. If you can't be present, you will be able to discuss findings with the vet on the phone. In either case, you will be sent a standard form detailing the horse's description and age and what the vet found at each stage of the examination. At the end of the form, the vet will give an opinion on whether the findings are or are not likely to prejudice the horse's use for a particular purpose. If the horse is not recommended for purchase, the vet may not send you a detailed report unless one is specifically requested.

*A vet will assess a horse's movement as part of the pre-purchase examination procedure.*

It is standard practice for a vet to take a blood sample from the horse, which will then be stored for six months. This is so that, if you take the horse home and he immediately turns into a lunatic or goes lame, the blood can be tested for the presence of medication that could have been used to mask a problem or make him appear quieter. Never be embarrassed about this part of the procedure, because it protects the seller as well as the buyer – and, of course, if any seller refuses to allow it, you have to wonder why!

There are always people who query the value of some parts of the vetting procedure, in particular flexion tests, where each limb in turn is flexed and held for a short time and the horse is trotted away immediately the limb is released. What they forget, or choose to ignore, is that a vet can tell the difference between a stride or two of lameness resulting from the limb being bent and held, and indications of an underlying problem. Vets are not 'out to fail' horses, they are being paid to pass an informed opinion.

Another thing to remember is that a vet can only give an opinion of the horse on the day of the examination, not make a prediction as to whether he will stay sound forever. In the same way, although a vet will point out any physical defects or blemishes, this is not the same thing as predicting whether a horse will win in the show ring, or has the potential to become an advanced dressage performer.

### INSURANCE

The moment you pay for a horse, he becomes your property, so get on your mobile and arrange any insurance cover you have decided to take out before you drive home. The three essentials for most owners are mortality cover, vets' fees and public liability. Mortality cover is a standard part of all horse insurance policies and means that if the horse dies or, in the opinion of a veterinary surgeon, has to be put down, the insurer pays out the sum insured. Vets' fees are essential, because the costs of diagnosis and treatment can run into thousands of pounds: if your horse needs surgery for colic, you will be facing a bill of £3,500 plus. Third party liability is also essential, whether it is obtained through an equine policy or, in the UK, as part of a British Horse Society membership package.

The best way to find a good insurance company or broker is to talk to those who advertise regularly in the equestrian press and to ask other horse owners about their experiences. Vets are not allowed to recommend companies, but will be able to tell you which are easier to deal with. When you make inquiries, does the person at the end of the phone seem knowledgeable about horses and talk in plain language? Someone who talks jargon you don't understand or seems to lack equestrian knowledge would not be the best person to deal with in an emergency.

When owners have problems related to insurance, it's usually because they didn't read their policy documents properly – which is lesson number one – or because they don't understand the terms and conditions. Some of the commonest problems relate to understanding the following terms and issues.

*PROPOSAL:* the form you fill in when you apply to insure your horse.
*POLICY DOCUMENT:* the written contract between you and the insurance company setting out the terms of insurance.
*EXCESS:* the flat fee or proportion of the claim you pay every time a claim is paid out.
*MARKET VALUE:* if a horse dies or is put down, the insurers will pay out the sum insured or the market value, whichever is the *smaller*. General advice is to insure the horse for the sum you paid for him, as it would be difficult to argue that this is not his market value. It could be said that if an insurance company accepts your proposal in the first place, it has also accepted the sum you have proposed as the market value. That said, there is no point in trying to over-insure. If you feel a horse has increased in value after some time in your ownership, perhaps because you have achieved good

*If good competition results increase your horse's value, talk to your insurer before renewing your policy.*

competition results, or an unbroken 3-year-old has become a well-educated 4-year-old, ask your insurer to approve a higher valuation when you renew your policy.

*MORTALITY COVER:* this does not cover what is referred to as 'economic slaughter' unless specifically agreed with your insurer. If your horse cannot be ridden but could be retired, you cannot claim the insurance payout if you choose to have him put down. You may feel you would never take that option, but not everyone can afford to keep a horse in retirement and if you cannot guarantee his future, it may be better to have him put down than risk his welfare.

*VET FEES:* check that these are not limited by the value of the horse, as a colic operation costs the same for a £1,000 pony as for a £20,000 event horse. Realistically, you need cover of £5,000 per incident to hopefully cover diagnosis and treatment, including surgery. There may be cases where bills are higher, but standard policies are usually limited to £5,000. The other thing to check is that the cover limit is set *per incident*, not *per year*, so that if you are unlucky enough to have two serious but unrelated problems you will still be covered.

*TACK AND SADDLERY:* if you keep your tack at home, you may find that you are already covered for theft and damage on your household contents policy. In any case, check whether your policy pays out the actual value or a replacement value. There can be a big difference, as if your £1,000 saddle is stolen two years after you buy it and you are covered for actual value, this will be considerably less than the purchase price.

*LOSS OF USE:* this is the most expensive area of horse insurance and will be uneconomical for most people. It applies to permanent, not temporary, loss of use and so will apply only if the horse is permanently incapable of doing *the job for which he is insured*. For instance, if you insure him for show jumping, dressage and hacking and he has an accident that means he will be able to hack but not jump, you will receive the difference between the sum or a proportion of the sum insured – depending on your policy – and his residual value.

There are ways of keeping down the cost of insurance premiums, but they have their pros and cons. For instance, the higher the value of the horse, the higher the premium will be, so you could insure your horse for less than his market value and take the risk that if he died or had to be put down, you would lose the difference between the sum insured and the purchase price.

Check whether you are better off taking out a 'pick and choose' policy rather than one which includes options you may not need. Many companies will also offer lower premiums if you ask to pay a higher excess on veterinary fee claims. For instance, if you opt to pay the first £500 of every bill rather than, say, £100, you will still be covered for major problems. Some British companies and brokers offer better rates for members of affiliated Riding Clubs or the British Horse Society. Unfortunately, the idea of a 'no claims bonus' is virtually unheard of and discounts for horses who are security marked are also rare.

**WELCOME HOME**

So you've bought your horse, told all your friends and family about him, prepared his stable at his new home and arranged for him to be delivered. This is hopefully the start of a fantastic partnership – so try to make sure it gets off to a smooth start. No matter how quiet and experienced the horse, he has to get used to new surroundings, new equine friends and a new owner. At the same time, you have to get used to the excitement and responsibility of looking after and riding a horse without the security blanket of an instructor telling you what to do all the time – though you should make sure you have someone to help you and give you confidence.

Travelling a horse safely is dealt with in Chapter 11. For now, make sure that your horse is either delivered by his previous owners or fetched by a professional transporter. Many dealers will either deliver a horse as part of the deal or recommend a transporter. Private owners may want to see his new home – if they haven't already visited before agreeing to sell him – but neither you nor your new horse wants the trauma of them weeping into his mane whilst they say goodbye. If a friend offers to fetch him, be careful, as even you paying for the fuel may mean they are transporting for 'hire and reward' and as such, may be contravening their insurance and even breaking the law.

If possible, arrange for your horse to arrive in daylight so he can start to get used to his new surroundings. A good livery yard will be used to welcoming new arrivals and may even have an isolation zone. It should at least be possible for him to be stabled for an hour or two with hay to nibble and at least one other horse in view. Let him settle and dissuade well-meaning visitors who are anxious to see your new purchase.

It's a good idea to have a worm sample taken straight away (see Chapter 9) and base your worming programme on the results, though yards have different policies and some will insist that all new arrivals are wormed immediately. You should also be aware of the risk of bringing in infections such as ringworm or strangles. A knowledgeable yard owner will be aware of this and ensure that the horse and anyone in contact with him takes appropriate preventive measures; this is where an appropriate isolation zone is so valuable.

If he is to go out with a group of horses, he should ideally first be turned out with the quietest of them before being introduced to his 'herd' and gradually establishing his place in the hierarchy. Some people like to turn horses out with protective boots on at first, but these can cause problems if used routinely; if dirt gets trapped between the boot and the leg, it can result in rubs and possible infection.

As you handle him and watch him out in the field over the next day or two, try to assess his state of mind. Make sure he has plenty of good quality forage (see Chapter 5) but in general it's best not to give hard feed until you start working him; if other horses on the yard are fed at a particular time, give him a short-fibre 'forage feed' with a few sliced carrots or apples. In general, you should be able to ride him for the first time a couple of days after his arrival; look on it as a 'getting to know you' ride and choose safe surroundings with an instructor or experienced friend who will boost your confidence.

# 4. TACK AND RUGS

Once you've bought your horse, the next most expensive purchases will be essential tack and rugs. If you're lucky, you may be able to buy them as part of the deal with the horse and as long as they are of good quality and fit correctly, this is well worth doing. Condition and fit of the saddle is particularly important and there are fitting guidelines later in this chapter, but the safest bet is to consult someone who holds the Society of Master Saddlers' saddle fitting qualification (see Useful Addresses Appendix.)

If you have to kit out your horse from scratch, concentrate on good-quality basics rather than trying to buy everything at once. As you progress in your career as a horse owner, you will find that there is always something new and tempting to buy – but it's easy to waste money, not only by getting your priorities wrong but by buying 'bargain' goods that don't last and may even be unsafe.

Although there are lots of mail order and internet sites – including the ubiquitous Ebay – it's often best to buy from a good local saddlery. A good retailer should be able to give you advice on how to make the most of your budget, and you can see what you're buying.

*A double bridle with a plain cavesson noseband. Note how the broad, flat noseband complements this show cob's attractive but workmanlike head.*

## BASIC SHOPPING LIST

To equip an all-round riding horse, you'll need:

Nylon headcollar and lead rope for
  everyday use
Saddle, girth, stirrup irons and leathers
Two numnahs, if used
Bridle and bit
Martingale, if required
Set of brushing boots

Travelling equipment – tail bandage;
  travel boots or leg bandages and pads;
  leather headcollar (for safety reasons as
  well as smartness)
Two lightweight, waterproof, breathable
  rugs that can be used indoors and out.

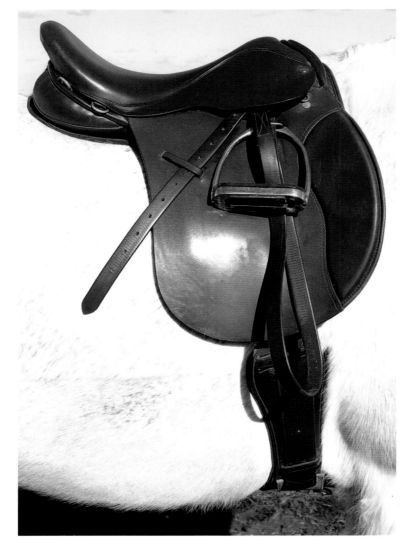

RIGHT *A new
generation of
synthetic saddles,
such as this
Thorowgood T6
synthetic saddle,
looks good and is
easy to look after.*

LEFT *A well-fitting
general-purpose
(GP) leather saddle
that is suitable for
hacking, schooling
and jumping and
would be suitable for
riders wanting to
have a go at most
activities.*

## IN THE HOT SEAT

A SADDLE MUST FIT the horse and the rider so that both of you are comfortable. The horse takes priority, because a badly fitting saddle can cause pain, resistance and sometimes permanent damage, but the saddle must be well designed and suit your conformation as well as his! A general-purpose saddle is the best option for first-time owners and will allow you to hack, school and jump small courses in confidence. Later, you might want to buy a dressage or jumping saddle, but you don't need to specialize when you start out.

If money is tight, find a saddler who will fit and sell a good second-hand leather saddle or a new synthetic one; the latest generation of synthetic saddles are smart and serviceable. The saddler should explain the basics of fit so that you know when your saddle needs adjusting or

*If you use a numnah or saddle cloth, make sure it is designed so it can be pulled up into the saddle gullet and will not press down on the withers.*

even changing for another: horses change shape dramatically as they gain or lose weight and build up or lose muscle tone.

Traditionally, saddles are flocked with wool and many riders and saddlers remain happy with this. Others prefer to ride on air; airbags are fitted in the panels and inflated with a special pump. You can opt for airbags alone, a mixture of air and conventional flocking or, in some cases, a pad incorporating air and foam under a traditionally flocked saddle.

Although there may be situations when a numnah or pad can be used to alleviate a problem temporarily, it can't turn a saddle that fits badly into one that fits well – and if you use too thick a pad under a well-fitting saddle it can cause problems, as it's the equivalent of asking someone to walk comfortably wearing three pairs of socks and their normal shoes. Check, too, that anything used under the saddle is designed so it does not press down on the withers but stays up in the saddle gullet all the way along.

## BARGAIN PITFALLS

When you're shopping for tack, you'll hear lots of stories about the bargains to be had at auctions, including online auctions. Browsing Ebay can show what look to be plenty of good buys and many of them may be just that – but unless you have the knowledge to assess a saddle's condition and fit, you could end up wasting your money and possibly damaging your horse's back. You're far better buying from a retailer who knows how to do this, or employs a fitting specialist. Anyone who holds the Society of Master Saddlers' saddle fitting qualification has proved they know how to do this.

### FIT FOR PURPOSE

Rather than assuming that your saddle needs checking once a year and that you don't need to worry until the date comes round, learn to recognize when you might need a professional eye cast over it. Anyone can learn to do this – it's simply down to observation, so you can co-opt a friend or family member to help you make regular checks. If you have to be the observer, the rider should be as close to your height and weight as possible.

Most saddles are built on a frame called a tree. This should follow the profile of your horse's back and be the correct width, so you have as wide a bearing surface as possible and the horse's movement is not restricted. Don't buy a second-hand saddle that hasn't been professionally checked, as a damaged tree will damage a horse's back. Some saddles are sold with interchangeable gullets that allow the width to be changed quickly and easily.

The saddle should be level from front to back, so the rider is balanced and not tipped forwards or backwards. If the tree is the right width and profile for the horse, your saddler should be able to correct the balance of the saddle by adjusting the flocking.

The panel should be in contact with the horse without pinching. When you ride, the saddle should not bounce up and down or swing from side to side at the back, though there will always be some *slight* movement.

From behind, the saddle should sit evenly and not be over to one side. However, lop-sidedness is often down to the rider rather than the saddle. If you mount from the ground rather than using a mounting block or a leg-up, you're more likely to pull the saddle over. Also, a rider who puts more weight on one stirrup than the other, or who has uneven stirrup leathers, will move the saddle sideways.

The saddle gullet should clear the horse's back all the way along, especially under the rider. It's sometimes said that you should always have three fingers' width between the pommel and the withers, but it isn't always possible to achieve this. However, this is where you need the advice of a good saddle fitter who will take into account the design of the saddle and the work your horse is doing. As a basic check, stand in the stirrups and put one finger between the pommel and the withers: if your finger gets pinched, the saddle will definitely come down too low.

*Treeless saddles, such as this one designed by Heather Moffett, suit some horses and riders.*

## FIT FOR YOU

If your saddle does not complement your proportions, or is badly designed, you won't be able to ride in balance. This will have a knock-on effect of making your horse unbalanced and probably also uncomfortable, which is another reason for calling in a knowledgeable fitter who can assess you and your horse together.

For instance, if you are relatively long from hip to knee and your knees come over the knee rolls, you'll be uncomfortable and insecure. The length of the flaps and size of the seat also make a big difference to the rider's position and comfort and the stirrup bars should not be so far forward that you are always struggling to bring your legs back into the correct position.

Your saddle should help you: you shouldn't have to fight it to achieve a correct position. If you have a physical problem which makes it difficult for you to sit centrally – something which can affect riders of all ages, either through injury or the normal wear and tear of everyday life – a knowledgeable saddle fitter will often be able to adjust your saddle to compensate.

Although saddle fitting still relies heavily on the eye of the fitter, high-tech pressure analysis systems – not yet widely available, owing to their high cost – allow the operator to see what is happening underneath the saddle with a rider on board and to identify pressure points. Work

## TREELESS SADDLES

Over the past few years, treeless saddles and those with partial trees have become increasingly popular. Some enthusiasts claim that they are the solution to every fitting problem, but most experts say that they may not be suitable in all cases and that each horse and rider partnership should be looked at with an open mind.

*Sophisticated pressure analysis equipment linked to a computer enables a specialist fitter to identify pressure points under a saddle that could cause problems.*

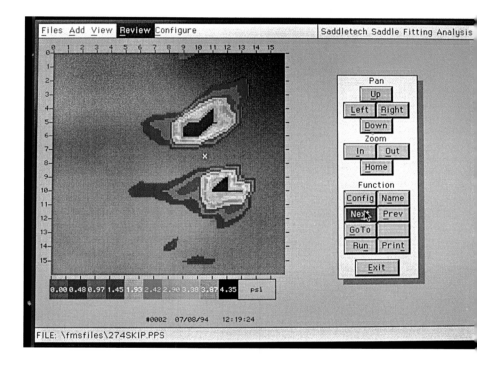

carried out with potential candidates for the British Olympic teams has shown, not surprisingly, that the rider's balance and weight distribution play an essential part in achieving a comfortable horse. Whilst saddle design and fit are vital, so is riding ability!

### STIRRUPS AND GIRTHS

Don't compromise on quality when choosing stirrup leathers, irons and girths, as your safety depends on them. Follow the traditional advice of leaving the levers at the end of the stirrup bars down, as this will make it easier for the leathers to be released if you fall and find that your foot is caught up – but don't rely on this measure alone.

Stirrup irons must be the right size for the rider's feet; allow 12 mm (½ in) clearance on each side of the widest part of your boot to ensure that your foot can be freed easily but not slide too far forward. Safety stirrups minimize risks even further; one of the most popular designs is the bent leg safety iron, which has become accepted in all disciplines, even the conservative world of showing. Traditional safety stirrups with detachable rubber rings on one side are not suitable for riders other than very small children, as greater weights impose too much stress on the metal.

A synthetic or leather girth which incorporates a small amount of 'give' throughout its length must be more comfortable for the horse; research from Australia shows that girths which are over-tightened restrict the horse's stride and some 'give' will help to minimize the risk. Some designs have elasticated ends and those with elasticated inserts at both ends are preferable. Girths with just

*This horse wears a girth incorporating a stud guard to prevent injury if he tucks his front legs up so high that the studs in his front shoes come in contact with his belly.*

one set of elasticated ends can result in the saddle slipping to one side. If you are compelled to use them, perhaps when riding someone else's horse, ensure that the elasticated ends are on the offside so that when you tighten the girth via the nearside buckles, you are less likely to over-tighten.

A girth should be long enough to allow plenty of adjustment on both sides. If you ride on a dressage saddle with long girth straps and a short girth – designed to minimize bulk under the rider's legs – make sure the girth is long enough not to cause discomfort to the horse. If his elbow catches on the buckles as he moves, the girth is too short; this might sound obvious, but it is a mistake even professional competitors sometimes make.

## BRIDLES AND BITS

A GOOD-QUALITY leather bridle that is well looked after will last for years and makes a great investment. Again, it must fit well; standard sizes don't always allow this and you may have to mix and match bridle parts in different sizes to keep your horse comfortable. Basic criteria are:

● The browband must be long enough to ensure that the bases of the horse's ears are not pinched between it and the headpiece. On some bridles, the noseband strap runs on top of a shaped, padded headpiece (rather than underneath a flat headpiece, as with traditional designs) to afford greater comfort and avoid poll pressure.

● You should be able to fit four fingers between the throatlatch (pronounced throatlash) and the horse's face.

● The top of a cavesson noseband, the simplest design, should not rub the facial bones. It should be fastened to allow two fingers' width between it and the horse's face.

● Reins must not be so long that there is a danger of them looping round a foot. This is something to watch out for particularly with children.

● Many riders use nosebands which fasten below, or above and below, the bit. These are designed to prevent the horse opening his mouth too wide, but if they are fastened so tightly that he can't open his mouth at all, he will be uncomfortable and resistant. Remember that, to accept the bit, he needs to be able to move his jaw. The nosebands below are in common use and perfectly acceptable – but even if you feel you need extra control for hacking and jumping, experiment with using a plain cavesson for schooling in a safe area. You may find that your horse is more comfortable and actually goes better.

*FLASH:* comprises a cavesson noseband with an additonal strap fastening below the bit.

*DROP:* adjusted lower on the nose, though high enough not to impede the horse's breathing, and fastens below the bit.

*GRAKLE:* sometimes called a crossover noseband because of its X-shape. This fastens above and below the bit: a high-ring Grakle can be useful if a young horse tends to open his mouth too wide but is also teething, as it minimizes pressure on areas which are sensitive at this time.

Not all nosebands are acceptable for all disciplines, so check rule books when necessary. This applies particularly to dressage.

## BEAUTY AND THE BEAST

A well-chosen bridle can complement the shape of your horse's head. The golden rule is that the more workmanlike the head, the more workmanlike the bridle should be. Cobs and hunter types look better with broad, flat nosebands and browbands whilst Thoroughbred types suit more lightweight bridles. However, lightweight should never mean flimsy and leatherwork should always be substantial enough to be strong.

Fashions come and go and one rider's delight is another's nightmare. If you like the idea of a browband which has your initials or your horse's name spelled out in diamante letters, or a bridle with pink edging on the noseband and browband, by all means go for it: but check up on competition etiquette first or you and your horse will stand out for all the wrong reasons.

### A BIT AT A TIME

If your horse seems comfortable and goes well in the bit he was wearing when you tried him, there is no reason to change it. At the same time, it's worth appreciating that a change of bit might help if, as you get to know each other, you find you have a communication problem. There is no such thing as a 'magic bit' that will miraculously transform every horse into one who works beautifully, but sometimes a minor change can help make the conversation between you and your horse clearer. For instance, some riders who tend to tense and fiddle with their hands when riding a horse in a snaffle with fixed cheeks, such as an eggbutt, stay softer through their arms and hands when using a loose-ring snaffle. Similarly, a horse who backs off the rider's hand when ridden in a loose-ring snaffle often gains more confidence from a fixed ring one.

But – and it's a big but – there are some things that should always be remembered when deciding what bit to use:
- A horse will only accept the bit if his mouth and teeth are in good condition and he is ridden correctly. It used to be said that wolf teeth – small, shallow-rooted vestigial pre-molars – should be removed as routine, but many dental specialists now believe that the best course is only to take them out if they interfere with the action of the bit.
- A bit must be the right size for the mouth, and correctly adjusted.
- Your horse's mouth conformation will have an effect on the type of mouthpiece he is most comfortable with. In particular, a horse with a fat, fleshy tongue will not have room in his mouth for a thick mouthpiece and will be more comfortable with a thinner one. Ponies' mouths often have short bars, which will not leave enough room for a thick mouthpiece.

*A well-fitting bridle with a Flash noseband.*

● A bit that is theoretically mild, such as a snaffle with a wide bearing area, will have a severe action if the rider is rough or unbalanced.

● You don't need to feel inadequate if you feel happier using a different bit for faster work and jumping. It's better to use a potentially stronger bit gently than to pull at a horse who is wearing a theoretically milder one.

● Don't confuse a strong horse with one who is on the forehand and out of balance. A horse who feels 'heavy on the hand' will feel much lighter when he and his rider learn to carry themselves in balance. Lessons with a good trainer will often be much more effective than simply changing a bit.

● Don't be tempted to use a double bridle to try to achieve an educated outline. A horse comes on to the bit when he is working from behind and in balance and a double bridle should only be used to add finesse to your communication when he has already achieved that.

● Don't be a fashion victim. There are excellent, much publicized designs which seem to suit many horses, notably the KK Ultra snaffle with an angled, central lozenge, and the Myler range. But if your horse is happy, comfortable and performs well wearing his current bit, don't decide that you must use one of these just because famous event rider A or international dressage star B says they are the best thing since sliced bread.

● If you or your trainer feel that a change of bit could help resolve a schooling problem and a possible solution is expensive, contact one of the many 'bit libraries' advertised in magazines and websites such as *Horse and Hound* (www.horseandhoundonline.co.uk) and arrange to try before you buy.

● Different riders have different preferences to the feel of a bit, as do horses. For example, some riders find that a fixed-ring bit tempts them to 'fiddle' with the reins whilst others want to take a stronger than ideal contact on a loose-ring bit to get a more definite feel. Listen to your horse and to your instructor!

● Some bits and nosebands are not permitted for competition (especially dressage), so check the relevant competition rules.


### SIZE, ADJUSTMENT AND CONDITION

Bits are measured as in the accompanying photograph. To find out if a jointed bit is the right size for your horse, straighten it gently in his mouth and check that there is no more than 1 cm (about ⅖ in) clearance on each size. A straight bar or mullen-mouth bit should have the same or slightly less clearance; in both cases, there should be no risk of the bit pinching because it is too small or moving excessively from side to side because it is too big. The commonest mistake is to use a bit that is too big, which means that a jointed mouthpiece will hang too low in the mouth.

A jointed bit that is adjusted at the correct height in the mouth will wrinkle the corners slightly, without pulling the mouth into a false smile. However, take the mouth conformation into account – if the horse has loose, fleshy lips, the wrinkling will be more pronounced when the bit is correctly in place. A mullen or straight bar mouthpiece should fit snugly into the corners of the mouth.

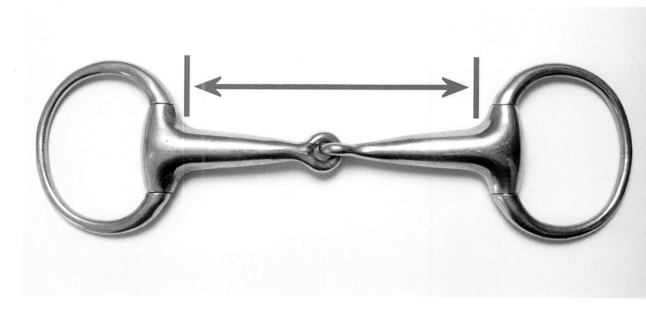

*The correct way to measure a bit mouthpiece – here, an eggbutt snaffle.*

Check bits regularly for signs of wear. Rough edges or sharp protrusions round the holes of loose-ring snaffles can cause discomfort and not all materials will stand up to a horse's teeth. Rubber- and plastic-covered bits should have a central metal core so that if a horse does chew through, you aren't left without control.

### USING A DOUBLE BRIDLE

A double bridle offers the ultimate in fine-tuned communication and should be used for finesse, never in an attempt to supply extra brakes. A horse must be working correctly in a snaffle before a double bridle is introduced. It comprises two bits, a small, thin snaffle called a bradoon and a curb bit, each available with a variety of mouthpieces. A double bridle has an extra piece called a sliphead to take the second bit and is used with two pairs of reins. The rider must have the skill to be able to use each rein independently. A double bridle should only be used with a cavesson noseband, never with one which fastens wholly or partly below the bit. Some riders use a crank noseband, which is designed to fit extra tightly, but if you feel you need this, you also need to ask yourself whether your horse's schooling and/or your riding is at the stage where a double bridle should be used at all.

Adjust the bits carefully, fitting the bradoon first and the curb second. As with snaffles, loose-ring bradoons should be very slightly wider than eggbutt ones to ensure that there is no pinching, whilst curbs should fit snugly into the corners of the mouth. A loose-ring bradoon usually needs to be 6 mm (¼ in) wider than its curb partner. As a guide, a curb should be 2.5 cm (1 in) above the tushes in a gelding and 5 cm (2 in) above the corner teeth in a mare.

The curb chain comes into contact with the back of the jaw when the curb rein is used. It should be fastened so that there is no risk of it twisting and should touch the jaw when the curb cheek is drawn back to an angle of 45 degrees. Riders often fasten a curb chain too loosely, thinking that they are being kind to their horses. In fact, the opposite applies – before it comes into effect, the cheek will be pulled further back and the mouthpiece will slide upwards.

Most horses take kindly to a double link metal curb chain, but sensitive ones may be happier with a rubber-covered, leather or elastic one. However, it is worth checking current rules before using these alternatives in competition.

### PELHAMS AND KIMBLEWICKS

These are useful bits belonging to the curb family and some horses and ponies go well in them, though they are not permitted for dressage. Pelhams are popular in the show ring and in this discipline they are always used with two pairs of reins. In theory, the pelham combines the action of a double bridle in one mouthpiece, with the top ring acting as a snaffle and the bottom as a curb. In practice, they have a far less precise action. Some riders prefer to use roundings when jumping; these are leather couplings which buckle to the top and bottom bit rings on each side and allow the use of a single pair of reins. They blur the action of the bit still further, but if your horse performs well with this set-up and you don't want to have to manage double reins when jumping, don't knock it!

The kimblewick was invented specifically for show jumping and goes in and out of fashion. In theory, the curb action is stronger when the reins are fastened to the bottom slot (if there is more than one on the bit ring) or when the rider's hands are lower. Logically, there is so little leverage from a kimblewick compared to the longer cheeks of a true curb or a pelham that its effect remains limited – however, some horses go well in them.

Strictly speaking, you should not use any kind of noseband which fastens below the bit in conjunction with a bit which employs a curb chain, as one interferes with the action of the other. However, some riders, including those competing at top level, use a Flash or Grakle noseband with a pelham or kimblewick.

### BITLESS AND COMBINATION BRIDLES

Bitless bridles – a term which is often used to cover everything from designs capable of applying powerful leverage to the nose and outer jaw area to what are basically rope headcollars – can have a valuable role to play. For instance, one school of thought suggests introducing a young horse to ridden work using the nose as a control point so that he can become accustomed to a rider's weight without unwanted pressure on his mouth. This can work well in safe surroundings, but most riders would want to introduce a bit as soon as possible and anyone educating a young horse should be capable of using a bit correctly and without force. It is also important to realize that, in the wrong hands, a bitless bridle can act with considerable force and may cause damage.

*This event horse is ridden in a Myler combination bit, which acts on the nose as well as on the mouth.*

*Bitless bridles are sometimes useful for horses who are fussy or resistant in the mouth, or who are teething – or who simply go best in them.*

If you decide to go bitless, ride in a safe, enclosed area until you have established your new communications system and remember that you need to be even more aware of using your weight aids and to ask for changes of direction in plenty of time.

Horses who are fussy or resistant in the mouth, or who are uncomfortable because they are teething, may respond well to a bitless bridle. Combination bits with special nosebands or attachments – notably the Myler combination and the Mikmar bit – offer 'dual controls' and have been used successfully by several leading show jumpers and by event riders in the show jumping and cross-country phases.

## MARTINGALES AND BREASTPLATES

MARTINGALES ARE INTENDED to give extra control by preventing the horse raising his head too high. A well-schooled horse should not need one for working on the flat – and martingales are not permitted in dressage competitions – but many people feel happier using one when jumping or hacking, or when riding a young or inexperienced horse. Even so, they should not be regarded as standard: if you don't need one, don't use it.

A standing martingale attaches to a cavesson noseband or the top part of a Flash noseband and as such, has no interaction with the reins and bit. It should never be attached to any form of noseband that fastens below the bit, or to the drop strap of a Flash. Adjust it so that it reaches into the gullet when pushed up, shortening it a hole or two if necessary.

A running martingale works via the reins and therefore influences the position and action of the bit. The textbook method of adjustment is to ensure a hand's width between the rings and the withers when the straps are pulled back towards the withers, but this can give a false fit if the horse has a particularly straight or sloping shoulder. A better way is to adjust the length until the rings reach into the gullet when both straps are held along the underside of the neck.

A bib martingale is basically a running martingale with the straps connected by a V-shaped leather insert. It is designed to prevent a horse grabbing at the rings; some riders prefer to use it when they need to open gates whilst mounted, either out hunting or hacking, as there is less chance of it getting caught up. Adjust it the same way as a normal running martingale.

An Irish martingale is the odd one out, as it isn't really a martingale at all – simply a strip of leather with rings at each end through which the reins pass. It fits under the horse's neck and is sometimes used in racing to prevent the reins being thrown over the horse's head.

A breastplate or breastgirth is sometimes used to help prevent the saddle slipping back. It should be looked on as a safety precaution, not as a way to try to keep an ill-fitting saddle in place, but is recommended for hillwork and cross-country.

### SAFE STOPS

Whatever type of martingale you use, fit a rubber stop at the junction where the neckstrap joins the section which runs to the girth to prevent it dangling between the horse's front legs when jumping. If you use a running or bib martingale, it is also essential to use stops on the reins to prevent the rings sliding too far down.

## LUNGEING AND LONG-REINING

AT SOME STAGE you will certainly want to lunge and perhaps long-rein your horse to add variety to or improve his work, or as part of a fitness regime. Whilst you don't need to buy lots of lungeing equipment the moment you buy your horse, do buy a good-quality lunge rein and a lunge whip. Cotton or webbing lunge reins are easier to hold than many nylon ones – though you should still always wear gloves. Even the quietest horse can spook and pull the rein through your fingers, with painful results for bare hands.

It's possible to lunge a quiet horse using a headcollar, but a proper lunge cavesson with a padded, reinforced noseband and attachment rings gives more control. Lungeing from the bit gives even more control, but use this method with respect and only when you've mastered basic lungeing techniques. The most popular method is to pass the lunge rein through the inside bit ring, over the horse's head and clip it to the offside, remembering to change the fastening when you change the rein.

Side reins are commonly used to encourage the horse to accept and work into a contact on the bit. They can be plain leather or nylon, or have an elastic or rubber insert to allow a certain amount of 'give'. Ask your trainer's advice about which type would suit you and your horse best.

Although side reins are standard equipment, they should be used with respect. Always warm up without them, to allow the horse to stretch, and fit them fairly loosely to start with. Eventually, they should be at a length which allows a light contact when the horse is working in an outline appropriate for his stage of schooling – don't over-shorten them to try to get him to bring in his head.

Long-reining can be carried out using two lunge reins or, if you prefer, long lines made from rope. The latter have been made popular by some modern trainers but are actually about as traditional as you can get – farm workers used rope plough lines when working heavy horses in the field.

## TRAINING AIDS

### AIDS FOR HORSES

Training aids or gadgets? The terminology depends on your point of view, but the wider view is that the definition of a training aid is anything that is literally an aid to training rather than an attempt to cut corners. It should be used not to try to coerce the horse into carrying himself in a set outline, but to help him achieve the posture and balance that he as an individual is capable of. Whether equipment is designed for use when lungeing or ridden, the same principles apply:

- Make sure that the horse does not have any physical problems – though there may be situations when a vet or other suitably qualified professional working under veterinary supervision recommends using a particular training aid as part of rehabilitation.

- Introduce all equipment carefully and considerately and fit it so that it has a minimal effect to start with. This gives the horse time to get used to the feel and the action and to avoid an explosion because he is frightened or feels restricted.

- If you have never used a training aid before, get someone who works with it successfully to help you.

- You will be asking a horse to use unfamiliar muscles, so work him for very short periods only. Remember that his new posture may lead to slight stiffness the next day, so be prepared to work him one day and perhaps hack out or simply turn him out the next.

- A horse can only carry himself and work on the bit if he has the musculature that enables him to do so. This does not happen in days, or even weeks.

## AIDS FOR RIDERS

There are training aids for riders, too. One of the simplest and most useful is the balance strap, a leather strap about 25 cm (10 in) long which clips or buckles to the D-rings on the front of the saddle. Holding it or simply slipping a thumb under it helps you keep an upright position when riding on the flat and therefore keep in balance with the horse. It can also be useful if a horse throws a buck, as sitting up instead of tipping forward can make the difference between staying in the saddle and ending up on the floor. You can use a balance strap when competing in dressage.

The traditional neckstrap, which can be no more than a spare stirrup leather buckled round the horse's neck, isn't as helpful for security but can be used to help slow down a horse without relying on the reins. Give a quick pull and release on the neckstrap as, for instance, you ask the horse to half-halt or go forward to a downward transition.

Other ideas are said to help give a stable, correct leg position. They include elasticated straps which link the irons to the girth, and angled stirrup irons.

*A balance strap can help a rider keep an upright position and its use is permitted in competition.*

## EXPERT QUOTE

*'A balance strap also helps horse and rider feel the benefit of a steady contact. It is very important that the hand is kept still; this is much nicer for the horse'.*

ULLA SALZGEBER, OLYMPIC DRESSAGE RIDER

## TOP TEN TACK MISTAKES

- Bits that are too big. If the mouthpiece of your bit is too long, it won't sit correctly in the mouth – and if it has eggbutt, full or D-cheeks, it will bang against the sides of the mouth. If you are worried that a loose-ring bit will pinch fleshy lips, don't use too big a one; use rubber bitguards or swap to a T-bar snaffle, in which the rings run through a T-shaped sleeve.

- Girths fastened too tight. This can restrict your horse's stride length: in general, you should be able to fit three fingers between the girth and your horse.

- Stirrup irons too small. There should be a 12 mm (½ in) gap between the widest part of your boot and each side of the iron to make sure your foot can't get trapped if you fall. Appropriate safety irons give greater protection.

- Saddle placed too far forward. Make sure it doesn't impinge on the horse's shoulder-blades as they move back.

- Numnahs that pull down on the withers. Often caused by fixing straps in the wrong place; get them re-positioned or choose a numnah or pad that doesn't require straps to hold it in place.

- Reins that are too long. If your horse or pony has a relatively short neck, make sure your reins aren't so long that you could catch your foot in the loop.

- Nylon headcollars left on in the field. Unless they are designed to be 'field safe', with breakaway sections or fittings built in, they could get caught up – and might not break before your horse gets injured.

- Flash nosebands where the cavesson part is too flimsy. It will only slide down the head, which means that the bottom strap will also be wrongly positioned. Choose a noseband with a fairly wide, substantial cavesson.

- Nosebands fastened too tight. You should be able to slide a finger under any part of the noseband which fastens under the bit – if you can't, the horse can't flex his jaw and if he can't flex his jaw, he can't work truly on the bit. You should also be able to slide at least one finger between a cavesson noseband or the cavesson part of a Flash and the horse's face.

- Browbands that are too short. This pulls the headpiece on to the base of the ears, causing pinching.

## BOOTS AND BANDAGES

THERE ARE MANY TYPES of protective boots and bandages designed for use when working or travelling a horse; this chapter covers the first category and travelling gear is discussed in Chapter 11. But before you rush out and spend a fortune on the latest high-tech leg protection, look at your horse's conformation and movement, the type of work he will be doing and, depending on the time of year, environmental factors. It may seem tempting to use boots all the time, even when he is turned out – and some owners do – but if they are worn for long periods in muddy conditions, trapped dirt may cause rubs and infection. In general, the sensible approach is to use boots when jumping, doing fast work, if a horse is unbalanced through lack of schooling or inexperience, or if his movement predisposes him to striking one leg with another.

## TYPES OF BOOT

There are three basic types of boot.

***Brushing boots*** have a reinforced strike pad on the inside of the cannon bone area. They are a useful general-purpose boot and essential for horses who tend to brush one leg against another.

***Tendon boots*** are particularly useful when jumping. Although they offer some protection against blows, they are unlikely to give support to the tendon area.

***Overreach boots*** can be useful when hacking or schooling young and unbalanced horses who tend to strike the heel of a front foot with the toe of a hind shoe. However, some top event riders feel they should not be used when jumping, particularly cross-country, as there is a risk that if a horse treads on a boot when travelling at speed he could trip or even fall. If you feel your horse needs overreach boots, look for designs which are shaped to minimize the risk of this happening.

Boots are usually sold in pony, cob and full sizes. Check that you have the right size for your horse's leg conformation – for instance, a Thoroughbred with slender limbs may only need cob-size boots. They should be long enough to protect vulnerable areas, but not so long that they interfere with joint movement. Fit them so that they are snug enough to stay in place, but not so tightly that they cause pressure problems. As a rough guide, you should be able to slip a finger between the boot and the horse's leg at top and bottom.

Modern materials make boots easy to keep clean, either by hosing them off and leaving them to dry or machine washing. Fasten Velcro or hook and eye straps before washing to prevent them getting clogged up with hair and other debris.

## EXERCISE BANDAGES

Leg bandages have become fashionable again, particularly in the dressage world, and will sometimes be marketed as 'wraps'. But although some manufacturers claim that their products can be used without padding underneath, most vets advise caution. Bandages that are too tight – and this is more likely to happen when they are used without protective padding – can cause serious tendon damage.

For information on using bandages for travelling, see Chapter 11.

## THE RIGHT RUGS

Buying rugs can, if you let it, become a quick way of spending a lot of money. But before you become overwhelmed by all the outdoor and indoor rugs, coolers, exercise sheets, thermal rugs, flysheets and all the permutations on them, divide your shopping list into essentials and extras. If you're on a tight budget, put two lightweight, waterproof, breathable and machine-washable rugs that can be used indoors and out on top of your list; some owners still prefer to use stable rugs indoors and waterproof ones outside, but fabrics designed for outdoor use are tougher and easier to clean and modern turnout rugs weigh no more than indoor ones. Also, as climate change has blurred the defining lines between the seasons, rugs that are waterproof and breathable make it easier to protect your horse against wind and rain without the risk of him getting too hot if the weather changes dramatically within a short time.

In summer, flysheets made from lightweight mesh can offer useful protection from insects. However, these will usually not be enough to help animals who suffer from sweet itch, an allergic reaction to the saliva of the biting midge Culicoides. In these cases, a specialized design called the Boett blanket is often recommended.

Thermal rugs which transfer moisture from the coat through to the top layer of the fabric are excellent for drying off wet or sweating horses in cold weather. When temperatures soar, a sweating horse should be cooled down by washing off and walking, repeating the process when necessary. A lightweight cooler rug will then help to finish the process.

Summer sheets – thin, cotton rugs – are useful for keeping off flies and keeping a stabled horse clean in warm weather. They can also be used under bulkier rugs to provide a clean layer next to the coat; it's easier to wash and dry a summer sheet regularly and it will keep the lining of the top rug clean. Even better, buy a rug with a detachable, lightweight lining that can be washed alone, as this will minimize the number of straps and fastenings you have to deal with.

Exercise sheets that fit behind or under the saddle help keep your horse warm and dry when you are hacking out in cold weather or standing waiting to compete on a clipped horse; for competition, use a rug which can be removed without having to take off the saddle. A fluorescent, reflective exercise sheet can help keep you and your horse safe on the roads even when you don't need protection from the weather.

## HIGH TECH, HIGH FASHION

Modern rugs incorporate advanced fabric technology and you'll find everything from materials incorporating silver – used in hospitals to help combat the killer bug MRSA – to fabrics designed to military specification. You'll also see some frequently used terms on the labels.

*DENIER:* this measures the weight and density of the yarn in a fabric. In simple terms, the higher the number, the denser and tougher the fabric.

*HYDROPHILIC:* some rugs include fabric coated with a hydrophilic (water-attracting) coating. This attracts excess moisture, whether water or sweat, and the difference in temperature between the external air and that inside the rug draws the moisture through a breathable outer fabric to the outside.

*RIPSTOP:* nothing can stop even the toughest fabrics ripping under the ultimate strain, but ripstop fabric has been modified to contain tears as far as possible.

*WICKING:* this term describes the way some fabrics transfer moisture from the inside of the rug to the outside surface. You can see the effect most clearly on a good thermal wicking rug such as Thermatex; if you put one on a wet or sweating horse, he will dry off underneath whilst beads of moisture sit on the outside of the rug and eventually evaporate.

## FIT AND FUNCTION

Although you tend to get what you pay for when buying rugs – and the more expensive ones usually have better quality fittings and tend to last longer – a rug will only be effective and comfortable for your horse if it is the right size. This may sound glaringly obvious, but a lot of people buy rugs that are too big and then wonder why they slip and cause problems such as rubs and pressure points. When the fastenings are adjusted correctly, the body of a correctly sized rug will start just in front of the withers and end at the top of the tail. If it has a built-in neck cover, this should not restrict the horse when he grazes.

To find out what size you need, measure from the centre of the horse's chest, along the body to the hindquarters. It should be deep enough to finish below the belly line but not so deep that it hangs round his knees!

Horses, like people, don't always come in standard shapes. Broad-chested, short-bodied types such as cobs are sometimes difficult to fit; one answer is to have a rug made to measure, which some companies will do for a small extra cost. Another is to use a chest extender, a rectangular insert with clips that fasten to those on the rugs and provide extra room at the front.

Stretch hoods and bodies help to keep horses clean and inhibit coat growth, thus cutting down on clipping. Although most horses accept hoods, they should be introduced carefully and in safe surroundings.

### WARNING!

Ill-fitting rugs or ones which are left on for long periods can cause pressure points and injuries. White hairs in the withers area are more likely to be the result of damage from rugs than from saddles. All rugs should be removed and put back on twice daily, even when a horse or pony is not being ridden – not only to avoid pressure points but to enable you to check the horse's general well-being.

### CLEANING UP

ONCE YOU'VE INVESTED in valuable tack and horse clothing, look after it. Few people have time to strip and clean tack every time it's used, but it is important to wash off bits and prevent dried saliva causing rubs and, for the same reason, to wipe off any mud or dirt. Numnahs and boots must also be kept clean.

Once a week, clean tack thoroughly and check for signs of wear and tear on stitching and leather. When necessary, use a good leather balm or similar preparation – once a month is usually enough. If leather tack gets wet, let it dry gradually at normal room temperature. Don't put it in front of a heater or radiator or it will dry out too quickly and become brittle.

Keep the linings of bulky rugs clean by using a liner or summer sheet underneath. Smaller sizes may fit into a domestic washing machine but you may need to send large rugs to specialist rug wash companies; many saddleries offer this service. Alternatively, use a household power washer. Make sure that any cleaning agents are compatible with the rug fabric.

Tack and rug theft is all too common, so mark all items with your postcode. Engraving tools are cheap and easily available and can be used to mark everything from bit rings to stirrup irons.

# 5. FEEDING

THE HORSE EVOLVED as a grazing animal, designed to live on grass and other plants. Yet walk into any feed store and you'll see bags of feed and tubs of supplements for every eventuality – feed for youngstock, performance horses, older horses, horses who might be intolerant to various ingredients and so on. So when feeding ought to be relatively simple, why has it become seemingly complicated and how on earth is the average owner supposed to work out how to do the best for his or her horse?

The answer is that, whilst scientists now know more about horses' nutritional demands than ever before, it is essential to base any feeding plan on the horse's physical and mental demand for a diet that is based mainly on good quality forage. In fact, good feed manufacturers stress this themselves. In many cases, good forage and a broad-spectrum vitamin and mineral supplement will be all that is needed to enable a horse or pony to work and remain in correct condition; in the case of animals in true hard work or those with specific needs, extra fuel will be necessary. However, it's important to realize that one of the biggest problems in the horse world echoes that in our own – too many are overweight and even obese. The results are the same in both cases: physical problems that can affect and even end a horse's working life.

So before you start working out what to feed your horse, assess his condition and workload accurately. The best way to assess his condition is to use a system called condition scoring, which is explained in Chapter 9, and to use a weight tape every couple of weeks. Whilst this may not be

*Forage should form the main part of every horse's diet.*

strictly accurate, it will show whether your horse is gaining or losing weight. When you see a horse every day, minor weight fluctuations aren't usually noticeable to the naked eye and your horse may be piling on the weight without you realizing it. Weight gain is usually potentially more harmful than weight loss. (It is not necessarily a problem if your horse weighs a bit less in winter than in spring and summer, when grass is more nutritious, but these seasonal fluctuations should be fairly minor – if a horse becomes outright skinny in winter, and fat in summer, there is something wrong with your regime.)

It is also important to check that your horse's mouth and teeth are in good condition and that he is on an effective worming regime (see Chapter 9). If a horse can't chew properly, he will not get the full value from his food; he may also be more at risk of getting colic. Similarly, if he has a worm burden he will also be at risk from colic – and other problems as well.

The other factor that must be taken into account is that the horse is designed to eat most of the time – given the opportunity, he will spend about two-thirds of his entire time grazing. This isn't because he is greedy, but because his digestive system is designed to cope with 'trickle feeding' rather than taking in larger, less frequent amounts. He therefore has both a physical and a psychological need to chew.

## WORKLOAD

Most owners greatly overestimate their horses' workloads. The following guidelines show that most animals are in light or medium work even when ridden every day, and that relatively few are in true hard work. However, they can only be guidelines – someone who rides a horse in for two hours before a dressage test or showing class is obviously upping the workload considerably. Similarly, if you are unwise enough to jump your horse in four classes at a local show and end up in the jump-off each time, he could be working harder than a horse competing in one or two low-level affiliated classes at a competition.

*LIGHT:* hacking; the basic levels of dressage; show jumping at unaffiliated level and up to about 1.15 m (3ft 9 in); sponsored rides and endurance rides at a slow pace and up to about 25 km (15 ½ miles); unaffiliated one-day events; showing.
*MEDIUM:* the lower levels of affiliated one-day events; show jumping at around 1.2 m (4 ft); endurance rides up to 80 km (50 miles) ; affiliated dressage at Elementary to Advanced Medium level; fast canter work in preparation for racing.
*HARD:* affiliated three- and four-star three-day events; endurance race rides; racehorses in full training and racing; hunting three full days per week in demanding country.

*Horses who are fit enough to race, such as these point-to-pointers, are in hard work.*

## HOW MUCH?

ONCE YOU HAVE assessed your horse's condition and weight (see Chapter 9), you can decide how much food he needs overall each day. Don't get hung up on number crunching, though – use your common sense as well by taking into account how your horse looks, feels and behaves.

In general, a horse who does not need to lose weight needs to consume the equivalent of 2–2.5 per cent of his bodyweight daily, which in the case of a 550 kg (1,200 lb) horse would be between 11 kg and just under 14 kg (24–31 lb). Forage – grass and hay or haylage – should make up as much of the diet as possible and, in some cases, all of it. The forage portion should never fall below 50 per cent and will normally comprise 75–100 per cent of the total ration. Grass will provide between half and all the horse's forage needs, depending on how much time he is in the field. When he is stabled, perhaps overnight, he will need hay or haylage to keep his digestive system working and allow him to chew.

YOUR HORSE will need extra forage when grass has a low nutritional value – normally during the winter months – and when he is stabled. This can be in the form of good-quality hay or haylage. Hay is grass that is cut and baled when dry; haylage is grass that is baled when some moisture remains, then bagged or wrapped to keep out the air. It is not the same as silage, which ferments to a much greater extent in the bale and can lead to digestive problems and the risk of potentially fatal botulism. Silage is fed to cattle successfully, but is not recommended for horses.

So do you choose hay or haylage? It depends on your horse and pony and on the quality of forage available, but the pros and cons below may help you to decide.

HAY

**Pros:** higher in fibre than haylage; cheaper; usually has a lower nutritional value and so can be fed in larger quantities.

**Cons:** needs to be stored under cover; it can be difficult to find hay with a minimal dust and mould spore content, so nutritionists now advise that all hay should be soaked for short periods. (Forget the old advice of soaking hay overnight, as this leaches out the nutrients – unless, of course, you are trying to get weight off a fat animal whilst keeping him content. Instead, soak for between ten minutes and one hour, depending on the quantity. Submerge the hay in clean water, then drain and feed whilst still wet. If it dries out before it is consumed, the danger from dust and mould spores returns.

HAYLAGE

**Pros:** usually has a higher nutritional value than hay, though many manufacturers now make haylage suitable for animals who require a lower nutrient value; doesn't need to be soaked; can be stored outside.

**Cons:** more expensive than hay; lower in fibre; if bales are punctured or something goes wrong in the baling process, haylage may go mouldy. If you see any mould, discard the whole bale – your supplier should replace it.

Because haylage is highly palatable, many horses eat it quickly. In some cases, you may need to slow down the eating rate by feeding it in a small-mesh haynet. There is no reason why you can't feed both haylage and soaked hay mixed together to give the extra fibre, though a lot of horses will carefully pick out all the haylage first.

If necessary, buy haylage with a lower nutritional value or substitute low-energy, high-fibre feed for part of the ration. The more you cut down your horse's fibre intake, the more you increase the risk of digestive disturbances and perhaps colic.

*Haylage is grass that is baled whilst some moisture remains, then bagged or wrapped.*

*Feeding horses from the ground means that their teeth wear in a natural pattern and they are less likely to build up undesirable muscle on the underside of the neck.*

Most people feed hay or haylage in a net because it is more convenient and causes less wastage. However, it's far better for your horse to be fed from the floor, because this mimics grazing action and so creates a more natural pattern of wear on his teeth. From a schooling point of view, it also means you are encouraging him to keep the muscles on the underside of his neck relaxed. If you find your horse is trashing a lot of hay in his bed, look at one of the commercial hay containers which are fixed to the floor.

## WARNING!

Whatever forage you buy, make sure it comes from a reputable maker or supplier with a good reputation and extensive knowledge of horses. The biggest danger of forage from an unknown source is that it may contain ragwort, which means you could be slowly killing your horse with every mouthful he consumes. Ragwort that has been cut and baled is not obvious to the naked eye.

### FORAGE FEEDS

There are lots of forage feeds that can be used as well as hay or haylage. They may occasionally need to be used to replace long-stem forage; for instance, very old horses and ponies who find it difficult to chew can often manage short-chop feeds or high-fibre nuts soaked to make a mash. Short-chop feeds are also useful to mix with compound feeds to slow down the horse's eating rate and make his meal last longer, to act as a carrier for medication or to keep a horse who doesn't really need or can't have extra feed happy when his friends are fed.

These feeds range from molassed chaff, chopped straw or a mix of chopped straw and hay coated lightly with molasses, to dried grass and alfalfa. Check the energy levels (stated on the bag), as they vary; for instance, whilst alfalfa (lucerne) is a valuable addition to many horse's diets, you would not want to feed it to a laminitic or overweight animal, as the energy value would be too high.

**TOPPING UP THE FUEL TANK**

IF YOUR HORSE WORKS well and maintains the correct condition on a 100 per cent forage diet, all you need to think about is making sure that he receives enough vitamins, minerals and micronutrients – see the section on supplements and additives later in this chapter. However, you may need to supply extra fuel in the form of hard feed, especially in the winter when grass is scarcer and has lower nutrient levels. This is when compound feeds, straight cereals and other additions such as soaked sugar beet are used.

Compound feeds are formulated to give a balanced ration, either as cubes or coarse mix. Cubes are usually slightly cheaper, but most horses are just as happy to eat them as coarse mix. Mixes might look more visually appealing to us and there may be the occasional picky eater who turns up his nose at cubes, but if you want to save money, start off with the latter. There is a huge choice of compound feeds available, but it's important to feed one that is suitable for your horse and his workload. Feeding a competition horse mix won't turn a happy hack into a successful event horse!

Straight cereals, usually oats or barley, are still fed in some yards and rolled oats in particular are a traditional horse feed. Whilst cereals are an ingredient of compound feed (where they will have been through a special cooking process, if necessary, to make them more digestible) the main disadvantage of feeding them as part of a home-made feed regime is that their nutrient levels will vary between batches. They also need supplementation to balance nutrient deficiencies; for instance, you could feed oats with one of the widely available oat balancer products.

Compound feeds, on the other hand, have guaranteed nutrient levels and are a much easier way to feed. However, they will only supply all your horse's needs if fed at the manufacturer's recommended minimum daily quantity. This is usually 2.5–3 kg (5½–6½ lb), which in many cases will be far too much – so if you feed less than the recommended daily minimum, add a broad-spectrum vitamin and mineral supplement at half the recommended daily amount.

### FEELING HIS OATS?

As mentioned earlier, oats are a traditional horse feed and, in theory, their relatively low starch content and high levels of fibre make them the most suitable cereal for equines. So why do they have such a bad press in terms of generating excitable behaviour? And is it really deserved?

We don't really know the answers, but the most likely explanation is that because the starch in oats is more easily digestible than the starch in other cereals, they provide 'fast-release' energy rather than 'slow-release'. As most of us ride our horses fairly soon after feeding them, we're probably getting on board just as they are getting the benefit and literally feeling their oats!

So will feeding oats as part of a balanced diet add sparkle to a lazy horse? Some nutritionists feel that this is an acceptable strategy, but there are many cases when it could be counter-productive. For instance, if your horse is lazy and overweight – or lazy because he is overweight – adding extra calories isn't the answer. The only real answer to motivating a 'lazy' horse is to get him fitter and improve his schooling, teaching him to react more quickly to lighter aids.

### WHAT'S ON THE BAG?

All feeds and supplements must carry a statutory statement. This includes information such as the species of animal it is made for; a 'best before' or 'use by' date; the net weight; all ingredients in descending order of weight; the analytical constituents and a range of additives, including colours, preservatives and some vitamins. Manufacturers are not allowed to claim that a feed product prevents, treats or cures a disease – which is why you see so many phrases such as 'supports joint health'.

The analytical constituents are not ingredients, but are values obtained from analysis of the varied feed by different methods. A lot of people worry when they see a reference to ash, but feed does not contain ash. The term refers to a mineral residue that is left when, during analysis, the feed is burned at a very high temperature.

## USEFUL EXTRAS

Most nutritionists say that it is advisable to add one or two tablespoons of salt per day to your horse's diet, even if he is getting concentrate feed as well as forage. Some owners prefer to provide free access to salt licks in the stable and field, but the risk of these is that the horse either may not use them or may be so enthusiastic about them that he takes in too much.

Electrolytes are substances which maintain the balance of fluids in the body. The three most important are sodium, chloride (which together constitute salt) and potassium, which are lost in sweat. For this reason, commercial electrolytes are often recommended for hard-working horses who have been sweating heavily.

Sweating is the horse's natural way of regulating his body heat, but sometimes – particularly in times of combined heat and humidity – this system of thermoregulation doesn't work, because the sweat does not evaporate quickly enough. Whilst human sweat is less concentrated than body fluids (hypotonic) a horse's sweat is the opposite. Because it is more concentrated (hypertonic) a horse can lose considerable amounts of essential body salts during hard work or prolonged periods of sweating in hot and humid conditions.

Although free access to water and his normal diet will eventually restore the balance, a horse who is working hard over several days – for instance, an eventer or endurance horse – needs extra help. Ask your vet's advice about which commercial electrolytes are the most useful.

Soaked sugar beet pulp is a by-product of sugar manufacture and is a very useful fibre feed. It must be soaked in water, otherwise it will swell during the digestive process and may cause colic or even a ruptured stomach. Traditional sugar beet pellets need to be soaked for at least 12 hours, but a new generation of products is ready for feeding after 15–20 minutes. The other advantage of these quick-soaking sugar beet feeds is that they won't ferment in hot weather.

Sliced apples and carrots are a real treat for most horses. They can also be used to tempt fussy feeders.

Linseed adds calories, makes feed palatable, gives a gloss to a horse's coat and is traditionally fed in hunting and showing yards. It must be boiled for 20 minutes to destroy the hydrocyanic acid in the seeds, then simmered for several hours until a jelly forms. Alternatively, use dried linseed meal.

Bran used to be a staple in every horse's diet, then was condemned as the worst thing you could have in your feed room. There are still varying opinions as to whether it is good or bad; the biggest problem is that horses need twice as much calcium as phosphorus in their diets, and as bran is low in calcium and high in phosphorus, you need to feed a calcium supplement to compensate if you feed bran.

When horses worked hard all week and had Sundays off, they were traditionally given a bran mash on Sunday night, which acted as a laxative. However, this in turn goes against one of the golden rules of feeding, which is that all changes to the diet should be made gradually. Perhaps the best way to look at bran is that it can be useful if your vet suggests you give your horse a bran mash in a situation where its laxative properties are desirable.

---

### HOW TO MAKE A BRAN MASH

Put about 1 kg (2.2 lb) of bran and a handful of salt in a bucket and pour over enough boiling water to produce a damp, crumbly mixture – you don't want it to be sloppy. Add some molasses, sliced carrots or apples (or apple juice) for palatability, stir and cover. Leave for about 15 minutes until it is warm but not hot, then feed.

---

## FEEDING FOR WEIGHT LOSS OR GAIN

THE FOLLOWING are general guidelines – a veterinary perspective on feeding for weight loss is given in Chapter 9. If your horse needs to lose or gain weight, it's important to do it sensibly. Just as crash diets or gorging aren't healthy – or, in the long term, effective – for us, so you need to use strategies that will not compromise your horse's well-being.

Slimming down a fat horse doesn't mean leaving him for hours with nothing to eat, as this would compromise both his digestive system and his need to chew. The most likely result would be a bored, bad-tempered horse who is susceptible to colic. Instead, look at what you feed him. Stick to the rule of providing plenty of forage, but choose hay that has a low nutritional value, such as a crop that has more stem and less leaf. Soak it overnight to reduce the feed value further, but retain the entertainment value for your horse. You could also feed oat or barley straw instead of hay, if you can find it.

You will probably need to restrict the amount of grass your horse eats, but don't restrict his turnout. If possible, fence off a small area with temporary electric fencing and have it grazed down by another horse. Turn out your fatty on what's left, if necessary providing hay or straw as above. When the area can no longer support grazing, move him on to another area that has previously been grazed. Another approach is to use a grazing muzzle such as a Greenguard muzzle. This allows the horse to take in tiny amounts of grass as he forages and, of course, to drink: never use a solid muzzle, as there have been cases of foals in particular putting their noses in troughs and literally drowning in their muzzles.

Your fat horse won't need any compound feed, but you can provide vitamins and minerals via a supplement mixed into a handful of unmolassed chaff, or a low-calorie balancer pellet. Feeding carrots – very low in calories and with a high water content – will help keep him happy, especially when other horses are being fed.

With horses, as with humans, the best way to lose weight is through a combination of diet and exercise. If he is a riding or driving horse, increase his work gradually and, if necessary, start by walking him out in hand or long-reining. Lungeing is useful, but is hard work, so this too must be built up gradually. Finally, don't over-rug a fat horse. Use a thin turnout rug, if necessary, to avoid the risk of rain scald in bad weather, but let him burn off some of his excess fat to keep himself warm.

If you think your horse is too thin, first double-check! So many horses are overweight that it's sometimes easy to think that a horse is underweight when he is actually in correct condition. If you're sure he is underweight, get his teeth checked by a vet or qualified dental technician and arrange for your vet to take a worm count.

To put on weight, you need to increase the intake of calories. Provide ad lib, nutritious forage such as leafy hay or haylage and either give him more of his current compound feed – remembering to stick to the 'little and often' rule – or substitute one of the many conditioning feeds for part of the ration. If you add a different feed, introduce it gradually over several days. Adding sugar beet or oil to his diet will also add calories. Vegetable oil is particularly good and though you should start with a small amount per feed, it can gradually be increased up to a daily maximum of about 50 ml (2 fl oz) per 100 kg (220 lb) of bodyweight.

If your horse is bright, alert and happy in his work and you know that he has no dental or parasite problems, don't force-feed him. Some horses, like some people, are naturally energetic and naturally slim. When was the last time you saw a fat athlete?

## FEEDING CONTROVERSIES

EQUINE NUTRITION probably has as many controversial areas as you'll find in the human field. Over the past few years, one of the biggest controversies has been whether or not horses react adversely to sugar, with some owners maintaining that their horses become excitable if fed soaked sugar beet or molasses, or even believing that they are allergic to sugar. Logic suggests that as grass contains a high level of sugars, this is impossible – though there is also general agreement that large amounts of refined sugar could be unhealthy for horses as well as people.

Some people believe that molassed sugar beet can cause behavioural problems, but it may be that the horse in question is getting more than he needs from his overall diet and that adding sugar beet has simply tipped the balance. If you are convinced that eliminating it from your feed room solves your problems, go ahead, but rather than lose a valuable source of fibre, try unmolassed sugar beet. This is also a better option for good doers.

Food intolerance is big news in human nutrition and, not surprisingly, has translated to horses. Whilst no one would argue that it is impossible, it is unlikely that it is as common as some manufacturers seem to believe. If your horse becomes 'fizzy' or unpredictable when you increase his hard feed, the answer is usually simple – give more forage and less hard feed. Skin reactions should always be investigated by your vet and most vets say that reactions to food are very rare.

*Supplements may be useful in some situations.*

## HYGIENE AND STORAGE

ALL FEED AND FORAGE should be kept clean and dry in a cool place and be protected as far as possible from rats, mice and birds. Keep all feed rooms and barns as clean as possible, sweeping up spilled feed. Hay should be stored under cover, though haylage can be kept outside whilst bagged or wrapped. Compound feeds must be kept in suitable containers; proper galvanized feed bins are ideal, but expensive. For the average owner, buying two or three bags of feed at a time, metal dustbins are an economical answer. Plastic ones may be a lot cheaper, but won't stand up to rodents' teeth.

Wash out all buckets and mangers daily. Even if your horse has water left in his stable from overnight, empty it, clean the container and refill with a fresh supply. Water becomes tainted from the ammonia in waste, particularly urine, and may mean that a horse won't drink until he is desperately thirsty – by which time, he will already be dehydrated (see final section this chapter).

## SUPPLEMENTS

SUPPLEMENTS – or complementary feeding stuffs, as officialdom now calls them – have always been an accepted part of horse management. Fifty years ago, grooms would add an egg or a bottle of Guinness to a horse's feed to give him a 'tonic', or feed dried nettles to bring out the dapples in a grey or bay coat.

Today's supplements are usually more high-tech and certainly have higher prices. 'Nutraceuticals' has become the feed room buzzword and the line between products that support health and those that may actually go further sometimes seems blurred, perhaps in part by clever advertising and marketing. There are mixed views on whether nutritional science has reached the stage at which every horse or pony, whatever his age, type or job, could benefit from extra nutritional support, or whether a lot of owners are spending money unnecessarily. Perhaps the answer lies somewhere in the middle.

Whilst some understanding of what can help particular problems relies on anecdotal evidence, there is also new research. For instance, research by Dodson and Horrell has found that, whilst spring and summer grazing may enable horses to maintain weight and condition and provide enough energy and protein for light to medium work, it may not provide all the nutrients horses need: it may be deficient in one or more of the key vitamins and essential minerals such as chloride, zinc, copper, selenium, magnesium, sodium and phosphorus.

Occasionally, anecdotal evidence suggests that certain approaches can work with some horses even when there is, as yet, no scientific research to prove it. One example is that many owners, including top-class professionals, are convinced that feeding a magnesium supplement promotes calmness. However, it is important to look at your horse's overall diet and lifestyle before reaching for a supplement, and also to take into account his natural temperament.

There are supplements designed to help in all sorts of situations. Broad-spectrum vitamin and mineral supplements are, as mentioned earlier, designed to supply those that may be lacking in the horse's diet; alternatively, you could use a feed balancer – highly concentrated essential nutrients formulated into pellets and fed in small quantities instead of, or in some cases alongside, conventional compound feed.

Other products are more controversial and include those formulated to support joint health (often marketed for horses and ponies showing signs of stiffness); healthy hoof growth; to encourage calmness in excitable animals and to have a beneficial effect on mares who are unpredictable during the breeding season. One of the latest ideas to come on to the market is the use of products containing antacids to try to reduce crib-biting and wind-sucking. Whilst the products are new, the idea isn't: in the nineteenth century, grooms placed lumps of chalk in their charges' mangers to try to bring about a beneficial effect on the digestive system.

Nutritional support can be useful and sometimes vital, but don't fall into the trap of using supplements without due consideration. The first step in trying to solve a problem should always be to ask your vet's advice and/or to look at your overall management. A supplement designed to support and maintain joint health won't help if your horse is actually suffering from a foot abscess or has strained a tendon or ligament, and a product for grumpy mares won't be of any use if your mare is reacting to a badly fitting saddle or even has an ovarian tumour. Get a proper diagnosis first, then consider nutritional support in addition to any treatment your vet recommends.

Nor is feeding an antacid to try to stop your horse crib-biting likely to work if you restrict his forage and turnout: a horse only produces saliva, which is a buffer to stomach acid, when chewing – and eating forage necessitates a much higher chewing rate than eating low-fibre feeds. Just as important, it is generally accepted that crib-biting is a reaction to stress and the best way to alleviate stress is to turn a horse out in the field rather than stable him.

## WARNING!

Don't assume that because a product is marketed as 'natural' you don't have to take any precautions. Exceeding recommended dosages, giving supplements (herbal or otherwise) as well as medication without checking with your vet, and feeding more than one supplement at a time can lead to problems. Remember, too, that some substances are prohibited under competition rules. For instance, if you use a supplement containing valerian in the hope that it will help your buzzy event horse perform a better dressage test and this shows up on random testing, you will be facing serious disciplinary measures.

Rules on prohibited substances are updated all the time and it is not enough to accept a manufacturer's claim that, for instance, a product is permitted under FEI rules – the onus is on you to check, which can be easier said than done. If you can't be sure exactly what a product contains, don't use it.

### PROBIOTICS AND PREBIOTICS

Advances and fashions in human nutrition often cross over to the equine feed industry. Over the last few years, probiotics have become a buzzword in human health; supermarket shelves are packed with products containing live bacteria and they are heavily promoted as the answer to everything from stress to irritable bowel syndrome. In turn, that has sparked huge interest in probiotics and prebiotics for horses – so even though they have been around for a long time, they too are finding new converts.

Probiotics and prebiotics both help maintain a healthy balance of micro-organisms in the horse's digestive system, but work in different ways. The micro-organisms, which include bacteria and fungi, are called micro-flora and break down fibre in the hindgut so that the nutrients from it can be absorbed. In simple terms, a probiotic is a live product that can colonize the gut and should be used in situations where bacteria need to be replaced: in an extreme example, your vet may feel that a probiotic could be beneficial if a horse has had laminitis or colic surgery. A prebiotic, which cannot colonize the gut but which can help maintain the balance of the micro-flora, might be used if a horse gets excited when travelling. Prebiotics are now sometimes included in feeds.

In general, probiotics are fed over a shorter period. Whilst a prebiotic doesn't have to be a permanent addition to the diet, some people do use one all the time because they say that whatever they do, their horse has loose droppings. You can feed a prebiotic for a longer period than a probiotic because you're only feeding the bacteria that are already there, you're not adding to them. Some products incorporate both probiotics and prebiotics in a belt and braces approach.

Don't assume that because your horse or pony has loose droppings, all you need to do is add a probiotic or prebiotic. Again, the first step is to look at your management and perhaps discuss the problem with your vet. Is your horse suddenly grazing on wet spring grass, guaranteed to get things moving? If you have changed his diet, either feed or forage, has it been done too quickly? Could the problem be related to a worm burden, in which case your vet will arrange to carry out a worm count? (See Chapter 9.)

Ideally, horses' digestive systems shouldn't need extra help if they are getting a balanced diet. In reality, they face stresses ranging from weaning to competition – as well as challenges to the system that are necessary for their welfare, such as worming and, when necessary, medications such as antibiotics. At such times, extra support can give real benefits. However, products formulated to support the digestive system *should not be used as an excuse for continuing bad feeding practices*.

Racehorses, often fed high-starch, low-fibre diets and given minimal if any turnout, are often held up as an example of the worst way to keep a horse. Unfortunately, the commercial reality is that trainers need – or feel they need – to get a high level of energy into their horses without feeding much fibre. One consequence of this is that some racehorses become susceptible to gut disturbances, and prebiotics, probiotics and other substances may be given to prevent or alleviate these. Encouragingly, some trainers are seeing the benefit of turning out their horses and increasing the amount of forage.

The key times to think about feeding a probiotic or prebiotic are:

- When foals are weaned.
- When mares are covered.
- When a horse moves to a different yard.
- After worming.
- After receiving antibiotics.
- To alleviate travelling and/or competition stress.
- When older horses cannot digest fibre as well as they used to.
- When a horse is fed a high-starch diet.

## BUZZWORDS

The more research you do on feeding horses, the more often you will find particular words and phrases coming up. Here are some of the most prevalent.

*ANTI-OXIDANTS:* compounds that mop up free radicals – highly reactive, unstable molecules – and thus protect the body from their effects.

*BIO-AVAILABILITY:* this means the ease – or otherwise – with which nutrients can be used by the body.

*BIOFLAVONOIDS:* these occur naturally in many plants. They act as anti-oxidants and improve the circulation.

*CHONDOPROTECTIVE AGENTS:* these are thought to slow down the degenerative processes of arthritis. The best known are glucosamine and chondroitin sulphate.

*DIGESTIBLE ENERGY:* this describes the estimated amount of calories in a feed (including forage) that can be absorbed and used by the horse. 'Used' can mean for growth or maintenance as well as work.

*DIGESTIVE ENHANCERS:* this term is usually applied to probiotics and prebiotics.

*ENERGY DENSE:* a concentrated source of energy in a reduced volume of feed.

*EXTRUSION:* a form of cooking which makes cereals more digestible.

*MICRONIZATION:* another form of cooking which makes cereals more digestible.

WE'VE ALL BECOME much more aware of how important it is to keep our bodies hydrated: if you don't keep a bottle of water on your desk, you're in the minority! It's also vital for your horse and he should have a permanent, unlimited supply of clean, fresh water indoors and out. Whilst racehorse trainers may remove the horse's water supply for a short period before a race, the general advice now is that horses, like people, should be allowed frequent small drinks during long periods of exercise. Endurance riders have to make sure that their horses drink regularly throughout a competition, if necessary encouraging fluid intake by offering very sloppy soaked sugar beet or adding apple juice or mint cordial to water.

Most horses will drink between 20–45 litres (about 4⅓–10 gallons) a day, but this varies according to factors such as weather conditions, workload and the moisture content of the rest of their diet. Every horse should be allowed to regulate his own water intake. Even a 2 per cent level of dehydration will affect a horse's performance and this won't be picked up by the commonly recommended 'pinch test'. (Pinch and release a fold of skin at the base of the neck; it should spring back into shape immediately and if it doesn't your horse is badly dehydrated.)

Field troughs should be cleaned out regularly and, if they freeze over in winter, the ice must be broken regularly – if there is enough breeze to move the water, you may find that floating a plastic ball in it helps prevent ice forming. Some horses are reluctant to drink from water containers on the stable floor and are happier with ones which are mounted on the wall. Automatic waterers might seem like a luxury, but they don't allow you to monitor how much your horse is actually drinking.

*Some horses prefer to drink from water buckets mounted on the wall when stabled rather than from buckets on the ground.*

FEEDING CAN BE A complex subject, but the good news is that feed companies do the work so that horse owners can keep it simple! The golden rules below will help make sure your horse is getting the right fuel to keep him healthy and happy, but if you want help formulating a ration for a particular horse, it's often worth ringing one or more of the big feed companies' free helplines. Although they will obviously make recommendations based on their own products, they should follow the same principles; for instance, all highlight the importance of forage. Alternatively, there are a handful of freelance nutritionists who are not allied to particular companies (though by the nature of their profession, they may have done work for them). They will, of course, expect you to pay for their advice.

The golden rules are:

- Feed according to your horse's weight, condition and temperament.
- Make sure that his teeth are in good condition and that you are following an appropriate regime to combat worms (see Chapter 9).
- Make sure that good-quality, clean forage makes up the greater part of his diet.
- Make sure that he always has access to clean, fresh water.
- Mimic nature and preserve his digestive health by allowing him as much grazing time as possible, taking into account any health problems or risks such as laminitis. If he needs compound feed, work to the 'little and often' principle. Don't feed large meals in one go; the maximum a horse should be offered in one meal, apart from forage, is 2–2.5 kg (4½ –5½lb).
- Weigh all feed to start with, including forage, so you know exactly how much he is getting. The easiest method of weighing hay and haylage is to put it in a net and use a spring balance; remember to take into account the high water content of haylage. Weigh compound feed in level scoops, using kitchen scales, or invest in a high-tech feed scoop with a weighing mechanism built in.

Once you know how much of a particular feed a scoop holds, or how much hay and haylage a net holds, you probably don't need to weigh every feed, every day. But do weigh at regular intervals to make sure you're not over- or underfeeding.

- Feed by weight, not by volume. A scoop of one feed will not necessarily weigh the same as a scoop of another.
- Feed according to the work your horse is doing *now*, not what you anticipate *he will be doing*. Increase the work then, if necessary, increase the feed.
- Make any changes to the diet gradually. If you introduce a new compound feed, add a small amount whilst subtracting the equivalent amount of the old one. Continue doing this over a period of several days until you have made a complete switch. Take the same approach with a new batch of hay or haylage, gradually mixing in the new with the old.
- Supplements can be valuable, but if you think your horse has a physiological problem, start by getting veterinary advice.

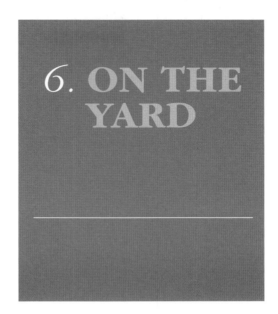

# 6. ON THE YARD

R OUTINE CARE of your horse takes a lot of time – and these days, many of us are rush hour riders. But whilst busy owners need to work out a system that makes sure they don't waste precious minutes, any time you spend with your horse is valuable. It not only allows you to assess and protect his health and welfare, but to get to know him. Horses, like people, have different personalities; some enjoy lots of attention whilst others prefer to keep to their own space. You should expect your horse to treat you with respect, but make sure you behave in the same way.

Most people would agree that horses do not have the same relationship with their owners as dogs do, but they definitely have their likes and dislikes. Professional riders who don't have time to be responsible for the day to day care of horses on their yard appreciate the skills and input of their grooms because they are the ones who notice when a horse might be off colour, or is slightly grumpier than usual. So from the moment you walk on to the yard, focus on your horse and what you are doing, not about problems you might face at work or on your return home.

At the same time, you need to set priorities. If time is short and it comes down to a choice between grooming and exercising, the latter should come first. As long as you pick out your horse's feet and clean off any mud or dirt from areas where tack rests, it doesn't matter if the rest of your horse bears evidence of his rolling, or if his mane and tail are full of shavings from his bed. This doesn't mean that grooming isn't important. It is, as is explained in the next chapter – but don't confuse therapeutic benefit with cosmetic appearances.

*Does your horse look bright and interested when you see him first thing in the morning, or does his demeanour suggest something could be wrong?*

## KEEPING TIME

Now and again, it's also worth doing a personal 'time and motion study', not only by looking at the way you do things, but by watching other people. Even non-horsy friends and family members may have ideas to help you make the most of your time.

● One enterprising riding school owner advertised for ladies who wanted to lose weight to come and muck out her stables, pointing out that this would provide healthy exercise in a friendly atmosphere. You could always try a similar approach, even if it means paying mercenary teenagers to pick up piles in the field.

● Can you save time in the week by multi-tasking at weekends? If you use haynets, fill enough to last the week and you've saved yourself a daily job. Call in the same mercenary teenagers and you've saved even more time.

● Do more than one job at a time. Don't stand there watching water buckets fill when you could be doing something at the same time.

● Keep up to date on products that could make your life easier and look for ideas from other sports and activities. For instance, if you have to carry water buckets to fill up field containers, try a roll-along water barrel with a handle, designed for caravanners.

It's also important to make sure that you don't put yourself or your horse under undue pressure: if you've only got half an hour to ride because you've got an important meeting ahead of you, don't choose that session to work on something that you and your horse have been finding difficult – go for a short hack or lunge him instead, because chances are that, if you try something complex, you'll run out of time and not be able to finish on a good note.

**FIRST IMPRESSIONS**

NOTHING'S NICER than walking on to the yard and seeing your horse's head looking over the stable door – even if he's thinking of you more as a provider of breakfast than looking forward to your company. First impressions are important; don't just rush in and feed him – or, if someone has already done that, start mucking out – because you need to check that nothing untoward has happened since last time you saw him. Start with his overall demeanour; does he seem his usual self, or is he grumpier than usual, dull or showing obvious signs of discomfort, such as sweating? The more you get to know your horse, the easier this will become and, of course, he may take time to settle in a new environment.

As you go into his stable, give him and his surroundings a look round; this soon becomes second nature, but it is important. Don't walk in on automatic pilot because you had a late night – because that's the day you'll miss the fact that he has a swollen fetlock or a small cut. Has he eaten all his supper and hay or haylage, or is there feed left in the manger? If he normally eats every scrap of hay and has left half of it, could he be harbouring the start of colic, or a virus?

Is his bedding in its normal state – which can vary from clean and tidy to a total mess, depending on your horse? Check the quantity and consistency of the droppings: if there are noticeably fewer than usual, or even none at all, or what's there is in the form of small balls that haven't broken as they hit the floor, check your horse's demeanour and temperature and keep an eye on him, as he may be developing impacted colic (where impacted food causes an internal blockage.) Loose droppings may just mean that he's eaten wet grass, which has a laxative effect, but diarrhoea can point to problems such as worm damage.

Take him out of the stable and notice how he moves. Does he move freely, or are there signs of stiffness? Many horses will stop and stretch out a hind leg, which is perfectly normal. Older horses may show signs of stiffness after having been stabled for a few hours; if this is something new, get him checked out by your vet, as it may be the first signs of arthritis or may be linked to an injury. Both cases need proper diagnosis and treatment. Use your ears as well as your eyes: has he lost a shoe, or does one footfall sound different from another, pointing to a loose shoe that needs to be checked?

Tie him up and take off his rugs, if worn. Look him over from head to foot and run your hands over him, feeling for any lumps, bumps and indications of heat in his body and limbs. It really pays to know what's normal for your horse, because that's the only way you can tell when something is abnormal, so make sure you know the location, appearance and feel of anything that was picked up on a pre-purchase examination, such as splints or scars from old injuries. Replace his rugs and pick out his feet, checking the condition of his feet and shoes.

## REMOVING A LOOSE SHOE

If your horse's shoe is very slightly loose, you may have time to ask your farrier to make an emergency visit. In the meantime, don't work him. However, every horse owner needs to know how to remove a shoe so that, when the inevitable day comes and you find your horse with one that is so loose he is in danger of pulling it partly off and injuring himself – perhaps by standing on a nail – you can take preventative action.

Every yard should have the basic tools to remove a shoe: a buffer, a hammer, a pair of pincers and a rasp. At the very least, you need a rasp and a pair of pincers. If you need to buy these yourself, ask your farrier, as he may be able to help. Your farrier is also the person to ask for a practical demonstration in removing a shoe. Most will be happy to show you as, if you know the correct way to do it, you are less likely to cause him or your horse problems.

You will need to hold the horse's leg against your own, so if possible, protect yourself from injury by wearing a pair of full-length suede chaps.

The basic steps are:

● Put the edge of the buffer under the clenches (the ends of the nails that have been turned over on the outside of the hoof) and tap them up with the hammer. If you don't have a buffer, use a rasp to file off the clenches.

● In an ideal world, you will now be able to pull out all the nails, putting each one down where your horse won't stand on it when he puts his foot down. However, you may find you have to loosen the shoe further, using the pincers. Work on each side to loosen, then pull the shoe off from the toe.

## BEDDING AND MUCKING OUT

MOST YARDS (other than those providing full livery) will expect you to muck out first thing in the morning. Even if you have the option of doing it later, it's the best system – droppings left in the stable for a long period attract flies and insects, and wet bedding releases ammonia fumes. The sooner you can get waste material out of the stable and on to a suitably sited muckheap, the better for your horse and his neighbours.

Many racing and competition yards still muck out with horses tied up in the stable, because they believe it is safer. However, this practice is bad news for your horse's health, as you are releasing dust and spores into the environment when he has no choice but to inhale them and are thus compromising his respiratory system. Either tie up your horse outside or, if this is impossible or unsafe, can you turn him out whilst you muck out, perhaps in an outdoor arena?

There is now a huge range of bedding materials available and the one which works best for you will depend on availability, storage space, price and ease of disposal. Another important factor is that you need to protect your horse's respiratory health, so use materials and management methods to minimize dust and spore content. If your horse has recurrent airway obstruction (RAO) talk to your vet about management: in some cases, you may need to keep him out 24/7 and if he needs to be stabled, use rubber matting on its own or with a minimal amount of suitable bedding to soak up urine.

Rubber matting is popular with many owners, with good reason. You'll often see it at veterinary centres and hospitals, where it is important that stables can be cleaned thoroughly between one occupant and the next. It is warmer and softer than a concrete floor, so not only is it useful for horses prone to stiffness, it minimizes the risk of capped hocks and elbows if your horse likes to dig up his bed. Some manufacturers recommend using a minimal amount of bedding in all cases, or even none at all, but it's usually better to use the same quantity as on a concrete floor. This is because some horses are reluctant to stale (urinate) if there is a risk they will get splashed and, if droppings get kicked all over the floor, your horse and his rugs will get filthy. Also, unless you have state of the art drainage in your stable, you need bedding to soak up urine. Waste products which run under matting build up to create not only a foul smell, but a breeding ground for flies and insects.

Although most matting systems are fairly easy to lay, some mats are heavy. If the manufacturer recommends taking them out and hosing down/disinfecting the floor at regular intervals, check that you are actually going to be able to manage this. Some systems are sealed to the floor, which is great when they work – and not so great if the sealing breaks down.

Bedding materials to consider as well as or instead of rubber matting range from the traditional to the high-tech. Try talking to owners who use various kinds and find out how they manage them and whether their stables are similar in design to yours. You also have to factor in your horse's personal habits – some are a dream to muck out and deposit all their droppings in one particular spot, whilst others spread them far and wide.

Wheat straw is a traditional choice for bedding and is still used on many yards. It is relatively cheap, but because it is not as absorbent as some materials you need to make sure that your stable has good drainage. Another disadvantage is that it tends to be dusty and some horses will munch their way through their bed; wheat straw is indigestible and is sometimes implicated in colic (see

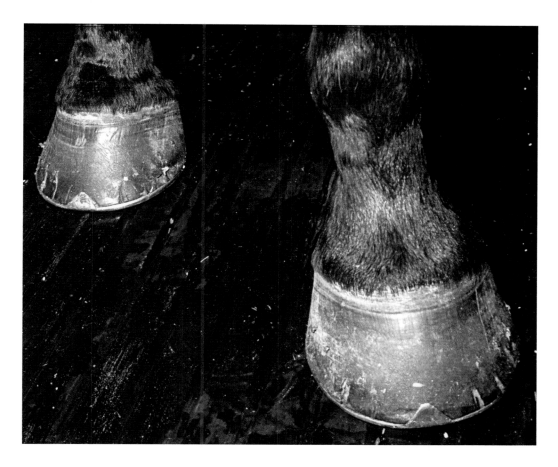

*Rubber matting, laid on concrete stable floors and often used in conjunction with other bedding, adds warmth and minimizes concussion.*

Chapter 10). However, short-chopped, dust-extracted straw that has been packed in plastic-wrapped bales may be a healthier alternative from the dust and moulds point of view. Some products are treated with additives such as eucalyptus oil to discourage horses from eating their beds – though the occasional one refuses to be put off. Straw breaks down easily, but a yard with several horses will be faced with a substantial muckheap to dispose of and if you have to pay for it to be taken away, this could cancel out initial savings.

Dust-extracted wood shavings are another traditional favourite. Some are a by-product of the building industry whilst others are specifically made for the purpose from sustainable woodland. Shavings are readily available and reasonably economical, but some dust extraction systems are more effective than others. Don't buy shavings intended for poultry, as they have a high dust content. Shavings break down reasonably well and produce smaller muckheaps than straw.

There are several highly absorbent wood fibre products on the market, some of which are used in a dry state and some which should be sprinkled with water. Wood fibre is not the cheapest option, but produces a small muckheap.

Dust-extracted chopped hemp, flax and misocanthus (elephant grass) are popular with some owners. As with shavings, the effectiveness of dust extraction can vary. These natural products result in small muckheaps that break down quickly.

Shredded paper and chopped cardboard have the obvious advantage of being dust free to start with, though – as with any bedding – dust from the horse's coat and tiny pieces of droppings that dry and crumble eventually work in. They can be heavy to handle when wet and may also be difficult to dispose of. Also, in windy weather it's difficult to prevent bits of shredded paper escaping and blowing everywhere.

---

### HOUSE-TRAINING YOUR HORSE

You house-train your dog, so can you house-train your horse? It's possible – some owners do in fact teach their horses to stale (urinate) into a bucket by catching them as they are about to perform and giving them a reward when they do. Eventually, the horse will stale 'on command' before or just when he comes in.

However, whilst you may want to use this method if you know that your horse always stales as soon as he comes into his stable, it probably isn't a good idea to carry it to the extreme. For instance, if you get to the stage where your horse will only perform into a bucket, what happens if he needs to stale whilst he's travelling? And if you ever need to find him a new home, not everyone may want a potty-trained horse.

---

### MAKING THE BED

To muck out efficiently, you need the right tools:

A well-balanced wheelbarrow

A skep (pronounced skip) – a large rubber or plastic tub, useful for picking up droppings when not doing a full muck out

Rubber gloves

A fork suitable for the bedding

A plastic shovel

Stable and yard brooms.

Just as keen cooks have favourite implements, so stable hands have their individual preferences; the important thing is to choose equipment you can handle easily without putting undue strain on your back, and to use the correct lifting and pushing techniques. For instance, a four-pronged fork is best for mucking out a straw bed and a two-pronged pitchfork makes shaking out new bales easier, but for shavings and other materials a lightweight shavings fork, which has a greater number of prongs set closer together, is the answer. Consider not just the weight, but also the balance and the length of the handle. For instance, if you're tall, you don't want to be bending over too far. If you're left-handed or have any physical problems, look out for tools designed to make your life easier; these include ones with special handles to allow them to be used one-handed. However, when working one-handed make sure you don't try to cope with loads that are too heavy, which could cause back or arm problems.

Some racing stables still use traditional muck sacks rather than wheelbarrows; these are large, heavy-duty canvas squares with handles on each corner. Soiled bedding is forked into the middle and the sack is gathered up and carried over the groom's shoulder to the muckheap. As these are neither pleasant to use nor back- and shoulder-friendly, they can't really be recommended.

There are three methods of mucking out and maintaining a bed: a complete daily clean out, semi deep-litter and deep litter. The healthiest option for your horse is to muck out completely each day, taking out all the droppings and wet patches, turning over the banks and adding fresh bedding. This is the only acceptable way to manage straw beds.

However, with some highly absorbent materials, you may be able to operate a semi deep-litter system by taking out droppings and obvious wet patches daily and doing a full muck out twice a week. Full deep litter, where only droppings are removed daily and fresh bedding is put on top of wet for several weeks or even months at a time, is a threat to your and your horse's health owing to the build-up of ammonia and moisture. As well as affecting his and your respiratory systems, standing on wet, dirty bedding will predispose your horse to thrush, which attacks the frog and surrounding area in the foot. The only way deep litter bedding can work is if you use a special enzyme system.

### ENZYME TIME

A system developed in Italy uses harmless bacteria and enzymes to turn urine in shavings or other suitable bedding into a colourless, odourless liquid and to accelerate the breakdown of any tiny pieces of dung that escape your fork. A deep bed is set up and maintained with regular applications of liquid and powder products over two weeks; during this time and afterwards, all you need to do is take out droppings and add roughly one bale of bedding per week. The enzymes and bacteria work together to break down harmful substances and mucking out time is cut to a minimum.

Each bed lasts about 18 months. The top layer is then taken off and saved to start a new one and the bottom layer dug out. There is no unpleasant smell and the bedding can be put straight on the land as fertilizer. Muckheaps are much smaller and the system is said to be environmentally friendly.

Whatever system you use, the best way to maintain a clean, healthy bed is to pick up droppings as often as possible. The easiest way to do this is to don your rubber gloves and do it by hand – it isn't unpleasant. Owners who keep their horses at home should try to take out any piles last thing at night: you'll reap the benefits by finding a cleaner bed in the morning.

*When mucking out, keep wheelbarrow loads manageable, as shown here, or you will put unnecessary strain on your back.*

Don't skimp on bedding materials when making a bed from scratch. Some manufacturers give optimistic guidelines on the quantities needed and it's better to be generous than to find your horse with a capped hock because you begrudged an extra bale of shavings. Opinions vary on whether bedding should be banked round the sides of a stable; the idea is that this helps to prevent a horse getting cast (stuck against the wall) if he rolls or lies in an awkward place. This is debatable, but it probably helps prevent draughts. Don't leave an expanse of bare concrete at the door, because that's where your horse stands to look out; if you don't want to lay bedding up to the door, at least fit rubber matting.

## WASTE DISPOSAL

If you keep your horse on a livery yard, getting rid of manure will be the owner's responsibility. But if or when you keep a horse at home, it's a real responsibility for you. Not only does it need to be sited where it can't cause annoyance to neighbours or be a potential fire hazard, you also need to arrange for regular disposal. This is when bedding materials that produce less waste become much more attractive.

Burning muckheaps is not just unacceptable; it's usually illegal under local by-laws. If you're lucky, you may find a local farmer who will collect manure or even leave you a trailer to put muck and bedding on that is collected when full. Realistically, most yards now have to pay for manure to be collected and so need to try to minimize the size of their muckheaps and keep them tidy.

And why not put worms to work? You can buy these hard-working wrigglers and watch your muckheap reduce in size until you're left with what is effectively compost – an efficient and environmentally friendly solution.

## WORKING WITHOUT PAIN

LOOKING AFTER HORSES is hard work, with lots of lifting, pushing and carrying. It's important to protect your health – and at the same time, improve your riding and safeguard your horse – by maintaining a decent level of fitness, as explained in Chapter 8. At the same time, check the way you carry out routine tasks to make sure that you are not putting undue strain on your body, particularly your back.

Lifting weights up to 25 kg (55 lb) or more is a fact of life for horse owners, but keep lifting to a minimum by using a trolley or a barrow to move that sack of feed rather than lugging it across the yard. When you have to lift something, place yourself as close to the load as possible, then bend your knees. Keep your back straight as you lift and tighten your abdominal muscles – join a Pilates class to learn how to build your strength in this area. If you're shifting a weight to a higher level, do it in stages or work with a partner.

More horse-related injuries occur on the ground than in the saddle and many could be avoided simply by wearing the right clothes and staying alert. Boots with protective toecaps can save a bruised or broken toe if your horse treads on your foot; being aware of your horse and the surroundings so you are not in the wrong place at the wrong time is equally important. Wear a hat whenever appropriate; some yards now insist that this is essential when turning horses out and bringing them in – and it's common sense to wear a hat when lungeing, long-reining or clipping a horse who might let fly with a hind leg, even just out of high spirits.

Keep your wits about you and, no matter how reliable your horse, try not to take him for granted or take short cuts. It might seem like the sign of a perfect partnership to be able to bring him in from the field with just a lead rope looped round his neck, but what happens if a bird flies out the hedge and spooks him, leaving you with no control? A headcollar and gloves not only give you more influence; they will save you from painful rope burns if he jumps to one side. If you know he's feeling full of himself, use a controller headcollar or lead him in a bridle – and never wrap a lead rope round your hand or slip a lunge rein loop over your hand. If you do, you could end up with a broken hand or wrist – or even be dragged underneath a frightened horse, with appalling consequences.

## KEEPING CLEAN

WHEN YOU'RE WORKING around horses, you're dishing the dirt – so if you need to go straight on to work, make sure you can clean up first. Arriving with hay in your hair and/or smelling of *Eau de Merde* probably won't advance your career prospects! Some livery yards have all mod cons for owners as well as horses, including hot showers. If facilities are more basic – cold water and getting changed in the tackroom – take a vacuum flask of hot water and keep bottled soap and a nailbrush at the yard. Cleansing wipes are also useful and if you've worked up a sweat, don't forget the anti-perspirant...

Overalls are useful – and essential if you have to change at work. If you have to arrive in old jeans, you can at least ensure that they've stayed clean.

# 7.
# GROOMED FOR SUCCESS

IN A PERFECT WORLD, every horse would get a thorough daily grooming (unless he lives out 24/7 – see later this chapter). As we saw in the previous chapter, there may be days when time constraints make this impossible, but there are some jobs that must be done every day to keep your horse healthy and allow you to check for problems. Most horses enjoy a thorough grooming, so try to fit it in as often as possible.

**THE RIGHT KIT**

EVERY HORSE should have his own grooming kit, to lessen the risk of passing on infections such as ringworm. Wash grooming tools regularly in water with a little horse shampoo added; clean off grease deposits by rubbing the bristles on a piece of clean towel.

Choose grooming equipment that is easy to handle. Modern designs include brushes with flexible backs or finger grips and boomerang-shaped brushes that are easier to hold if you have difficulty gripping. There are also small grooming tools for smaller hands – children often can't manipulate full size brushes.

Some big, busy yards use electric grooming machines. Although these save time and labour, they aren't as good as the real thing. Also, a grooming machine won't pick up signs of heat or swelling that would be noticed when grooming by traditional means.

*If you want to leave your horse with a full tail rather than pulling or shaping it, you can plait it for special occasions, if appropriate.*

Every owner builds up a collection of favourite grooming tools, but the following lists of essentials and extras might help your choice.

## ESSENTIALS

**HOOFPICK,** incorporating a small brush if preferred.

**RUBBER CURRY COMB** or similar groomer.

**DANDY BRUSH** – traditional designs have stiff bristles and may be suitable for gentle use on thick coats and legs coated in dried mud, but are too harsh for horses with thin or clipped coats. Use a flick brush, sometimes called a whisk or flick dandy, instead. This has long, softer bristles and is used to flick away dust raised on the coat.

**BODY BRUSH** – short bristles go through the coat to remove grease, and brush through the mane and tail.

**METAL CURRY COMB** – used only to clean grease from the body brush, never on the horse.

**FLY REPELLENT** when appropriate.

**COTTON WOOL PADS** to clean eyes, nose, mouth and dock. These are far more hygienic than sponges, even when the latter are kept separate, as they can be thrown away after each use and thus help prevent the spread of infection.

**STABLE RUBBER** (a clean cotton or linen tea towel does the job) for giving a final polish.

**TRIMMING SCISSORS** with rounded ends.

## EXTRAS TO ADD LATER

**HAIRBRUSH** designed for human use – a favourite with professional grooms to use on manes and tails without breaking the hair.

**FACE BRUSH** – a small, soft brush with goats' hair bristles to use on the face.

**CACTUS CLOTH** – a loosely woven cloth with mildly abrasive fibres to help remove stains. Cactus cloth mitts (like mittens) are easier to use on awkward areas.

**PULLING COMB** – a metal comb with short teeth if you want to pull (thin and shape) manes and tails the traditional way by pulling out a few hairs at a time.

**SHAPING COMB** from the dog-grooming industry – a kinder way to shape tails if your horse dislikes the pulling process.

**HOOF DRESSING** – if you want to use a cosmetic preparation, ask your farrier's advice. Some oils and dressings dry out the horn, which is undesirable.

**SHAMPOO** – use a shampoo formulated for horses, not washing-up liquid, which is too harsh. Some people use 'cheap' shampoo for human hair, but it doesn't work out any cheaper. If you have a grey or coloured horse with a white tail, shampoos with brightening agents help to turn dingy yellow tails into bright, white ones.

**MANE AND TAIL CONDITIONING SPRAYS** – used every few days, these can help prevent tail hair tangling. They also help keep the tail cleaner, as dirt comes off more easily.

## GROOMING ROUTINES

If your horse or pony lives out all the time, or you need to save time before you ride, follow this four-step method:

*1.* Bring him in and tie him up, remove any rugs and give him an all-over visual and hands-on check to pick up any signs of heat, swelling or injury on his head and neck, body and limbs.

*2.* Pick out his feet, using the hoofpick from the toe to the heel; some hoofpicks incorporate a small brush for clearing dirt off the underside of the foot and round the clenches. Save time on sweeping up by picking out direct into a skep or bucket. Check the condition of shoes, nails and feet: are there any risen clenches or does one foot feel warmer than the other? If so, take the appropriate action.

*3.* Brush off any dried mud in areas where tack or your legs will rest. Wet mud should either be left to dry, then brushed off, or washed off with cold water when appropriate, then dried. If your horse needs to wear boots and his legs are covered in wet mud, hose off with cold water, not warm, to keep the pores of the skin closed. Then pat dry with a towel and use thermal leg wraps to dry them off quickly. Don't put boots on wet or muddy legs or you could set up rubs and skin infections.

*4.* Use dampened pads of cotton wool to clean the outside of each eye, the nostrils, mouth and dock. Use a separate pad for each eye, one for the mouth and nostrils and another for the dock. This minimizes the risk of spreading infection.

*Picking out your horse's feet enables you to remove dirt and any stones that have become lodged and (if he is shod) to check the condition of his shoes.*

*Use a separate pad or piece of cloth to wipe each eye, to avoid spreading infection.*

## QUARTERING

Quartering is the traditional term for giving a stabled horse a quick brush over before you ride. It gets its name because you are grooming a quarter of the horse at a time, folding his rug (if worn) back and forwards to keep him warm. Start by carrying out steps 1 and 2 above, then unfasten his rug and fold it in half so that it covers his back and quarters.

Working on the uncovered area, use a flick brush to flick off any dirt or dust and remove any bedding from the mane, brushing it through and if necessary 'laying' it with a damp water brush to encourage it to lie correctly. Brush the face gently and clean the eyes, nostrils and mouth.

Fold the rug forwards and use your flick brush again. Remove any stable stains with a cactus cloth, damp sponge or cloth, if necessary using a stain-removing product. Replace and fasten your horse's rug, remove bedding from his tail and separate the hairs with your fingers or brush through with a soft body brush. If your horse has fine or sparse mane and tail hair, avoid brushing except when necessary so you don't lose any more.

Whether you are giving your horse a quick brush over or a full groom, the most effective way to work is to use the hand nearer to him – so when you're working on his nearside, hold the brush in your left hand and, on the offside, switch it to your right hand.

## THE REAL McCOY

A full grooming is a workout for you and your horse. Done properly, it will take about 20 minutes and at the end of it, you'll feel as if you've worked hard. Your horse will not only look smart, but should feel both relaxed and invigorated – because done properly, a thorough grooming is the equivalent of a massage. It can also incorporate stretching exercises, as explained later in this chapter.

Whilst quartering is done before you ride, the best time to do a 'proper' groom is after exercise, because although you will, of course, have cooled down your horse, the pores of his skin will still be open. This means that grooming will spread the natural oils of his coat along the hair shafts, helping to keep the coat glossy and healthy.

### GROOMS WITH A VIEW

Different owners have different views on the value of spending time and effort on thorough grooming. Some believe it has no value beyond that of the cosmetic and say that it's what you put on the inside that counts, not what you do to the outside – that the only way to a healthy, shiny coat is through a correct diet. Others set great store by a daily grooming session, pointing out that it gives you the chance to spend time with your horse and pick up any problems. It is also something that many horses enjoy. The obvious answer is to combine correct feeding with a grooming routine that fits into your and your horse's lifestyle, thus giving him the best of both worlds.

*Use a flick brush as part of your grooming routine to remove loose hair and dust.*

Every owner works out a personal grooming system, but following the steps below is a logical base. Be considerate as you work; don't bang bony areas or use stiff brushes on sensitive places. If necessary, use your hand instead.

- Tie up your horse, outside his stable if possible, and check him over as detailed earlier. Pick out his feet and check the condition of his feet and shoes.
- Separate the mane hairs with your fingers and brush them with a body brush or hairbrush if necessary.
- Use a rubber curry comb or groomer in a circular motion to remove dried mud and raise grease and dust to the surface of the coat, starting at the neck on one side and working back, then repeating this on the other side. In cold weather, fold his rugs back and forward as explained in the section on quartering. Tap out any debris which accumulates in the curry comb as you go along. A rubber curry and/or a stiff dandy brush can also be used to remove dirt and dried mud on the legs.
- Now take your whisk dandy and use it in light strokes, ending with a flick of the wrist, to lift the dirt you have raised. Again, work from front to rear so that you are not depositing dirt on an area you've already cleaned.
- Next, it's time to literally use some elbow grease. Stand far enough away from your horse to allow you to put your weight behind each brush stroke – if you are small, or your horse is tall, you may need to stand on something safe to enable you to do this. Lay the brush flat on his coat, then lean your weight into each smooth, sweeping stroke. Use lighter, angled strokes in tricky areas where dirt can get trapped, such as the gullet and behind the elbows.

Don't put your weight behind the brush when brushing over the loins, as this is a relatively weak area, and be careful when grooming ticklish areas such as the belly. If necessary, use your hand instead of a brush and, if he still shows signs of resentment, be gentle and wear a hat when grooming to offer some protection if he cow-kicks. Horses who have been handled inconsiderately will often continue to show signs of resentment even when treated fairly, as they associate being groomed with discomfort.

After every four or five strokes with the body brush, clean it on a metal curry comb. Push the brush over the curry comb, away from you – this way, you won't scatter dust and grease over yourself as happens when you pull the brush over the curry comb towards you. Tap the curry comb on the ground so the debris falls out. Your horse's face can be cleaned with a body brush, small facial brush or a cloth.

- Separate tail hairs with your fingers. If you need to brush the tail, use a body brush so as not to break the hair. Hold the tail near its lower end and brush through the roots, then move up a little bit at a time. This way, you can tease out any tangles but won't create new ones. Using a small amount of de-tangler or conditioning spray every ten days or so helps prevent tangles from building up.
- Clean the eyes, mouth, nostrils and dock, then wipe the horse over with a damp, but not wet, stable rubber. Stable stains can be removed at an appropriate stage with a cactus cloth or a damp sponge or cloth; if necessary, use a stain-removing product and follow the manufacturer's instructions. If you need to wet the coat, wait until the end of the grooming session, or you'll be brushing grease and dust onto damp hair, where it will stay.

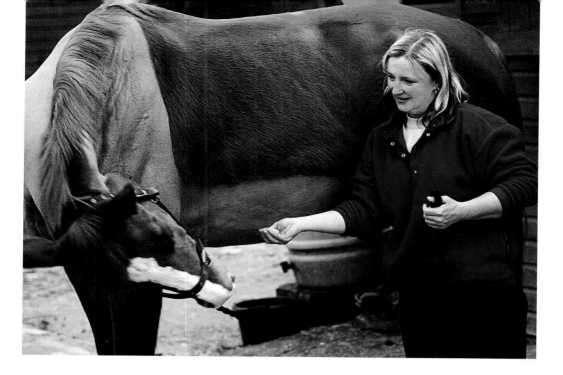

*Careful use of 'carrot stretches' as part of your grooming routine can encourage your horse to stretch his muscles.*

## STRETCHING IT OUT

Use grooming time to carry out some 'carrot stretches'. These will help keep your horse flexible through his neck, shoulders and back by encouraging him to stretch round or down to get his reward – a carrot is easiest to use, hence the name. Some stretches involve manipulating the limbs and it's best to get your vet or a qualified practitioner such as a chartered physiotherapist to demonstrate them to you, as it's important not to extend a joint beyond its normal range of movement, but there are two simple and beneficial ones.

● Encourage your horse to show lateral flexion by holding him on a loose rope so he is standing square. Holding a carrot in your other hand, move it back in line with his nose to encourage him to reach round; if he tries to 'cheat' by moving his back end, stop and put him back in position. He'll soon work out that, to get the carrot, he has to do it right. Build up gradually, first asking him to stretch round so his nose reaches just behind his shoulder, then, if he shows no sign of discomfort, asking him to stretch further back to his hip. Repeat on the other side and notice if he finds one side easier than the other; if so, don't try to force him to stretch as far on his stiffer side and ask your trainer's – or if you think there could be an underlying problem, your vet's – advice about exercises to improve his suppleness.
● To encourage him to lift his abdominal muscles and stretch the ones along his top-line and back, stand him as before and this time take the carrot down between his front legs.

## PRIVATE PARTS

If your horse is a gelding, you will probably need to clean his sheath occasionally. Some people do this frequently, but veterinary advice is that it should only be done if an excessive amount of smegma (waxy material that is the result of normal secretions) builds up. Frequent cleaning has the effect of stimulating the production of smegma, so you end up with a vicious circle.

When cleaning is necessary, wear disposable latex or plastic gloves and wash the area with lukewarm water. If there is a heavy build-up, you may need to use a little mild soap that does not contain colouring or perfume. Avoid commercial products containing antiseptics or detergent, as these can interfere with the balance of normal, healthy bacteria in the area and possibly lead to infection.

Both mares and geldings should have the dock area cleaned regularly with lukewarm water.

## BUZZ OFF

Changing climate patterns mean that flies and other insects can be an all-year-round irritation, so fly repellent is often more than just a summer necessity. Spray products that are environmentally friendly are the easiest way to give all-over coverage, but some horses hate the noise, the feeling or both. Desensitize a horse to the noise by filling a garden plant spray with water and spraying it from a distance to start with, gradually getting nearer. When he accepts the noise, try brushing him and spraying him with water between each brush stroke; for some reason, this settles many horses.

If you still don't feel it's safe to spray, wet a cloth in water and wring it out, then tip fly repellent on to it and apply it in broad strokes over large areas. This way, you use less repellent than if it's poured on to and soaked up by a dry cloth. Alternatively, use roll-on, cream or gel products – useful in their own right for applying to the head and face. It's wise to carry out a patch test first to make sure there is nothing in a product that would irritate your horse's skin, especially with formulations said to last several days.

Some owners swear by feeding garlic or other combinations of herbs to keep off flies. Research suggests that, in theory, a horse would have to consume a large amount for this to work, but if it works for your horse, who cares about the theory?

## BATH TIME

HORSES ARE OFTEN bathed before a competition to make sure they look their best, but unless you have access to luxury facilities such as special wash boxes and infra-red solariums to dry off the horse afterwards, giving him a full bath in cold weather may be impossible. You don't want him to catch a chill and should also consider his lifestyle: if he lives out all the time, he needs a certain amount of grease in his coat as a weatherproofing agent – though this shouldn't be compromised by 'special occasion' baths in warm weather.

Get everything ready before you start so you don't keep a wet horse standing around and increase the risk of a chill. A good bath time kit comprises:

- Shampoo formulated for horses. Some people prefer to use one of the cheaper shampoos for humans, but they don't usually work out any cheaper. Don't use washing-up liquid or any other cleaner containing detergent, as this will strip out oils from the coat and leave it dull as well as perhaps irritating the skin.
- Rubber curry comb and whisk brush to remove as much dirt and dust as possible before you start.
- Wash brush with sponge or nylon mesh body scrub to work in shampoo.
- Sweat scraper to remove excess water from coat.
- Clean towels.
- Thermal rug if necessary to transfer moisture away from the body.

Many yards will have a mixer tap that allows you to use lukewarm water via a hose. If yours doesn't, most horses don't object to being bathed in cold water on a hot day. If it's essential to bath your horse on a cooler day and you don't have all the mod cons, you'll need a constant supply of buckets of clean, warm water.

Groom out as much dirt from your horse's coat as possible, then wet the coat thoroughly. If you're using a hose, play a gentle flow on a front foot then work up his leg and shoulder and along his body. Don't take your horse for granted even if he's accustomed to being bathed – you aren't frightened of having a shower, but you still wouldn't appreciate it if someone suddenly directed a jet of cold water at you. Horses particularly hate getting water down their ears.

If necessary, give him a 'blanket bath', keeping a thermal rug folded over his back and quarters whilst you clean up the front end, then folding it over his shoulders and neck whilst you wash the back half. It's usually easiest to apply shampoo if you dilute it in a small amount of water first, though brightening or colour-enhancing products may need to be applied neat – check the manufacturers' instructions.

Apply shampoo with whatever applicator you prefer, starting at the neck. Include the mane, working shampoo into the roots and down to the ends of the hairs on both sides. Many horses really enjoy this as a form of massage and it's a technique you can incorporate into your grooming sessions. If you need to wash the forelock, take it gently back between the ears, as this makes it easier to keep shampoo out of the horse's eyes. Work down the shoulders and front legs, along the back and down the body. Don't forget the area behind the elbows where grease and dirt sometimes gets trapped in skin folds.

As always, keep yourself out of harm's way. Stand to one side, not behind your horse and bend or crouch if necessary – never kneel down, or you won't be able to get out of the way quickly enough if something untoward happens.

Once you've finished shampooing, scrape off the excess with a sweat scraper, then hose or wash off with clean water. Don't skimp on rinsing: carry on until your horse is squeaky clean and there is no trace of shampoo in his coat. Use your scraper again; you only need to apply a little pressure and your horse will resent it if you press too hard. Finish the drying process by rubbing with clean towels and put on a thermal rug if necessary. Walking your horse in hand or leading him out to pick some grass, depending on the weather conditions, will speed up the drying process.

**NO STRINGS**

The old-fashioned method of drying off a wet or sweating horse – which is occasionally still employed in some yards – was to use an anti-sweat rug made from mesh with large holes, rather like a string vest. Using one on its own, as often seen after races, did no good at all. To have any effect, these rugs need to have a thin rug on top so that a layer of air is trapped between the two. If you look in old books and magazines you may also see reference to 'thatching', where a layer of clean hay or straw was put along the horse's back and a sweat rug fastened over the top.

Although this method was reasonably effective, modern fabric technology means there is no need to go retro, as there are now materials which transfer moisture from the horse's body to the outside of the rug. But don't just put on a rug and trust to luck – if you need to leave your horse in the stable to dry off, make sure he's got hay or haylage to keep him occupied, and keep checking him.

**HEADS AND TAILS**

Unless your horse has bad stable stains on his face, you should only need to use a cloth or sponge soaked in plain water, then wrung out, to wipe over the head area. This means there is no risk of getting shampoo in his eyes and causing discomfort and irritation. If you do need to remove stains, try a cactus cloth mitt – easier to use in this area than a flat cactus cloth – or a cloth soaked in shampoo solution. Don't risk stain-removal products getting in the eyes.

Tails (and manes) can be washed separately or as part of a full bath. When bathing your horse, leave the tail until last, as you can keep your horse warm by putting a thermal rug on if necessary whilst you deal with it. Wet the tail hairs thoroughly from the dock right to the ends, using a bucket and wash brush/sponge or, if your horse accepts it, a hose. Alternatively, hold up a bucket of water and dunk the long tail hairs in it; again, be careful when doing this for the first time and stand to one side, not directly behind your horse.

Apply shampoo and work well into the roots all the way down the dock, then continue down to the ends of the long hairs. Rinse thoroughly, squeeze out excess water and then grasp the tail below the dock and swing the long hairs round in circles. If you haven't tried this before, do it when his tail is dry first – you don't want your horse taking off in fright because he thinks his tail has turned into a helicopter.

**CLIPPING, TRIMMING AND PLAITING**

IF YOUR HORSE grows a thick winter coat and you want to keep him in moderate or hard work, you'll need to clip him. This may be necessary in a mild winter even if he is only doing light work. But before you get carried away by the idea of turning a hairy monster into a strimmed and trimmed picture of elegance, be realistic. The more hair you take off, the more you'll have to compensate in bad weather through careful rugging and feeding. If he lives out all the time, it isn't fair to remove all his natural protection, no matter how efficient and expensive his rugs – and it's downright lazy to take off all his coat because you can't be bothered to follow the lines of a less drastic clip that leaves hair on his back, loins and perhaps all or part of his neck.

If you haven't clipped a horse before, or don't know how your horse will behave, think about paying a professional to do it whilst you watch and pick up tips. If the person you bought him from warned you that he wasn't the easiest to clip, it's definitely best to call in a professional who is used to handling horses and may be able to persuade him that the experience isn't so bad. However, don't pretend ignorance: tell your clipper that you've been told the horse might be difficult so that he or she can allow extra time, and be content with a minimal clip to start with.

## TOO HOT TO CLIP?

Some horses are awkward to clip and a few can be downright lethal. In most cases, it's because they've been badly handled or subjected to discomfort, perhaps from blunt clipper blades that pull the hair. Desensitizing techniques such as using a grooming machine to accustom the horse to noise and getting him used to vibration by holding small trimming clippers against him will solve all or most of the problem in most cases – the proviso being that the person who works with the horse is experienced and calm, with a recognized reputation. If you're inexperienced, this is a 'Don't do this at home, folks' scenario.

Some horses are nervous only about being clipped round their heads, probably because the skull acts as a sound box and increases the noise and vibration. Using small, quiet, battery-powered clippers often helps, or you may want to investigate the pros and cons of using a twitch. This is a restraining device used for short periods only on the top lip; although it looks bad, research shows that it works on an acupressure point to release endorphins – natural 'feel good' chemicals – into the system. The fact that many horses nearly fall asleep when a twitch is applied correctly seems to back up these findings.

A twitch should be applied so that it does not touch the nostrils and secured so it can't become a dangerous weapon if the horse throws his head up. *If you feel you need to use one, do so under expert supervision.*

Alternative routes are to call in your vet to sedate the horse before he is clipped or, if he grows a fine to medium coat rather than a thick one, to start rugging him up before it starts coming through. However, you need to be careful that he isn't at risk of overheating.

### TYPES OF CLIP

There are several classical styles of clip, all of which can be adapted or combined to suit your horse and his circumstances. For instance, a trace, chaser or blanket clip can be high or low. (If you buy a clipped horse in winter, make sure you don't get taken in by an optical illusion. A clever clipper can minimize conformation faults by, for instance, setting back a blanket clip so it makes a long

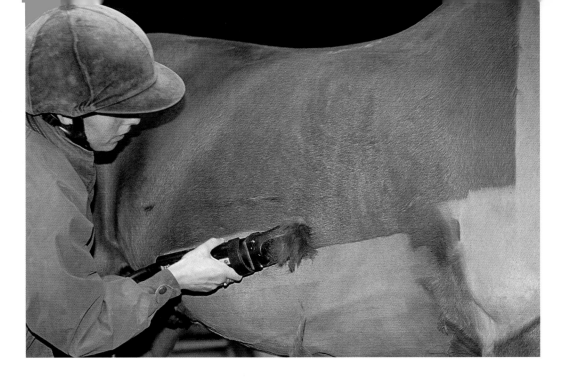

*It's sensible to wear a hard hat when clipping a horse, especially one who is ticklish or nervous and may strike out.*

back appear shorter. In the same way, you can make the most of your horse's shape – or mar it – by the clip you choose.)

The golden rule is to clip cautiously – you can always take off more hair, but you can't put it back. The main types of clip are:

*FULL CLIP:* everything goes, including the leg hair. Not recommended unless thought necessary for show horses.

*HUNTER CLIP:* all the hair is clipped off except for that on the legs and in the saddle area. It's best to leave a saddle patch to avoid rubbing and absorb sweat: either clip round a numnah or leave a lozenge shape under the saddle seat.

*BIB CLIP:* just takes off the hair on the front of the chest and the throat. A little can often make a big difference and this can be a great clip for hairy ponies in light work or animals who live out all the time.

*TRACE CLIP:* follows the lines of harness traces along the body and continues under the throat. One step up from a bib clip.

*BLANKET CLIP:* leaves hair on the back and body equivalent to the coverage of an exercise sheet.

*CHASER CLIP:* takes hair off the belly, lower body, shoulders and most of the neck. Allows for the head to be clipped. A variation of this clip, sometimes called the dealer clip because it smartens up a horse without removing lots of coat and is therefore popular with dealers, starts just behind the elbow and also allows most of the neck and head to be clipped.

## SAFETY FIRST

Clipping is potentially dangerous. For instance, a careless handler can get knocked over and there have been cases of horses' tendons being severed when they objected to or were spooked by the clippers. Think about when and where it will be done – you need a dry, light, safe area out of the wind and your horse should be clean, dry and relaxed. If you try to clip him when he thinks he should be getting his dinner, or other horses are getting theirs, he won't be too keen.

If you're using electric clippers, always use a circuit breaker; it could save your and your horse's life if, despite precautions to keep live cables out of the way, he treads on one. Extension leads must be placed where they won't get trodden on and plugs and cables kept away from and protected from water. Rechargeable battery clippers are great for small areas and trimming but they don't always hold their power long enough to complete larger clips.

Some people clip alone but it's easier and safer with a helper, not least because a helper can hold the horse, help keep him calm and hold up each front leg in turn if the area behind the elbow needs to be clipped. With an inexperienced or nervous horse or one whose behaviour is unknown, both clipper and helper should wear hard hats; long hair should always be tied back. The helper should always stand on the same side as the person doing the clipping, because if the horse spooks, he will usually move away from the clippers – so if you're on the opposite side, you stand a good chance of being knocked down or trodden on.

Always allow plenty of time and don't take the horse by surprise, no matter how experienced he is. Talk to him and run the clippers for a few seconds before starting, so he gets used to the noise. Begin on the shoulder area, which is usually less sensitive, but don't put the blades straight on to the horse. Put your hand on the shoulder and rest the running clippers on top, so he feels a muted vibration before the real thing.

## TRICKS OF THE TRADE

The best way to learn how to do a professional job is to watch a professional. Here are some tricks of the trade:

● Choose the right blades. Fine or medium are best for most horses, though you might need coarse ones for trimming the legs of a heavy cob.
● Clip against the direction of hair growth and make fairly long, sweeping strokes.
● Lubricate blades frequently with special clipper oil. Don't use household oil, as it may clog the blades and/or irritate your horse's skin.
● Keep a spare pair of blades, so if one pair breaks or blunts in use you don't have a half-clipped horse.
● Mark guidelines for where to clip with chalk and use a piece of string to make sure lines meet over the withers and round the quarters.
● If you don't want to clip out your horse's head in full, draw an imaginary (or chalk) line down each side of the face from the base of the ear to the corner of the lips and clip up to this. This gives a smart appearance without having to clip the eye area.

- Use your other hand to stretch out the skin around areas with creases in the skin, such as round the elbows.

- Don't clip all the hair from inside your horse's ears, because he needs it for protection. If he doesn't mind the clippers near them, neaten the outside edges to give a sharp outline.

- Too risky to clip round the ears? Close the edges together gently in your hand and trim the hair that pokes out with trimming scissors.

- If you clip the neck, take the blades as near to the mane as possible, but don't clip into the mane hair. Keeping just below the hairline, hold the blades at a slight angle so they will cut properly even though they may not be running against the lie of the coat.

- If you clip a bridlepath (take hair off where the bridle headpiece lies) be conservative. If you take off too much, you'll make his neck look shorter. The same applies to clipping hair at the withers.

- When trimming for the show ring, pay attention to breed society rules and see how top exhibitors interpret them.

- Clean and check your clippers after every use and follow the manufacturer's recommendations for seasonal checks and servicing.

- Get blades sharpened professionally. On average, a set will last between five full clips and ten partial ones, depending on the size of the horse and how clean he is to start with.

### MANE LINES

Show cobs are traditionally shown with hogged (clipped off) manes and many people feel that a hogged mane suits cob types whatever job they do. Use the clippers in three runs – first up each side of the neck, then up the centre. If you're hogging a long, thick mane for the first time, take off most of the excess hair before going for the final look.

### STAYING IN SHAPE

Unless your horse or pony is kept with a full, flowing mane and tail – a method of presentation for the show ring which applies to 'traditional' cobs, pure-bred Arabs and native ponies – you will want to do some shortening and shaping. Even when breed society guidelines stipulate that animals should be shown with a natural appearance, many exhibitors interpret this as meaning that manes and tails can still be shaped slightly – but be discreet. Fashion also comes into it; for instance, many exhibitors of pure-bred Arabs cut off a sizeable part of the mane at the top of the neck, believing this shows off a flowing neck. However, not everyone agrees.

The traditional method of thinning, shortening and shaping manes and tails is to remove excess hair by pulling it out. If done considerately – which means taking out four or five hairs at a time, pulling when the horse is warm so that the hairs come out more easily and spreading the procedure over several days rather than trying to do it all in one go – some horses don't

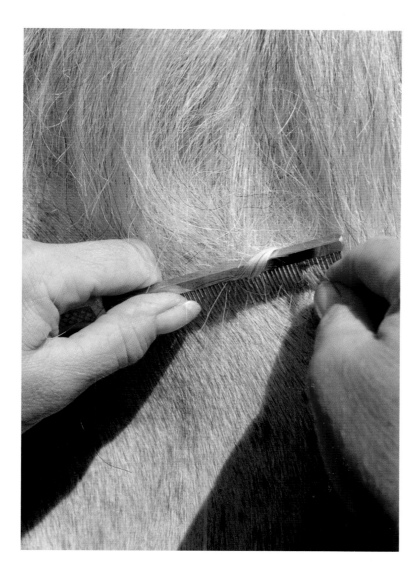

*When pulling a mane, only take hairs out from underneath and remove just a few hairs at a time.*

object and a few even seem to enjoy having their manes pulled. However, others obviously find it uncomfortable or even painful and you need to employ alternative techniques.

### HOW TO PULL A MANE

If you are pulling a mane so that it is easier to plait, it needs to be about 10 cm (4 in) long throughout and of even thickness. Comb it through so that it lies on the offside of the neck, then use either a metal pulling comb with short teeth or an ordinary nylon comb used for human hair to pull out a few strands at a time. Always take hair from underneath, not on top, or you will end up with a row of hairs sticking out at the top of the mane.

*A shaping comb which incorporates short blades can offer an easy and safe way to give the appearance of a pulled tail.*

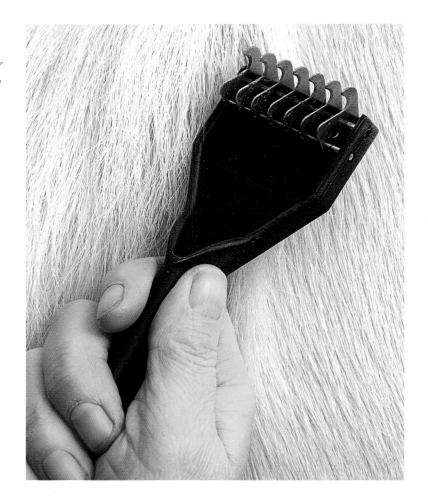

Taking a few hairs at a time, push the top layers up as if you were backcombing, wrap the selected hairs round the comb and pull out in one quick, upward movement. Continue up the mane, stepping back every now and then to assess the appearance. The forelock can be pulled in the same way.

Tails take more practice and put you at more risk. Using the same technique as for the mane, take a few hairs at a time from the sides of the dock, working down until you have the desired shape. If your horse has a thick dock with lots of hair, as is the case with many cobs, you may need to take a small amount of hair from the centre, but only do this if you have to as there is more risk of it sticking up.

To keep a pulled tail looking neat, you'll need to apply an elasticated tail bandage regularly, dampening the hair first. Don't dampen the bandage, or it will constrict as it dries: there have been horrific incidents of horses losing their tails because a bandage that is too tight has been left on for too long. In any case, you shouldn't need to leave it on for longer than two or three hours.

## EXPERT TIP

*'Clever hogging can improve the looks of a cob who has not quite perfect neck conformation. If he has a slightly weak, unmuscled neck, leave a bit more in the centre than at each end and if he's a show cob, hog him about a week before a show to allow for slight re-growth and add to the appearance of a better neck.*
*If he has a slightly too thick neck, hog him the day before and keep the line even.*
*Nothing looks worse than a greasy hogged mane.*
*Remove the grease by wiping along the neck with a cloth dampened with witch hazel.'*

LYNN RUSSELL, SHOW PRODUCER AND COB SPECIALIST

### A KINDER APPROACH

Many people now question whether it is fair to pull tails in particular, particularly as some horses clearly object and it may cause bleeding. It is certainly kinder to use one of the new shaping combs incorporating blades, originally designed for thinning the coats of some breeds of dog. As these achieve the same effect in skilled hands as pulling, why not use one instead? As with everything, practice makes perfect, but they are relatively easy to use and it is possible to get an effect matching that of a pulled tail. Combing down the sides of the dock takes off hair without giving sharp edges and gives a natural rather than a cut look.

Alternatively, you could plait a full tail, as explained in the next section. This takes time, patience and nimble fingers.

If your horse hates having his mane pulled, there are ways round this, too. Combing the underneath layers regularly with a metal comb or using a shaping comb described above – again, not on the top layers – will pull out a certain amount of hair to thin it and you can shorten it with trimming scissors or an old clipper blade. Only use trimming scissors with curved blades, so you won't accidentally prick your horse's neck with the ends. Hold them at an angle and work up the mane, alternately combing and snipping to give a level but natural-looking edge.

To use a clipper blade, comb through the mane, then backcomb the underneath layers and use the blade to nip off a few hairs at a time to the desired length.

*Choose the number of plaits carefully to suit your horse's conformation – achieving results like this takes practice.*

## WHISKERS AND WELFARE

The most controversial aspect of traditional turnout methods is removing whiskers from the muzzle, usually with clippers or scissors. Many competitors in all disciplines believe this accentuates the appearance of a horse's head, but it also has to be acknowledged that whiskers act as sensory aids. It has to be an individual decision and some horses seem more sensitive than others, but if you take off your horse's whiskers and he shows different behaviour when grazing or putting his nose in a manger or bowl, maybe he needed them more than you thought.

(Some people also believe that it is unkind to hog a cob's mane because this removes natural protection from flies. However, it can be argued that in this case, you can compensate by using a fly fringe or mask and fly repellent.)

## PERFECT PLAITS

Plaiting your horse or pony's mane, when appropriate for his breed or type, smartens his appearance for competition or hunting. To get a professional look, try the professionals' secrets:

- Plaiting a newly washed mane is more difficult, as the hair is slippery. Try to wash it a couple of days before a show.
- Sewn plaits are smarter and stay in place better than ones secured with rubber bands, but the latter will suffice when you're in a hurry.
- Choose the number of plaits to suit your horse's conformation – more plaits add an illusion of length of neck, but don't go overboard. The tradition of seven or nine along the neck is often disregarded now, but you shouldn't need more than eleven.
- Spray hair gel for humans at the top of the mane before you start plaiting to flatten shorter hairs that would stick out.
- If your horse lacks muscle on the top of his neck, set the plaits on top to give the impression of more substance. Plait, then push back as you roll up the plait and secure.
- Stable plaits help train an unruly mane to lie flat. Divide into sections, plait down and secure with bands. Leave in for several days.
- To plait a tail, take a few hairs from each side at the top. Cross them, then take a third section from one side to the centre to start your plait. Work down, taking a few hairs from each side in turn as you plait. Keep your plaiting tight so the side bars stay level, continuing until the centre plait is about two-thirds of the way down the dock, then continue it into a long plait without taking in any more side hairs. Double up the end plait and stitch for neatness.

# 8. FIT FOR THE JOB

To KEEP YOUR HORSE sound and healthy and increase his chances of working as well as possible, it's important to build and maintain his fitness. Every horse needs to be fit for his particular job, whether he is a hack or a three-day event horse. As it's pretty obvious that being in shape to do an hour's hack every day doesn't mean he could theoretically go round Badminton, a fitness programme must be tailored to the individual. The basis of getting a horse fit is always LSD (long, slow, distance work) but you can't simply get him fit from a chart. Life doesn't always go to plan – if he gets a viral infection or bruises a foot, you aren't going to be able to tick all the boxes on all the right dates.

So what does fitness actually mean? Perhaps the best definition is that a fit horse can do his job without undue stress. When you're talking about top-level competition, fitness work becomes highly specialized. An endurance horse would not necessarily be in the perfect state of physical tuning to play high-goal polo, just as marathon runner Paula Radcliffe would probably not be first through the tape in a 100 m sprint. The reason why specialized fitness is required for different disciplines at this level, whether you're talking about equine or human athletes, is that the disciplines have different demands.

These demands are often defined partly in terms of aerobic (with oxygen) and anaerobic (without oxygen) respiration. All disciplines use both forms of exercise, and you can't say that one is 'harder' than the other – but one will dominate. Aerobic exercise is of low to moderate intensity over a prolonged period: for example, endurance riding and most dressage. Anaerobic exercise is more intense, over intermittent periods, as with show jumping and polo.

*Every horse needs to be fit for his particular job – in this case advanced eventing.*

*Horses need to be got fit for a particular job, so a regime for a polo pony would be different from that followed for a dressage horse.*

However, whilst we can all learn from top riders' approaches, most of us don't specialize to the same degree. It's relatively easy to get a horse fit enough to take part in most activities at a reasonable level, which covers Riding Club clinics and competitions – dressage, show jumping and cross-country – as well as sponsored/endurance rides up to about 25 km (15½ miles). To a certain extent, everyday riding will build fitness, especially if you're doing a mixture of hacking, schooling on the flat and jumping, with lungeing and long-reining for variety or necessity.

At the same time, you can't sit back and assume that your horse will get fit as if by magic. You need to take a holistic look at his lifestyle to make sure that all aspects from feeding to environment are conducive to good physical and mental health. You also need to make sure that he is working correctly as well as putting in the physical effort, because getting a horse fit for a job won't necessarily make him successful at it. Whilst you might get a horse fit enough to run in a Pre-Novice event in 6–8 weeks, that won't guarantee that he will score a good dressage mark or jump clear.

One thing that is often forgotten is that a horse needs to be balanced and secure mentally as well as physically, taking into account his natural temperament. He might be physically capable of doing a job, but if he's anxious, stressed or bored, he won't come up with the goods.

## FITNESS FACTS

ALTHOUGH DIFFERENT riders may have different ideas about the finer points of getting horses fit, there are some facts which always hold true.

- It's easier to build peak fitness in a horse who has achieved it previously than to get a horse fit for the first time.
- You can't keep a horse at a permanent peak of his maximum fitness. Understanding this is one of the skills top riders use – they time their horses' schedules so that they peak at the correct moment.
- Some types and breeds of horse take longer to reach their physical maturity than others and this must be taken into account. For instance, Irish Draughts, Warmbloods and native ponies may not be fully mature until they are about 8 years old.
- A horse in his late teens who has maintained good levels of soundness and fitness throughout his life can be as supremely fit as one half his age. Look at Over To You who, as this book was in preparation, competed with great merit at his seventh Badminton at the age of 19 with his rider of 15 years, Jeanette Brakewell.
- It all comes down to details and no detail is too small. Ignore the fact that your horse seems slightly listless one day, or tell yourself that it won't hurt to do that show jumping class because a shoe is only slightly loose and you're setting yourself up for disaster.
- To get a horse fit, you impose gradually increasing levels of physical stress so that his physiological systems work harder and his response to stress improves. It doesn't take rocket science to work out that if you keep his work at the same level, his fitness will also stay at the same notch.

However, the build-up must be gradual and if you spot a problem at any stage it is important to back off. For instance, if a horse comes out the day after a schooling session seeming sound but slightly stiffer than normal, take him for a gentle hack and/or make sure he has plenty of time grazing in the field.

- We now know that mild stress helps develop healthy bone in growing youngsters. However, this has been misinterpreted by some people who assume that loose jumping yearlings, 2-year-olds and even foals is a good way to strengthen their limbs. By mild stress, researchers mean grazing – and at the same time, walking – and natural play behaviour. It does not mean forced exercise.
- At top level, you can get a horse *too* fit and impose unwanted wear and tear. This is unlikely to happen at lower levels, where it's more common to see horses out competing at weekends who simply aren't fit enough, but it's a risk that top event riders are now particularly aware of. Whilst competing is, in itself, a way of maintaining fitness, a horse only has so many miles on the clock. The UK foot and mouth epidemic of 2001 caused an about turn in attitude; until then, it was generally accepted that you had to run a horse in a certain number of events to keep his fitness up to scratch. But when, after a lot of events had been cancelled, horses came back to competition only to perform as well or better than ever, it underlined the fact that they hold fitness longer and better than had been appreciated. The attitude now is that if you want a horse to last at top level, you don't impose unnecessary strain on joints and tendons.

# EXPERT QUOTE

*'When you're working out a fitness plan for a three-day event horse, you have to start from your competition date and work backwards, so the horse hopefully peaks at the right time. Once a horse has reached peak fitness, it's easier to work back to it when they've had a break.'*

JEANETTE BRAKEWELL, INTERNATIONAL EVENT RIDER

## BUILDING THE BASICS

IF YOU WANT TO GET your horse fit from scratch, or improve his current level of fitness, give him an equine MoT test first. Hopefully, you will already have made sure that he isn't carrying an unacceptable worm burden, that he is well shod, that his mouth and teeth are in good condition and his tack fits well. Don't forget that the fit of his saddle will need regular monitoring and, if necessary, adjustment.

Be aware of any existing lumps or bumps on his legs, such as splints and windgalls, not only so that you can spot first signs of any new ones but so you can identify any changes. All top riders feel their horses' legs before and after exercise every day – no matter how much they trust their support staff, they know that the buck stops with them.

Ready to roll? Then divide your fitness programme into four stages. The guidelines below could be followed by a rider getting a horse fit for the first time, and can be adapted to suit your individual circumstances. If in doubt, stay at each stage until you are sure your horse is ready to move up to the next one.

## STAGE 1

The basis of any fitness programme for any horse is LSD work, starting with 2–4 weeks in walk only and gradually building up the distance covered. However, if you are getting a horse back into work who has been off for some time, then for safety's sake you might need to lunge or loose-school him for a short period on a safe surface before getting on. This means you are less likely to get bucked off and he can get rid of his surplus energy without the added complication of your weight, on the relative security of a surface on which he is less likely to slip. It isn't safe to take a chance and ride a horse coming back into work after a long period straight out on to the roads, because you are putting at risk yourself, your horse and other road users.

*Jeanette Brakewell and the wonderful Over To You, still eventing at top level at the age of 19, prove that older horses can still be fit and successful.*

If you are dealing with a horse who has been rested because of injury or illness, follow your vet's instructions. It may be necessary to give a horse who has been box-rested a mild sedative before turning him out into a small, enclosed area and, as he gets used to this, into the field. Vets know all too well that it's one thing to advise a client to walk a horse out in hand for a few minutes a day and another to do it in safety. Long-reining your horse can build a useful stepping stone between resting and riding, as well as adding variety to his work.

If you are lucky enough to be able to use a horse walker, this can help settle a horse mentally as well as building in walk work without the rider's weight. Horses seem to realize that they can't explode whilst the walker is going round and they get into the swing of it quite happily.

It's often suggested that you begin walk work with a half-hour hack, but apart from the safety reasons outlined above, this is impossible for most people. Unless you're fortunate enough to go straight out of the yard on to a short, circular route, it only gives time to walk up the road or track a short distance then turn back. This is a quick way to wind up your horse – because he'll inevitably try to speed up to go straight back home – and it can also encourage him to nap.

In this situation it's better to start off walking in an enclosed area. Very quiet horses might be fine when asked to walk round a field, but many will find the open space too tempting to walk quietly.

*A horse walker can be useful for helping to settle a horse coming back into work and to build the earliest stage of fitness without a rider's weight.*

Alternatively, choose a longer route that means you don't have to turn back on your tracks and get off and walk beside your horse for the home section. This was traditional practice in racing yards and still has its benefits – for a start, you'll be building your own fitness as well as your horse's!

If you're riding on the roads, always wear fluorescent, reflective gear and at least to start with, enlist an escort with a quiet, reliable horse.

## STAGE 2

After 3–6 weeks the horse who has started from scratch will be coping easily with an hour's walk per day. It should be an active, 'on the bridle' walk, not a slopping along on a loose rein amble. Introduce short periods in a school or schooling area, riding large circles and turns; if your horse's schooling is up to it, leg-yielding, shoulder-in and turn on the forehand will keep him listening. Bring in short periods of trot at this stage; this should be balanced but not rushed. A lot of riders like to work in a 'hound jog', a slow trot that keeps riders and horses up with hounds being exercised to get them fit for the hunting season.

Whether or not you should trot on the roads is a million dollar question that prompts different views. Certainly there will be times when you need to move on to a gateway or passing place to allow vehicles to overtake safely, or to trot on past a driver who has pulled in to let you pass on a narrow road, and it's sensible and courteous to do so as long as it's also safe. Be careful if roads are slippery and keep your brisk working trot for the school – controlled trotting may, according to some authorities, help to build bone density but too much concussion causes or highlights problems in bones, tendons and feet in a susceptible horse.

If you are lucky enough to be able to incorporate hills into your riding, trotting up a gradual incline will encourage your horse to push off from his back end. During this stage of fittening work you can also introduce short lungeing sessions and work over poles on the ground; pole work can be done in hand by leading or long-reining your horse as well as under saddle.

## STAGE 3

Periods of canter, both in the school and on suitable ground out hacking, can now be introduced. Concentrate on balance and rhythm: you want your horse to be lobbing along nicely, not throwing his head in the air and trying to go faster. However, avoid concentrated periods of cantering on the lunge, because you will put too much strain on your horse's joints, particularly the hocks.

Start to ask a little more of your horse in all respects, both in activity and accuracy, and use trot and canter poles as part of your flatwork regime. By now your horse should cope well with a two-hour hack and so be ready to go on a short pleasure ride or sponsored ride. He should also be capable of competing in a showing class or a low-level dressage test (as long, of course, as he is not a 'hot to trot' dressage horse coming back to competition at a high level, in which case you may want to compete *hors concours* at the next level down in some circumstances).

Be careful with the inexperienced horse being introduced to competition for the first time. Don't underestimate the tiring effects of travelling, the sights and sounds of a competition venue,

*Working over poles on the ground can be a useful way of adding variety to your horse's fitness programme.*

the general excitement of 'going to a party' and the effort of warming up. If you have to lunge him for half an hour before he's safe to get on, be prepared for his energy level to plummet suddenly thereafter and don't push him too hard.

## STAGE 4

This is the home straight: you will now be able to combine increasingly demanding schooling sessions with active hacks, lungeing and, if appropriate, jumping. Gymnastic jumping (gridwork) is valuable for all horses, building athleticism and sharpening their reactions. Most enjoy it and even if you don't consider yourself to be a jumping rider, remember you don't have to come higher than 45 cm (18 in) off the ground to see the benefits. Nor do you need an eye for a stride, as correct spacing will ensure that your horse is in the right place at the right time – if you don't

*Gridwork helps to build fitness and athleticism – and you don't need to build big fences to get results.*

trust your judgement, have gridwork lessons with a trainer who knows their stuff. Don't jump without having someone around, both for safety's sake and so you don't have to keep getting off to alter distances.

## STARTING AND FINISHING

Anyone who follows an exercise routine, either at home or at a gym, should be aware of the importance of warming up and cooling down. This is equally important for your horse. Always start a session in the school with a period of walk, allowing your horse as long a rein as possible whilst still maintaining control, rather than asking him to come straight into an 'up and round' outline. Follow the same principle as you introduce trot and canter, incorporating transitions and changes of direction so that he works from behind and comes into an outline appropriate for his level of experience, rather than you being tempted to shorten the reins too much and create a false outline. When you have achieved your aim in the school, allow him to loosen up the same way.

On a hack, remember the old maxim of 'walk the first mile out and the last mile in' and if appropriate, get off and walk the last mile back yourself. When lungeing, start and finish with a brief period on each rein without any training aids, including side reins.

## INTERVAL TIME

RIDERS TRYING to get horses fit without access to hills and slopes have a much harder job and usually find that the best method is to use interval training as part of their work regime. The basic principle is that the horse carries out set work periods over a specific time, with intervals at walk to allow for a partial recovery in between. Your horse should be at the end of Stage 3 before you introduce interval training and it should be carried out about every four days, not on consecutive days.

You need to be able to take your horse's heart and respiration rates before, during and after the work periods, which means you need either a stopwatch or a watch with a second hand or – even better – a heart rate monitor, which can be used without the need to dismount. Establish base heart and respiration rates when your horse is tacked up ready for work so you can compare them with readings during and after work. Don't take a base rate when he is standing dozing in his stable; doing this may give you a false reading, as some horses' rates rise slightly in anticipation of work.

### HEART RATE GUIDELINES
Approximate heart rate guidelines are:

RESTING: 35–42 beats per minute (bpm)
TACKED UP AND READY FOR WORK:
  40–65 bpm
ACTIVE WALK: 60–80 bpm
ACTIVE TROT: 130–150 bpm
CANTER: 120–170 bpm
GALLOP: 160–200 bpm
A RACEHORSE GALLOPING AT MAXIMUM
  RACING SPEED will record a heart rate
  of about 205–240 bpm.

The final piece of the interval training formula is the need to be able to establish and hold a set speed in trot and, later on, canter. The only way to do this is to find an area of safe footing – which can be anything from a hired gallop to good going at the side of a field – and mark out a distance of 400 m (440 yd).

Time how long it takes you to cover this distance at an active trot. Your aim is to ride at a speed of 220 m (240 yd) per minute, so if you get it spot on it will take you 1 minute and 49 seconds. Inevitably, you'll find you've gone a bit too fast or too slow, so practice until you've got a feel for the right speed and amount of activity and can reproduce it at will.

On your first interval training session, warm up in walk, and follow this with a 2-minute period of trot at your set speed. Follow this by walking for 3 minutes, which will allow a partial recovery, then trot for another 2 minutes. Now check your horse's heart and respiration rates, then immediately walk for 10 minutes and check them again. This allows you to see how your horse is responding to and recovering from the work.

Your horse may find the 2, 3, 2 minute walk and trot programme easy from the start, or at least soon afterwards. The next stage is to gradually build up the trot times and repetitions until he is coping well with three periods of trotting for 3 minutes followed by walking for 3 minutes. Finish on a final 3-minute trot period, stop and take his heart and respiration rates. Follow this with a 10-minute walking recovery period and check his rates again.

When he's coping well, it's time to increase the trot periods from 3 to 5 minutes – but decrease the repetitions so that you trot for 5 minutes, walk for 3; trot for 5 minutes, walk for 3; trot for 5 minutes, stop and take his rates; walk for 10 minutes and take the final readings. If he shows a good recovery rate, move on to the next stage.

This brings in canter work, but before you start, establish a time of 1 minute 8 seconds over your 400 m (440 yd) track, using the same method as you did with trot. When you've got it right, you'll be covering the distance at a speed of 350 m (383 yd) per minute. To give you some comparison, horses at the four-star Burghley Horse Trials are travelling at an optimum speed of 570 m (624 yd) per minute over the 6 km (3¾ mile) cross-country course.

When you increase the effort, you also need to increase the warm-up period, spending 20–30 minutes in walk and trot. When your horse is ready to go, make your first 1 minute 8 seconds canter. Next, trot for 3 minutes; repeat the canter; halt (making gradual downward transitions, not pulling up quickly) and take your horse's readings; walk for 10 minutes and take them again. This stage will show whether your horse's fitness is building correctly or you've anticipated things a little.

If he's coping well, gradually build up your canter times to the stage where he's cantering for 3 minutes; trotting for 3; cantering for 3; stopping for a rates check; walking for 10 minutes and stopping for the final checks. The fitter your horse becomes, the quicker he will recover to his normal

## RECOVERY RATES

When you have finished your horse's interval training session and he has been through the final 10-minute recovery period, the following guidelines will help you assess his response to the work and whether you are ready to go up a step, or if you have been a little ambitious and need to go back a stage.

*100 BPM* – your horse is working, but needs to work a little harder.

*120 BPM* – he has worked hard enough and also made a good recovery.

*150 BPM* – he has worked too hard for his stage of fitness. Go back a step.

*200 BPM* – this points to a significant degree of anaerobic respiration. This is too high, unless you have been deliberately carrying out anaerobic work; in this case, his heart rate should drop to around 120 bpm within a minute of stopping work. If you were not aiming for an anaerobic response, you have pushed your horse far too hard during this session.

Your horse's respiration rate should never be higher than his heart rate. If you find it is, stop the interval training session, let him recover and don't repeat it that day. Next time, go back a stage and make sure he recovers according to plan.

*Build canter periods over set distances as part of an interval training programme.*

base rates and the easier he will find the work. You may already find that your horse copes with his job; at this stage, you may be happy with his performance in and recovery from hacks or endurance rides up to about 25 km (15½ mile) incorporating canter periods, and lower-level competitions.

If you're aiming for a Pre-Novice horse trials or comparable effort, you will need to build his fitness further, timing the establishment of peak fitness with the competition. Using the interval training method, you can do this either by building up to three canter periods rather than two, and/or working in a stronger canter. This means going back to your 'test track' until you can consistently cover 400 m (440 yd) per minute. Start with two canter periods, then build to three.

Riders who want to go beyond this level increase the demands on their horses until they can cope with, perhaps, a total of three 6-minute canters in one training session. They also increase the warming up and cooling down times and incorporate longer periods of trot within them.

In theory, interval training can work for every horse. In practice, some never settle to it – they soon anticipate what comes next and become too excited to work without risk to themselves or their riders. If your horse is one of those who 'blows up', the safest approach is to follow a four-stage fitness programme and if possible, incorporate regular day trips to hillier areas. In some circumstances you may also want to investigate the possibility of using treadmill work or swimming as part of your horse's work routine, where facilities are available.

## VETTING FOR FITNESS

MOST RIDERS CAN ascertain a reliable picture of their horses' fitness using the approaches detailed in this chapter. But if you need real accuracy – or have a problem with your horse's fitness – you may want to call in your vet so that tests can be carried out. The most commonly used investigative techniques are blood testing and endoscopy and both are used as part of the standard routine on some racing and competition yards.

Blood testing analyses the proportions of the various cells in the blood. Endoscopy allows the vet to see what is actually going on in the respiratory system via a flexible fibre-optic tube inserted through one of the horse's nostrils. This may be linked to a video camera so you can see your horse's airways on screen.

High-speed treadmill work may also be used as part of investigations into respiratory problems and/or poor performance. This allows the horse to be worked at a set speed for a set time and the investigator can use equipment such as a video endoscope to see what is happening whilst the horse is working.

## HAPPY HACKING

HACKING USED TO be part of every horse's work regime as well as being an essential part of a fitness programme. For some owners, it was, and is, one of the most enjoyable ways to ride, even if those who list hacking as their main activity feel they have to apologize for it: 'I'm just a happy hacker' is a comment made with the same inflection as 'I'm just a housewife'.

*When riding on the road, make sure you wear reflective, fluorescent clothing and that the horse is walking out, not slopping along.*

Sadly, being able to hack in safety is not as easy as it used to be and in some locations it may be impossible owing to traffic conditions. There is also an inaccurate assumption amongst some riders that hacking is an activity only for riders who are not good enough or brave enough to compete. In fact, if you can control, give confidence to and get the most out of your horse in the open instead of just in a school, you are just as (if not more) courageous and competent than the rider whose horse goes from stable or field to arena or competition venue.

If you can hack in acceptably safe surroundings, either on or off road, make the most of it. You and your horse can benefit from the stimulus of being off home ground and, as well as avoiding boredom, you can build his ability to focus on you in the face of distractions. If you do compete, this will prove invaluable – you might be able to work in quiet surroundings at home, but what happens when you swap a familiar arena for one where there are loudspeakers, show stands, lots of other horses and so on?

Hacking should be productive as well as enjoyable. Your horse's movement should be active and both his response to your aids and your riding should match the standards you set when working in a school. Horses are often more forward-going out hacking, so it can give you a benchmark: if you know you can achieve a forward, balanced trot or canter out hacking, why

*Fluorescent, reflective clothing makes a huge difference as to whether or not drivers can see you.*

settle for less when you school? Similarly, if you can achieve good forward and downward transitions when schooling, expect the same when you hack.

If you are able to hack, remember to:

- Wear fluorescent and reflective safety wear, preferably in all weather conditions. The earlier a driver sees you, the more chance and time there is to slow down and/or give you time to reach a safe passing place.
- Thank considerate drivers with a smile and a nod. You don't have to take your hands off the reins if you feel it isn't safe to do so.
- Young or inexperienced horses should be hacked out with a reliable escort (both horse and rider) until they have gained confidence and experience.
- Take a mobile phone with you in case of emergency but don't have it switched on. If you're chatting on the phone, you're not concentrating on your horse or your surroundings.
- Make sure someone at home or on the yard knows where you are going and the approximate time you should be back, so if anything happens, someone knows where to look for you.

### CAN'T HACK?

If it really isn't safe for you to hack out from your yard, you have to find other ways of keeping your horse's life happy and varied. Plenty of turnout is even more essential and you need to think about strategies such as travelling out regularly to safer areas, introducing lots of variety into his work and, if you live and work in an urban area, even moving your horse to a yard which has off-road riding routes.

## EXPERT QUOTE

*'We always work on the horses' balance, on the quality of their paces and on getting them to move off the leg.*
*We're on the edge of Salisbury Plain, so we'll hack out, then pick a spot and have a little school – even do a few flying changes. Picking a windy spot with the trees blowing and asking your horse to concentrate is really good training for event horses, who are always competing out in the open.'*

CLAYTON FREDERICKS, INTERNATIONAL EVENT RIDER

Exercise physiology – the study of all the physiological systems used in exercise – is an important science that helps us understand more about the importance of fitness and the best ways of achieving it. Some of the latest findings from papers presented at the 2006 International Conference on Equine Exercise Physiology include:

- Inflatable cuffs used on the front legs could boost a horse's muscle response to training. The cuffs featured in a Japanese study based on KAATSU (a Japanese phrase meaning increased pressure) training. A group of Standardbred mares was trained at walk, once a day, six days a week over two weeks; half wore KAATSU cuffs and the other half acted as a control, being walked without them.

The cuffs are inflated to above arterial pressure, which restricts the blood flow to muscles and increases the response to training. Measurements of muscles and tendons taken before and after the 2-week training period showed an increase in muscle thickness of about 11 per cent in horses wearing cuffs, with no difference in the tendons.

- Racehorses do not lose fitness as quickly as some trainers fear if they are taken out of training. Some trainers may still pull a horse out of a race if he has lost even a couple of days work because of fears that he might have lost fitness, but it appears that, from a scientific point of view, these fears may be groundless.

- An earlier start to slower training may help young racehorses adapt to bone stress. We know that the third metacarpal bone thickens in response to fast exercise, but an Australian study has given a clearer picture. Researchers looked at 40 horses who started training at ages between 20 months and 3½ years, X-rayed their cannon bones and looked for a plateau in bone thickness. On average, it took 501 days – but one horse took 2½ years to adapt.

One horse in the study increased bone mass in the cannon bone by around 30 per cent over 600 days. Some of this is probably a result of growth, not just work, but it may be that starting slower training earlier would allow bone to be thicker and become better adapted before a horse goes into fast training.

- Maximum heart rate may be equated with age in horses, just as it is in people. Human athletes using heart rate monitors in training work to the equation that their maximum heart rate – colloquially called heart rate max – should be 220 minus age, so the heart rate max for an 18-year-old would be 202 beats per minute, and for a 60-year-old, 160 bpm.

It was found that with horses, heart rate increased in a linear fashion until about 220 bpm and then reached a plateau. The state of fitness and gender had slight effects, with mares reaching 228 bpm and stallions and geldings 225 bpm, but thse variations were so slight as to be of little significance.

So you can use the same equation for your horse as for yourself when training – but remember that, if you work a young horse at 200 bpm and then work a 15-year-old to the same heart rate, you will actually be working the older horse harder.

- How much effort does it take to jump? A Dutch study looked at horses jumping a 700 m (766 yd) course of twelve fences between 0.8 m and 1 m (2 ft 7in–3 ft 3 in) high and compared their heart rates during jumping with those going round the same course with the poles removed. As a control measure, half the horses went round with the poles out and then jumped and the other half performed the elements of the exercise the other way round.

The difference in heart rates, which went up to over 180 bpm, showed that jumping required about 20 per cent more effort. Whilst it's no surprise that jumping is harder work than cantering on the flat, we now know how much harder, at least at this level. Until now, we have known how much effort it takes for a horse to walk, trot and canter, but didn't know how much it took to jump.

**RIDER FITNESS**

HOWEVER MANY HORSES you ride each day – whether you're a one-horse owner or a professional regularly riding six or more – you need an appropriate level of fitness. Even if you spend most of your day riding, you can't assume that this will be sufficient to achieve the required level: it will play a major part, but it won't necessarily be enough. Whatever his job, your horse is an athlete. You should think of yourself in the same way and put as much care into your own lifestyle as you do into his.

There has been a lot of controversy about overweight riders. It would be unfair and unproductive to discourage anyone who is too heavy from riding – particularly as the work involved in looking after a horse and riding itself are great forms of exercise – but if your scales register more than you know is acceptable, you'll do yourself and your horse a favour by following a sensible weight-loss programme based on a mixture of diet and exercise. If you are seriously overweight or have any health problems or worries, ask your GP's advice before

*Skipping is a good way of building your own cardiovascular fitness and is part of top endurance rider Linda Hams' regime.*

## EXPERT QUOTE

*You should be an asset to your horse, not a liability. Riders should be considered as athletes: they need cardiovascular conditioning, strength, flexibility and core stability.'*

MARCUS ROBERTS, FITNESS CONSULTANT TO THE BRITISH EQUESTRIAN FEDERATION

starting any programme. It's also important to keep yourself as well as your horse hydrated: if you feel thirsty, you are already dehydrated and, in some situations, a danger to yourself and your horse.

Deskbound riders can find it particularly difficult to build up fitness, core stability and flexibility. Obvious but often forgotten strategies such as walking up the stairs instead of taking the lift, and walking briskly for half an hour during your lunch break will make a big difference and, if you're trying to lose weight, help shift some excess. If you're a gym fan, explain what you're trying to achieve to the trainer and he or she should be able to work out a suitable programme. And if you smoke – you already know the answer to this one!

Swimming, cycling and skipping are great for building cardiovascular fitness. So is running, but the advantage of swimming and cycling is that these don't put strain on your joints, whereas pounding the roads and tracks takes its toll. If you don't enjoy exercising on your own, you'll find most local authority fitness centres offer circuit training, Pilates, spin classes (working on static bicycles to music) and all-round exercise to music classes.

## THE POWER OF PILATES

Over the past few years, Pilates has enjoyed a real boom in popularity. This system of exercise deals with the whole body and offers many benefits, including lengthening short muscles, strengthening weak ones and promoting effective breathing. One of the key elements, which is so important for riders, is that it helps you build core stability, improve your posture and help protect yourself from back injuries.

Correct basic techniques are essential, so – at least to start with – find a qualified teacher rather than following a 'teach yourself' DVD. As with all systems, it's important to follow a good warm-up and cool-down series of exercises.

Yoga can also offer benefits for riders. Different types of yoga involve different approaches, but all should improve flexibility. However, research has shown that yoga does not build core strength and stability in the way that Pilates does.

# 9.
# PREVENTATIVE HEALTH CARE

THE TRENDY IDEA for twenty-first century equine health care is evidence-based medicine, usually abbreviated to EBM. This is a fundamental part of modern medicine and means making clinical decisions that are supported by the best available scientific evidence. In this way horse owners and their vets can review all the evidence available rather than relying on anecdotal stories for a preventative procedure or an alleged magic cure. It is not just the case that vets should aim to manage their patients using the best possible practice – horse owners, also, should allow their horses to be cared for properly using scientific rationale, rather than relying on random hearsay or outdated treatments with little scientific basis for their use. There are innovations being introduced all the time and it can be hard to distinguish the genuine from the bogus, but every effort should be made to avoid the gimmicks and gizmos and give your horse the best possible care.

To keep a horse or pony healthy, preventative medicine is essential. This comprises all the routine procedures that need to be carried out to keep a horse or pony in good health. It is also important to know when a horse is well and to recognize if he seems ill. This includes knowing that some signs of ill health may be more serious than others, and when or if you need to contact a vet.

*A vet checking a horse's heart. A horse's resting heart rate is slow compared to a person's, with a normal rate of 23–42 beats per minute.*

THERE ARE MANY USEFUL day to day management measures you can adopt to help ensure your horse stays healthy. Many of these have been discussed in earlier chapters, but the following is a summary of key points.

### KEEPING YOUR HORSE HAPPY

Horses are naturally grazing herd animals. If we confine them in stables too much, we limit their natural activity and social interactions and alter their natural diet. This can give rise to boredom, stress, digestive disorders and stereotypic behaviour. A regime that includes plenty of turnout and contact with other horses, plenty of forage feed when stabled and plenty of appropriate activity will benefit the horse both mentally and physically.

Stereotypic behaviour was discussed in Chapter 3 from the perspective of discerning it in prospective purchases, but there are some management issues (additional to minimizing stress and maximizing turnout) pertinent to avoiding its development that should be of special interest to owners involved in breeding and rearing youngstock. The stereotypies involving the mouth – wind-sucking and crib-biting – have been associated with feeds with high digestibility but little dietary fibre and seem particularly related to feeding methods. They often appear after weaning when foals want to suckle but are separated from their dam. At this stage, concentrate feeds are frequently increased, but this can cause problems because essentially foals' digestive tracts are adapted to cope with a diet of milk and grass. Concentrate feeds can cause increased acidity in the gastro-intestinal tract, which may lead to inflammation and ulceration of the gut lining in the young horse. Studies show that foals who received highly concentrated rations early in life are more likely than others to crib-bite – and foals kept in after weaning are also more likely to develop abnormal behaviour than foals kept at grass.

It should be noted that other abnormal behaviours (which are not technically stereotypic), such as pawing or door-kicking, may be reinforced by being given attention. Many horses carry out this 'bad behaviour' prior to feeding, and are subsequently 'rewarded' for the abnormal behaviour by being fed, and because of this it continues. Giving a horse priority at feeding time because he is 'making a fuss', does not come under the heading of 'keeping him happy'; it is simply reinforcing bad behaviour. It is better practice to let such horses 'wait their turn'.

### KEEPING THE STABLES CLEAN

The need to provide good ventilation and an environment as dust-free as possible was discussed in Chapter 2, and the benefits of maintaining a clean, safe bed of appropriate material were dealt with in Chapter 6. In summary, it is worth reiterating that most respiratory disease in the horse is either caused or made worse by inhaling a combination of dust, bacterial endotoxins (toxic substances produced by bacterial cell walls), and moulds or fungal spores. So keeping dust levels low, the air fresh, and avoiding dusty or mouldy forage and bedding are the order of the day.

*Wind-sucking is a form of stereotypic behaviour.*

## PROTECTING YOUR HORSE FROM AVOIDABLE INJURY

Their long, spindly legs and fast movement make horses prone to damaging themselves. Also, their natural instinct is to flee in the face of danger, regardless of what is in the way, or alternatively to kick out in defence and injure themselves or a companion. All this means that horses are quite prone to getting hurt somehow, so you need to minimize risks. Sensible measures include:

• Care with companions: a large number of horses crowded together in a small field, limited grazing, or introducing new horses to a group will increase the risk of injury.
• Turning out in a safe environment, e.g. good fencing with no barbed wire or poisonous plants (see Chapter 2).
• Ensuring that there are no dangerous defects of fittings in the stable, and that the stable yard is hazard-free.

In general terms, note that a horse who is fit and healthy will have more stamina and be less likely to fall and injure himself under saddle, whether hacking or competing. Similarly, balanced, fit, observant and competent riders can help to protect their horses.

*Ragwort is poisonous and horses should never be turned out on grazing like this.*

**KEEPING YOUR HORSE IN GOOD CONDITION**

ACHIEVING THIS INVOLVES many factors, including keeping him free from injury and disease, ensuring good dental health and parasite control (see later in this chapter) and providing an exercise regime that is appropriate to the demands you make of him. However, on a day to day basis, feeding (see Chapter 5) is a major factor. To reiterate a few points made there from a veterinary perspective, your horse will benefit from being fit and reasonably lean but, like people, many horses are now significantly overweight. Many horses (and even more so, ponies, who have evolved to be very efficient converters of food), gain weight very easily, usually through the simple combination of insufficient exercise and too much to eat. *It is wrong for a horse or pony*

*'The number of ILPH welfare cases concerning obese equines has risen by more than 10 per cent in the past 3 years. While it's easy to shock the public with pictures of extreme emaciation, few owners seem to recognize the welfare issues of the grossly obese horse.'*

PAUL TEASDALE, CHIEF FIELD OFFICER FOR THE ILPH

*to be overweight.* There is a higher risk of laminitis (see Chapter 10) and other serious lameness, such as developmental orthopaedic disease (which tends to happen in growing horses, when their rapid weight gain is a strain on their immature skeleton). Also, as with people, obesity puts extra stress on the organs and limbs.

Spring and, to some extent, autumn are the crucial times of year for weight gain because the lush grass contains high levels of carbohydrate, especially fructans. Any fat horse or pony should never be turned out for long, as they will only get fatter! (Laminitis is most common in ponies out on lush spring grass, but can also be seen in horses; not all laminitis cases are related to feeding.)

## CONDITION SCORING

As mentioned in Chapter 5, this is a system used to describe or measure a horse's physical state. There a variety of scoring systems that can be used, but the one described here works best for horses of all ages. All the systems work on the principle of assessing the animal's fat deposits – body condition only refers to stored fat, not to protein, vitamin, or mineral status. It should be noted that some variation in normal patterns of fat storage exists among different breeds of horses, but this does not negate the system or provide justification for significantly overweight horses.

The scoring system described goes from 1 (poor condition) to 9 (extremely fat condition). Horses should be maintained at condition scores of 5–6 for optimum health and performance.

To condition score a horse, first stand back away and look at a side view. First, look for noticeable ribs. If you see no ribs, the horse has a condition score of 5 or greater. If you can see ribs, the horse's condition score is below a 5. (If the horse has a thick coat, a closer examination and a proper feel of the rib area is required. It is important to rely on feeling areas such as over the horse's ribs, as shaggy winter coats or rugs may disguise thinness. Essentially, you should be able to feel but not see a horse's ribs.) Then pick up the tail head and compare to the scorecard (see Table 1).

# TABLE 1 BODY CONDITION SCORECARD

This helps one understand a horse or pony's health status, diet and exercise needs at a glance.

| SCORE | DESCRIPTION | FEATURES |
|---|---|---|
| 1 | Extremely poor | Animal extremely emaciated; spinous processes (the tops of the vertebrae), ribs, tail head, tuber coxae (point of the hip), and ischii (point of buttock) projecting prominently; bone structure of withers, shoulders, and neck easily noticeable; no fatty tissue can be felt. |
| 2 | Poor | Animal emaciated; slight fat covering over base of spinous processes; transverse processes (part of the bone projecting sideways from the lumbar vertebrae) of lumbar vertebrae feel rounded; spinous processes, ribs, tail head, tuber coxae, and ischii prominent; withers, shoulders, and neck structure faintly discernible. |
| 3 | Thin | Fat build-up about halfway on spinous processes; transverse processes cannot be felt; slight fat cover over ribs; spinous processes and ribs easily discernible; tail head prominent but individual vertebrae cannot be identified visually; tuber coxae appear rounded but easily discernible; ischii not distinguishable; withers, shoulders, and neck accentuated. |
| 4 | Moderately thin | Slight ridge along back; faint outline of ribs discernible; tail head prominence depends on conformation, fat can be felt around it; tuber coxae not discernible; some fat on withers, shoulders, and neck. |
| 5 | Moderate | Back is flat (no crease or ridge); ribs not visually distinguishable but easily felt; fat around tail head beginning to feel spongy; withers appear rounded over spinous processes; shoulders and neck blend smoothly into body. |
| 6 | Moderately fleshy | May have slight crease down back; fat over ribs spongy; fat around tail head soft; fat beginning to be deposited along the side of withers, behind shoulders, and along sides of neck. |
| 7 | Fleshy | Crease down back; individual ribs can be felt but noticeable filling between ribs with fat; fat around tail head soft; fat deposited along withers, behind shoulders, and along neck. |
| 8 | Fat | Crease down back; difficult to feel ribs; fat around tail head very soft; area along withers filled with fat; area behind shoulders filled with fat; noticeable thickening of neck; fat deposited along inner thighs. |
| 9 | Obese | Obvious crease down back; patchy fat appearing over ribs; bulging fat around tail head, along withers, behind shoulders and along neck; fat along inner thighs may rub together; flank filled with fat. |

It is unusual to find a horse who is very thin, with a low condition score. Possible reasons for a horse to be underweight are:

- Not enough feed or grazing.
- Inadequate care, possibly related to parasite infestation, dental disease, inadequate shelter in cold wet weather, or bullying by other horses preventing the thin horse from eating enough.
- Illness or injury.

If a thin horse does not improve rapidly with a better diet and improved management, such as treatment for worms and having the teeth checked, then a vet should be consulted.

## MONITORING WEIGHT

The very simplest way of monitoring weight is by checking the fitting of your horse's girth: does it need doing up or letting out an extra hole from normal? As mentioned in Chapter 5, you can use a weight tape (or even a long piece of string) to measure your horse's girth. Remember, however, that a weight tape will only provide an *approximation* of weight – it can be out by a significant margin, especially in fit, lean or odd-shaped animals, such as a pregnant mare or a donkey. A calibrated weighbridge is far more accurate.

Table 2 offers a guide to ideal weights for different breeds of various sizes, but please remember that *it is a guide* – young or elderly animals, or those of unusual conformation, may show differences from the figures given.

## TABLE 2 IDEAL WEIGHTS

| BREED/TYPE | APPROX. HEIGHT | GIRTH | BODYWEIGHT GUIDE |
|---|---|---|---|
| Dartmoor | 112 cm (11 hh) | 140 cm (55 in) | 200–250 kg (440–550 lb) |
| Welsh section A & B | 122 cm (12 hh) | 145 cm (57 in) | 250–350 kg (550–770 lb) |
| Welsh section C | 138 cm (13.2 hh) | 160 cm (63 in) | 300–400 kg (660–880 lb) |
| Cob/Welsh section D | 148 cm (14.2 hh) | 175 cm (69 in) | 450–500 kg (990–1,100 lb) |
| Thoroughbred | 163 cm (16 hh) | 190 cm (75 in) | 500–550 kg (1,100–1,212 lb) |
| Warmblood | 173 cm (17 hh) | 205 cm (81 in) | 600–700 kg (1,323–1,544 lb) |
| Shire | 183 cm (18 hh) | 220 cm (87 in) | 700–900 kg (1,544–1,985 lb) |

## HELPING YOUR HORSE TO LOSE WEIGHT

General guidance about feeding for weight loss and gain has been given in Chapter 5. The following is a summary of the key points about weight loss from a veterinary perspective.

- Other than in exceptional circumstances (see below) complete starvation is not appropriate: weight reduction must be gradual to avoid metabolic disturbances. Hyperlipaemia, a serious disorder of fat metabolism, is triggered by cutting the feed too drastically or by a period of starvation. It is particularly common in fat ponies and Shetlands.

- Modify the type and amount of feed gradually. *Sometimes* a vet may advise total starvation, for instance, when treating certain colic cases, but otherwise never restrict rations by more than 10 per cent within a week.
- Obtain professional advice from your vet and/or a specialist nutritionist, if required. There are horses and ponies who have medical conditions such as equine metabolic syndrome that make losing weight a particular challenge.
- Measure any feed to be given accurately (this means by weight, not volume) to determine appropriate rations.
- Give feeds that are low in fat, since fat is an energy-dense nutrient source, which will obviously increase weight. Most, if not all, feed for the fatty should be forage-based and any extra food should be low in energy and high in fibre.
- If a horse is not working hard, he may actually need nothing more than hay and grass, but make sure that the horse's vitamin, mineral and protein requirements continue to be met.
- Plenty of fresh water will help the horse's digestive and other systems to function efficiently. A change to a higher-fibre diet can cause impactions and colic, especially if water intake is inadequate.
- Since horses are grazers who eat almost continuously when at grass, limiting access to rich grass is an important way of preventing weight gain. Lush grass is high in calories and it needs to be restricted. Turning out in a sparse 'starvation' paddock can be beneficial and it is more equivalent than lush pasture to the natural mountain and moorland environment of many native ponies.
- When animals are stabled, increase eating time by using double or treble haynets, one inside the other, or haylage nets with small holes to reduce the amount pulled out with each bite. When seriously restricting feed intake, e.g. with a laminitic horse, your vet may suggest scattering the hay in amongst non-edible bedding, so the horse has to hunt for it and takes longer to eat it.
- Choose your forage with care. Hay will be better than haylage to encourage weight loss and the type of hay is important too. Use less nutritious hay, e.g. switch from alfalfa to grass hay. Hay made from older plants (i.e. late cut) has increased fibre content, a lower percentage of leaves and is less easily digestible and not as fattening. Consider soaking hay to leach out soluble carbohydrates, particularly when dieting a fat pony.
- Feed an overweight horse separately, so he cannot steal the other horses' feed.
- Balance the horse's diet against age and level of activity. Never feed more than a horse needs for the level of work he is doing.
- Increase the time and intensity of exercise as the horse's fitness improves. The more work a horse does, the more he will lose weight. Never feed more *in anticipation* of increased work.

*This foal is being treated with a wormer. Not all treatments are appropriate or necessary for foals and it is best to obtain your vet's advice.*

WORM CONTROL is very important. Different equine worm infestations produce many problems ranging from ill-thrift, loss of appetite, reduced performance, poor coat and loss of weight to potentially fatal conditions such as colic or diarrhoea. The main factors leading to infection are:

- Over-grazed pasture with too many animals, so that horses are forced to graze close to piles of droppings.
- Presence of horses who have high worm egg counts, i.e. are significantly infected and will infect others. This often means young horses, who are more frequently heavily infected.
- Warm, damp weather.

Even if a horse has no apparent signs of worms, you should consider proper parasite control. Your vet is best placed to give expert advice, designed to fit a horse's particular circumstances. General guidelines are available, often from manufacturers of wormers, but this information is no substitute for an individually designed worm control programme from your own vet.

Advice about keeping your horse free from parasites may include:

*PASTURE HYGIENE*: the frequent (at least twice-weekly) removal of droppings is a highly effective means of controlling the spread of worms between horses. It is tedious, but it works! (Harrowing of pastures is not recommended as it merely spreads parasites around the paddocks.)

*ROTATION OF PASTURE*: this allows infective eggs and larvae on 'resting' paddocks to die before they can infect another horse. Ideally at least 6 months rest is required, depending on the weather.

*MIXED SPECIES GRAZING*: cattle and sheep will act as 'biological vacuum cleaners', eating eggs and larvae which cannot survive in species other than the horse.

*APPROPRIATE STOCK LEVELS:* ideally, fields should contain no more than one or two horses per 0.4 hectare (1 acre). Increasing this number leads to horses grazing closer to dung piles and to close-cropped grass, so they are more likely to pick up worms.

*CAREFUL USE OF WORMING MEDICATION:* different treatments eliminate different parasites. Your vet will advise what is most appropriate. Always read medication instructions and ensure that you know what compound you are giving, as there are several brand-named products which have the same key ingredients. Follow instructions, so that wormers are not used more frequently than recommended and so that the correct dose is given for the size of horse.

*DIAGNOSTIC TESTING:* this is the most logical way of determining whether horses actually need treatment for worms. It can also be used to check that worm control programmes are working. There are two tests currently used:

1.   Faecal worm egg counts. These simply require you to submit a small (tablespoon-sized dollop) labelled 'sample of fresh droppings', with the names of both horse and owner added, to your vet or lab for analysis. This will assess the number of worm eggs present, which is useful for checking the parasite status of a particular horse and deciding whether or not he needs treatment. A result of less than 200 eggs per gram is acceptable and usually indicates that treatment is not required. It is sensible to tolerate *low* levels of worm infection, which are not harmful to your horse and may stimulate natural immunity.

2.   A blood sample can be taken by your vet and sent for a specific antibody test to check for tapeworms. This method is useful for horses with recurrent colic, but can also be used to screen healthy horses. It has been developed at the University of Liverpool (see www.diagnosteq.co.uk for further details).

It is best to take these samples just before the horse is due to be wormed to see whether treatment is required – although there is a view that if you test *soon after* treatment with a wormer you can find out whether it has worked.

### REASONS FOR FAILURE OF WORM CONTROL

1.   Lack of synchronization of dosing within an entire group. This is a common problem in big livery yards, where there is no coordinated control programme and untreated horses may re-infect the treated animals.

2. Under-dosing as a result of miscalculating the horse's bodyweight.

3. Introducing new animals into the grazing area without treating them.

4. Extending the interval between doses beyond the period of activity of the various wormers.

5. Using the wrong treatment, for instance, only certain wormers (containing pyrantel or praziquantel) are effective for tapeworms.

6. One wormer will not destroy all the immature or larval worms. A particular problem is that some forms of cyathostomins (small redworms) encyst or bury themselves inside the equine gut wall, where they are relatively inaccessible to treatment. They then hatch out at a later date and cause problems – particularly severe diarrhoea if many such worms emerge at once.

7. Since drug resistance is developing amongst worm populations, so some wormers may no longer be effective.

**TIP!**

If you are administering a wormer treatment, ensure that your horse eats it immediately. There have been cases of dogs being poisoned by eating leftover wormer powders or paste. Also, the treatment itself is less effective if left in the feed.

## KEEPING YOUR HORSE'S FEET IN GOOD CONDITION

As mentioned in Chapter 6, it is essential to pay careful attention to your horse's feet, because they are the commonest area for lameness problems. This attention should include:

- Daily hoof care such as picking out the feet, especially around the clefts of the frog.
- Ensuring that the bedding of stabled horses is clean and dry to avoid foot infections such as thrush.
- Regular visits by a registered farrier every 4–6 weeks to have the feet checked, trimmed and reshod, if they have shoes fitted. After 6 weeks, the shoe may not be falling off, but the toe will be getting long, so the horse is more likely to stumble and will be putting more pressure on other structures such as the navicular bone and surrounding soft tissues.

In the UK, there has been a recent trend towards barefoot trimming without necessarily involving farriers, but it is *always* best to use a qualified farrier who has been fully trained to understand a horse's feet. The difficulty is who to choose – personal recommendation is ideal, but otherwise the Farriers Registration Council maintains a register of British farriers (see www.farrier-reg.gov.uk) and similar registers may be available in other countries. Although the situation varies from country to country, and from breed to breed, few horses in the UK can cope with hard work on abrasive or hard surfaces without shoes. Also, the British climate is not that well suited to the horse's hoof working without shoes; although some breeds do cope with

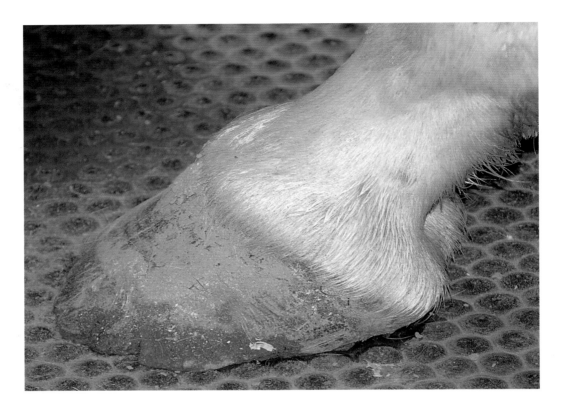

*A neglected foot with long toe and low heels – the commonest foot conformation fault.*

it reasonably well, others are less successful – and a lot will depend on the surface upon which they are worked, too.

'No foot, no horse' is a very true saying, so it is worth looking after all aspects of your horse's hooves. The shape and so-called balance of the foot are important in preventing lameness so, in the same way that decent running shoes are essential for any human athlete, a horse's feet must be maintained in the best possible shape for that particular animal.

## A QUESTION OF BALANCE

For a horse's foot, balance may be interpreted as the equal distribution of weight over different areas of the foot. More precisely, this is defined as equal medial to lateral distribution of weight, since more weight is normally placed towards the back of the foot. Front to back imbalance has been defined as a change in hoof alignment or as problems with heel support.

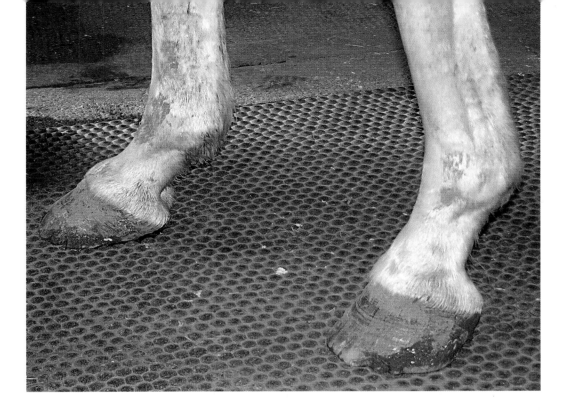

*Front feet that are not a symmetrical pair are another common fault best avoided.*

### FOOT PROBLEMS TO AVOID

● A 'low heel/long toes' shape, frequently found in the Thoroughbred type of horse. This results in collapsed heels and extra pressure on the back of the foot, especially the navicular bone and surrounding soft tissue structures. It will increase the chance of navicular syndrome developing, so avoid this. Frequently, the heels will gradually collapse as the balance of the foot deteriorates. Once a horse has collapsed heels, it is a difficult and lengthy procedure to correct this condition. It will take nearly a year for the hoof to grow down from the coronary band to the ground.

● A conformation fault best avoided is small feet in relation to the size of the horse, so that there will be too much weight on too small a surface area.

● Sheared heels, which is when there is a difference between the medial and lateral heel heights of more than 0.5 cm (⅕ in), i.e. the side to side balance is out of true.

It can be hard to spot the gradual changes in a horse's feet, so ask your vet and farrier if you have any concerns. Sometimes it can be beneficial for the vet to take properly positioned and carefully aligned X-ray pictures of the feet, particularly a sideways (lateromedial) and full frontal (dorsopalmar) view of the feet. Actually seeing where the bones in the foot are in relation to the hoof capsule can provide a lot of useful information for the farrier on how best to trim the foot and improve the overall balance.

## BALANCING FEET

Exactly how (or if) to change the foot balance will very much depend on what is wrong. Traditionally, the common foot imbalance problem of the long toe/low-heeled foot is corrected by shoeing the foot with a seated-out wide-webbed open shoe or an egg-bar shoe to provide extra length and width and thus give additional support to the overloaded heels. A quick fix is to fit heel wedges to build up the heels, but in the long term this may make things worse. The natural balance approach, using the four-point trim, is another popular therapeutic option. To trim and shoe a horse successfully is a skilled task, so appreciate your farrier. Always ensure the horses due to be shod are in, clean and ready in a well-lit dry area, so that the farrier can do the best possible job for you.

## KEEPING YOUR HORSE'S TEETH RIGHT

MANY EQUINE dental problems occur as a result of domestication. Diets fed to the domestic horse produce far less wear on the teeth when compared to natural grass grazing. Unlike humans, horses' teeth grow continually. This, combined with the standard practice of feeding hay in a net, or feed from a raised manger, means that most horses eat with their heads up, which is an unnatural position for a horse designed to graze at ground level. Consequently, they have different jaw movements that result in uneven wear of the teeth and the development of sharp hooks and points, which cause discomfort and usually require rasping. However, whereas a more minor defect may affect his performance, a horse has to have very bad teeth before he will fail to eat, since hunger will overcome minor dental discomfort.

As an owner, it can be difficult to know what needs to be done for your horse's teeth, and when, so it is important to rely on appropriate professional guidance. A proper diagnosis is essential prior to treatment of any dental abnormalities, so it is important to use experienced equine vets and qualified equine dental technicians (EDTs) to care for your horses' teeth. Over-treatment can lead to temporary difficulties in eating, reduced tooth life and unnecessary costs, so ensure that any dentistry is performed by a competent, qualified individual.

Signs of a sore mouth, that may indicate the need for professional investigation, include:

- Fussing or playing with the bit.
- Losing weight.
- Quidding (messy eating with food being spilt from the mouth as the horse eats).
- Reluctance to eat.
- Stiff-backed action, or even bucking.
- Tossing the head more than usual.

In the first instance, you need to be sure that your horse does indeed have a dental problem. For example, a horse who is losing weight may have other conditions such as intestinal or liver damage. If you are in any doubt as to whether your horse's signs are the result of a dental problem you should contact your usual vet for an appointment. He or she will then be able to check your horse and advise you accordingly.

*Inserting a gag in order to examine a horse's teeth.*

Ideally the first dental examination should be performed at birth, alongside the post-foaling check-up. This will pick up, at an early stage, abnormalities such as parrot mouth, wry nose and cleft palate. Any attempted treatments for these conditions will need to be started early, so prompt recognition of these abnormalities is required.

Thereafter, equine dental care is best performed on a little and often basis. Assuming that routine removal of sharp hooks is all that is required, horses up to the age of 10 years should be checked every 6 months. If routine care has been consistent every 6 months then this interval may be lengthened to 12 months for individuals with good dentition.

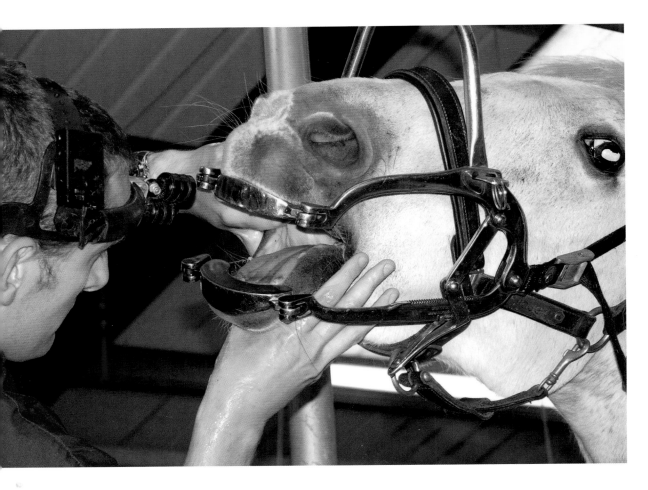

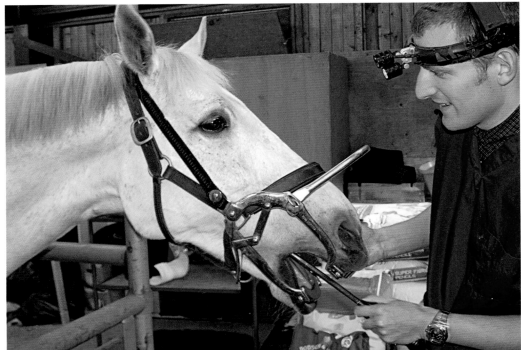

TOP LEFT *Examining a horse's mouth.* LEFT *Rasping the teeth.*
ABOVE *Completing dental records.*

## DENTISTRY TERMS

These terms are commonly used.

*ARCADE:* a row of teeth.

*BIT SEATS:* rounding off the front surface of the first upper and lower cheek teeth to make the horse more comfortable with the bit. It is widely believed that this does help, although scientific evidence to support this is minimal.

*CHEEK TEETH:* the premolars and molars at the back of the mouth, both top and bottom, which are the grinding teeth.

*DIASTEMA:* a space between teeth. This may be the normal space between the front incisors and the cheek teeth or an abnormal space that develops when a tooth is missing.

*INCISORS:* the top and bottom teeth (12 in total), found at the front of the mouth and used for grazing.

*TUSHES, OR TUSKS:* the canine teeth found between the incisors and the cheek teeth, which are more obvious in stallions and geldings but are smaller or absent in mares.

*WOLF TOOTH:* the first premolar that appears in front of the cheek teeth in around 25 per cent of normal horses. If small and correctly positioned they are unlikely to cause problems.

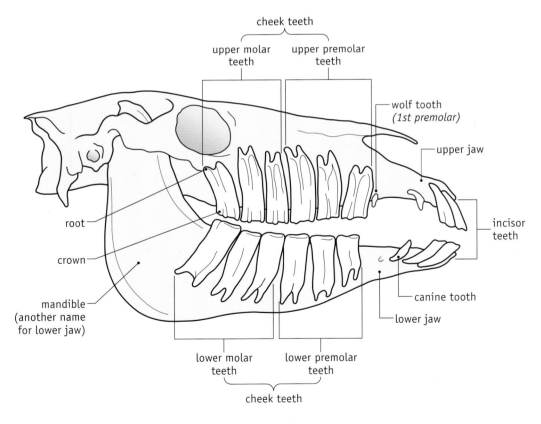

*Lateral section through an equine skull to show aspects of dentition.*

## My horse is due for a routine dental check-up. Who should I contact about this?

As a result of increasing demand, there are ever-increasing numbers of people offering equine dental services. Whilst some are very experienced and skilled, others have limited knowledge or training. In the first instance you should contact your usual vet, who should be able to advise you on local services that are available. If you wish to use the services of an equine dental technician (EDT), check out his/her credentials as equine dentistry is regulated in the UK.

Many technicians have gained training and certification abroad and the level and standard of training varies to an incredible degree. Those British-based EDTs who are working to the highest standards, and are prepared to work alongside your vet, have mostly been examined by the British Equine Veterinary Association and British Veterinary Dental Association. Having passed the requisite examination, they are eligible to join the British Association of Equine Dental Technicians (BAEDT). BAEDT members work to the highest possible standards, maintain a commitment to continuing professional development, are bound by a code of conduct and carry the appropriate indemnity insurance. Details of members can be found at the BAEDT website (www.equinedentistry.org.uk).

## KEEPING YOUR HORSE FREE FROM INFECTION

As with human disease, different diseases are prevalent amongst horses in different parts of the world. Fortunately, in the UK there have to date been only a limited number of contagious equine diseases (that is, infections that spread from horse to horse). However, with the increase in the international travelling of horses, horse keepers everywhere must remain aware of the potential threat from the emergence of new or 'exotic' diseases. The rapid spread of West Nile virus across the USA in recent years illustrates this potential threat and some parts of the world have problems with other serious viruses such as rabies.

Another potential concern is the spread of disease from horses to people – thankfully, in the UK, the commonest such problem is usually the self-limiting fungal skin infection, ringworm – but the situation is potentially more serious in other parts of the world.

### RESPIRATORY INFECTIONS IN THE HORSE

Respiratory infections are the most important types of contagious diseases that can spread among the horse population in Western Europe, and many other areas. These include influenza virus, equine herpes viruses and the bacterial infection, strangles. These diseases are very different, and preventive strategies therefore vary.

## TABLE 3 KEY FACTS ABOUT RESPIRATORY INFECTIONS IN HORSES

| DISEASE | EQUINE INFLUENZA | HERPES VIRUS | STRANGLES |
|---|---|---|---|
| CAUSE | Equine influenza virus. | Equine herpes virus. There are a number of different types, of which types 1 and 4 are the most important. | Bacteria: *Streptococcus equi*. |
| INCUBATION PERIOD | Short (2–3 days) and the virus can therefore spread rapidly among susceptible horses. | The incubation period is 2–10 days. | The incubation period is usually 3–14 days, but tends to spread round a group of horses more slowly than respiratory viruses. |
| SPREAD | Large amounts of virus are 'aerosolized' from infected horses by their frequent coughing. Infected horses can shed the virus for up to 10 days so it spreads rapidly from horse to horse. | Infection occurs by inhalation of the virus in aerosols (as for influenza) but does not always spread as rapidly. | The infection is often introduced into a yard by a carrier animal (the infection can persist for long periods in the guttural pouches with no apparent outward signs) or a mild case, which is not recognized as strangles. It spreads easily among susceptible horses. Although highly contagious, spread is slow compared with the respiratory viruses and requires direct contact between horses, or contact with contaminated equipment, tack, etc. The copious purulent discharges result in the rapid contamination of the environment. |
| SIGNS | •High temperature. •Harsh, dry cough. •Clear watery nasal discharge that then becomes thick and yellow/green. •Loss of appetite. •Depression. | Infection by EHV-4 usually results in respiratory disease, whereas infection by EHV-1 can result in respiratory disease, abortion, birth of sick foals and neurological disease. Respiratory disease is commonest in young horses (up to 3 years of age). | Typically, swellings of the lymph nodes around the head, which turn into abscesses – but not always. Other signs include: •Raised temperature. •Watery discharge from nostrils, which goes thick and yellow. •Dullness and depression. •Moist, soft cough. •Loss of appetite. Some horses are only mildly affected, which may allow the disease to spread unnoticed. |

| DISEASE | EQUINE INFLUENZA | HERPES VIRUS | STRANGLES |
|---|---|---|---|
| DISEASE DETAILS | Major outbreaks can occur occasionally, especially if the virus 'mutates' and changes its characteristics. These mutations are common in influenza viruses (in human as well as equine strains). This is why vaccines need to be 'updated' regularly so that the currently prevalent strains are included. Outbreaks are most common when large numbers of young, susceptible horses are brought together at sales and shows or for weaning and training. | Immunity following infection (and vaccination) is short-lived, and most horses become re-infected on numerous occasions throughout their lives. In older horses these infections are usually mild or may be sub-clinical (i.e. there are no obvious clinical signs). Latent infections within nervous tissue are also common. | The disease is particularly common in situations where young horses are kept close together with new horses moving in and out of the group, as occurs in many livery stables and dealers' yards. The disease is most commonly spread by direct contact between horses or by items contaminated by infected horses, such as water buckets. When an outbreak occurs it is recommended that the whole yard should be isolated, however there is no law that obliges people to keep infected horses quarantined. The strangles situation is often complicated by the existence of 'carriers' or 'shedders' – apparently healthy horses harbouring the disease. |
| VACCINATION | The extensive use of vaccines in the UK has significantly reduced the number and severity of equine influenza epidemics. | A vaccine is available which gives some protection and raises herd immunity. | A vaccination was available in the UK, but has been withdrawn in 2007. Check the current situation with your vet. |

## HOW TO PREVENT INFECTION BY CONTAGIOUS DISEASES

The most important measure to prevent equine disease spreading is prompt diagnosis, so that immediate precautions can be taken, such as isolation. It is therefore wise to be familiar with the clinical signs associated with the main infectious diseases and seek veterinary advice immediately if you suspect something is wrong.

If there is a rumoured outbreak of a contagious disease in the area, ask your vet about the risks and the measures that can be taken to minimize the chance of infection in your own horse. Always maintain high levels of hygiene in the stable, yard, trailers and horseboxes. Check with your vet concerning routine use of disinfectants and 'cleaning-up' following an outbreak of disease.

Although it is rarely done in practice, it is ideal to establish a quarantine procedure for new arrivals on to a yard. Isolation for 3 weeks is generally adequate, but at the same time it is important to minimize stress at all times and most horses do not like to be kept on their own, especially in a new environment. It is still sensible to keep new arrivals as separate from others as possible. Age segregation of horses, and segregation of pregnant mares from non-pregnant animals, is also advisable in certain situations, e.g. on studs.

## VACCINATION

For some diseases, such as influenza virus, the widespread use of vaccination plays an important role in prevention. It is important that a large percentage of the population is vaccinated in order to prevent epidemics. Although vaccination may not completely eliminate the risk of infection in an individual horse, it will reduce its spread, and is therefore a major component in the overall preventive strategy for the whole horse population. If suitable and safe vaccines are administered correctly by your vet, the benefits completely outweigh the risks of any side-effects.

There are four diseases for horses, for three of which vaccination is currently available in the UK.

### EQUINE INFLUENZA

Vaccination is compulsory in the UK for horses competing under the rules of racing and for those taking part in other events that utilize racecourses and associated accommodation. It is also now a requirement when competing under the rules of most other equestrian organizations. It is essential in these circumstances that the 'flu vaccination record is properly up to date, otherwise the horse will not be allowed to compete.

Equine influenza vaccine regulations as applied by most competition organizations within the UK are:

- Primary course: 2 injections 21–92 days apart.
- 'Six-month' booster: to be given 150–215 days after the second injection of primary course (or every 6 months for FEI competition horses).
- Annual boosters: within 365 days of the first booster. More frequent booster vaccinations may be indicated for high-risk horses (e.g. young horses in race training) or horses competing under FEI rules.

### TETANUS

Otherwise know as lockjaw, this is a frequently fatal disease of horses and humans; both should be protected by the very effective vaccine that is available. The disease is caused by toxins produced when spores of the bacteria, *Clostridium tetani*, multiply within a wound. Tetanus is frequently fatal, usually as a consequence of paralysing muscle spasms. Vaccination regimes for horses vary but they all involve a primary course of two injections 4–6 weeks apart, followed by boosters at intervals of 2–3 years. If an unvaccinated horse sustains a wound, tetanus antitoxin can be given to provide emergency protection.

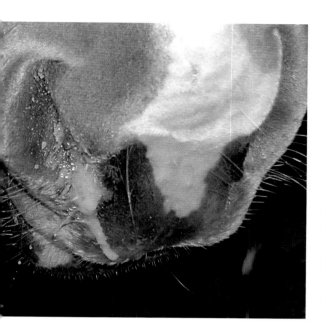 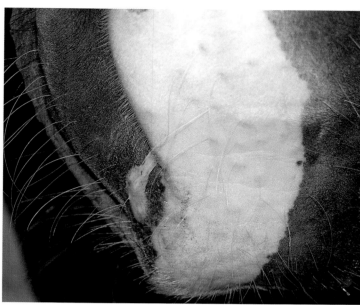

ABOVE LEFT *Strangles may produce a nasty nasal discharge.*
ABOVE RIGHT *Other infections and dust allergies may also present with a runny nose: it can be difficult to distinguish the various causes.*

## EQUINE HERPES

A vaccination against this virus is available. This has been shown to provide some immunity against infection by the respiratory and abortion forms of the infection, but it is not known to protect fully against the paralytic form of the disease.

## EQUINE VIRAL ARTERITIS (EVA)

This virus, which can cause fever, infertility and illness, is called 'pink eye' because of inflammation that occurs in and around the eyes. Stallions can become carriers of the infection; hence it is a concern for breeding establishments. Currently, any case involving a stallion or breeding mare in the UK is notifiable, meaning that DEFRA (Department for Environment, Food and Rural Affairs) should be informed if it is suspected. Although an EVA vaccination is not used routinely, it is available to protect stallions from becoming carriers of the disease. It is essential that any horse to be vaccinated is blood-tested first to confirm that he has not previously been infected.

## STRANGLES

A vaccine has been used in the UK, being given as a tiny injection inside the horse's upper lip. As immunity against strangles is not long-lasting the vaccination needs to be repeated frequently (every 3–6 months, depending on level of risk). At the time of writing it is unavailable, so check with your own vet as to the current situation.

## THE KEY TO KEEPING YOUR HORSE HEALTHY

WE ALL KNOW WHEN a horse is really ill, but can you tell if a horse is not quite right? The more that you know about what a horse is usually like, the easier it is to spot a problem.

### SIGNS OF GOOD HEALTH

It is important to be familiar with the signs of good health, so that any illness or abnormality can be detected in the early stages. A healthy horse or pony should have:

- A bright, alert attitude, with pricked ears, taking an interest in his surroundings.
- A good appetite.
- A shiny coat with healthy skin and salmon pink mucous membranes (gums).
- Clear, bright eyes with no discharge.
- Clean nostrils (a small amount of watery discharge is normal).
- Good condition without being fat.
- Droppings that are passed regularly and are not too loose or too firm.
- A body temperature of between 37 and 38.5 °C (98.5–100.5 °F).
- A pulse of 28–42 beats per minute.
- A respiration rate of 8–16 breaths per minute. The horse's breathing movements should be smooth and relaxed.

A responsible horse owner should know their horse's normal vital signs, namely temperature, pulse and respiratory rate.

### TAKING THE TEMPERATURE

There are special veterinary thermometers that can be purchased, although a human thermometer will do. The ideal is an easy-to-read digital thermometer and it is now possible to buy thermometers that take only a few seconds to obtain an accurate reading. These digital devices are far better than the old-fashioned glass version with narrow and hard to visualize mercury columns and the potential to break at a crucial moment. With horses, the process is not as simple as with people, so it's best to make it as easy as possible for all concerned. The routine approach to measuring a horse's temperature is to insert the thermometer in the rectum.

Ideally, grease the measuring end with some lubrication, such as a little blob of petroleum jelly (alternatively, saliva is always available). It is safest to have someone steadying the horse's head and reassuring him. Stand to one side of the horse's rear, run your hand over his quarters and then grasp the base of the tail firmly, lift it gently and carefully insert the thermometer through the anus. Keep hold of the tail so that the horse does not clamp it down, but also hang on to the thermometer, so you do not lose it! Stay standing to the side and be careful to avoid being kicked. Leave the thermometer inserted for about a minute, making sure you tilt it against the wall of the rectum, rather than it being in the centre of a ball of droppings. Then gently remove it, wipe clean with a tissue or cotton wool and read it. Afterwards clean it with cold water and disinfectant.

It is a good idea to get your horse or pony accustomed to the routine of having his temperature taken when he is well, so it will not be a problem if he is ever ill, and so that you know his normal temperature.

## MEASURING THE PULSE

It is simplest to feel a horse's pulse on the side of the face, where the facial artery passes under the jaw. Make sure that the horse is not eating and that his head is still when you do this. The horse's resting pulse is slow, so it can be difficult to detect. To find the pulse, run your fingers along the bony lower edge of the jaw. The pulsing artery will be felt as a tubular structure. If you press this lightly against the jaw with the flat of your first three fingers, you will feel the pulse. Count the number of beats in 15 seconds and multiply by four to get the pulse rate per minute.

If you cannot feel the pulse, feel for the heartbeat on the left side of the lower chest, where the girth would go, just behind the elbow.

Practise finding your horse's pulse after exercise, when it will be obvious. You may, in any case, want to be able to take his pulse at this time as a way of monitoring his fitness programme.

## MEASURING THE RESPIRATORY RATE

To check this, either place your hand close to the horse's nostrils to feel each breath, or count flank movements. On a cold day you will be able to see each time a horse breathes out.

As stated earlier, in respect of temperature, pulse and respiration, it is important to know what is normal for your own horse. However, it is useful to understand this not only in respect of 'normal' situations, but also in terms of how he reacts in different circumstances. For example, horses will often have increased pulse and respiratory rates if they are excited – there may be nothing actually wrong. This does not, of course, mean that you should try to invent a 'rationale' if your horse is clearly distressed; if you have any doubts about your horse's health, the best person to consult is your vet.

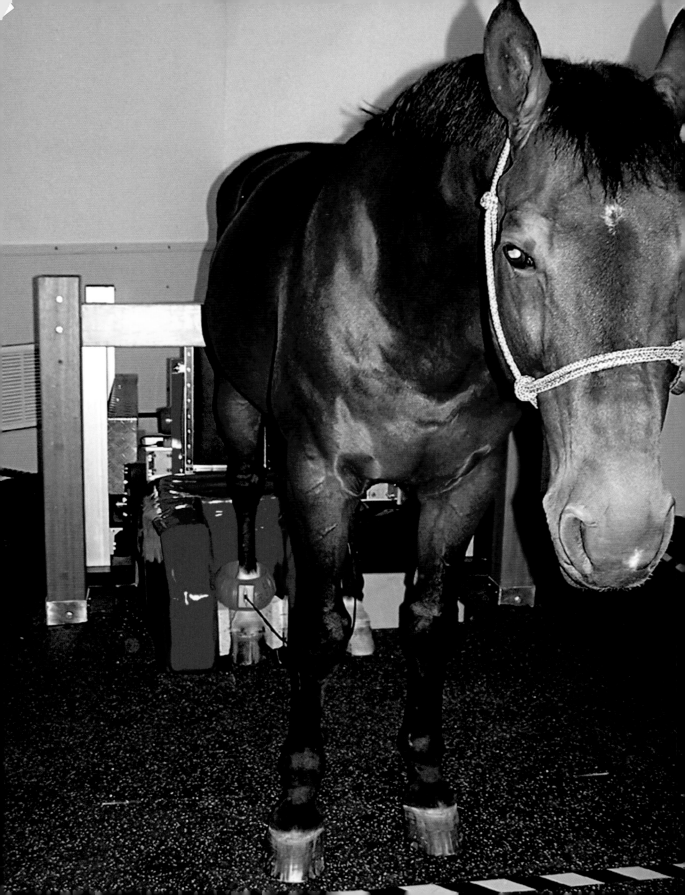

# 10. COMMON AILMENTS AND COPING WITH ACCIDENTS

Veterinary knowledge and expertise have expanded hugely over the last 20 years. New diseases and types of injury have been investigated and innovative and more effective treatments introduced. For instance, a few years ago equine Cushing's disease was dismissed as 'old age', but now it is frequently treated, with reasonable success rates. New keyhole surgical techniques have been developed and other surgical procedures, particularly operations for colic, have advanced significantly, in part because of better anaesthesia techniques. New methods of imaging have been introduced, including ultrasonography or scanning, nuclear scintigraphy (bone scanning) and magnetic resonance imaging (MRI). In short, it is tremendously exciting that there is now so much more that vets can do for horses in their care.

Despite the advances in technology, the horses and ponies remain the same – although in many cases they are living longer, so there are many more elderly animals who need fastidious care. Regular veterinary care is important for all horses and ponies, for routine procedures and preventative health checks, and veterinary intervention is, of course, essential in emergencies. It is therefore important to find a good horse vet with whom you can develop a working relationship, so that you can approach him or her easily for help. By discussing what might seem like a big issue with your vet, an apparent crisis may be rapidly resolved with proper professional advice and reassurance.

*Over the last decade, major advances have been made in diagnostic equipment, giving vets a clearer picture of their patients.*

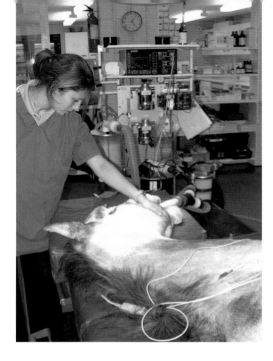

LEFT *Monitoring anaesthesia.*

## FINDING THE RIGHT VET

THE BEST WAY to find a knowledgeable horse vet may be word of mouth via other horse owners in your area. In some areas there may only be a limited number of vets who see horses regularly and your choice may be limited. Vets in practice are obliged to provide a 24-hour service for emergencies. It is important that the vets providing emergency veterinary cover have sufficient equine experience for your needs, so always check on the back-up available if your normal vet is away.

Vets train for 5 or 6 years before graduating and although they will have been taught the principles at vet school, it would be unreasonable to expect anyone to be an equine expert when they first qualify. However, if a young vet works in a good equine practice with support from more experienced colleagues, when needed, it can be beneficial all round. Be ready to judge the whole team, not just the first vet you meet at an equine practice.

Vets can take a number of post-graduate qualifications to increase their level of equine veterinary expertise. Certainly there are some excellent equine vets who have no post-graduate qualifications, but as a horse owner you are more likely to get a vet with more expertise and knowledge if it is someone who has succeeded in passing one or more of these testing examinations. Strangely, in the veterinary world, anyone can call themselves an equine vet without undergoing any form of specialist training. However, no one in Britain can call themselves a specialist equine vet unless they are registered with the Royal College of Veterinary Surgeons (RCVS) as a specialist. In order to qualify for specialist status, in addition to passing tough post-graduate examinations, a vet will have to show evidence of keeping up to date with new research and techniques by regular attendance at educational meetings, and making contributions to veterinary knowledge by publishing scientific papers describing new findings. This expertise ultimately helps provide the best treatment for your horse.

Vets generally list their qualifications on their practice letterhead and website. A vet must have a veterinary degree, the name of which differs slightly between the different veterinary schools both in the UK and abroad (e.g., BVSc, BVetMed, VetMB, DVM). All vets must pay a registration fee to the Royal College and thereby be a member (MRCVS), whilst some become fellows (FRCVS). Those vets with post-graduate qualifications will also use those initials (e.g. DipECVS – diplomate of the European College of Veterinary Surgeons; DEO – diploma in equine orthopaedics; CertEP – certificate in equine practice). If you want to find out about additional equine veterinary qualifications you can contact the Royal College of Veterinary Surgeons (RCVS), who have a useful website: www.rcvs.org.uk

If a practice in the UK is called a Veterinary or Equine Hospital you can be confident that it has met rigorous RCVS standards, both with respect to the qualifications of the vets employed there and the level of equipment required to meet hospital status. Just because a practice has an operating theatre that does not mean it is of a hospital standard, nor does it mean that the practice has a vet skilled in surgery, or the option of having your horse anaesthetized by someone with specialist training in anaesthesia. Horses are high-risk cases to anaesthetize as one in 100 can die under anaesthetic, so it is important that every risk is minimized. Similarly, just because a practice has the capability to perform a sophisticated diagnostic technique, such as bone scan, it does not necessarily mean that there is someone there experienced in the acquisition of top-quality images and interpretation of the scans. So it is important to ascertain that there is the human expertise available for your horse as well as shiny kit that looks impressive but is no good, if it is not used to the full.

Veterinary costs are another issue which has to be considered, since maintaining the equipment and employing the equine veterinary experts to utilize it does not come cheap. Horses by their very size and nature require large amounts of medicine and when major treatment such as surgery is needed, the practicalities mean a complex operating theatre set-up to accommodate such large, yet delicate creatures. In addition to the challenge of the surgery itself, the aftercare requires a large, dedicated team. For instance a dehydrated colic case will require more than 80 litres (nearly 18 gallons) of sterile intravenous fluids daily compared to the tiny 500 ml (less than a pint) drip that might be attached to one of us in hospital. Horse health care is an expensive business, which needs to be factored into your equine budget and, if necessary, covered by adequate insurance (see Insurance in Chapter 3).

**OTHER EQUINE HEALTH PROFESSIONALS**

In addition to acquiring a well-qualified equine vet, your horse will require the regular attentions of a skilled farrier (who will, if necessary, work in tandem with the vet to help remedy various types of foot problems and lameness) and there is a whole circle of other individuals who may become involved in maintaining your horse's health. Good horses are athletes and may require specialist input from several different people working together as a team with your vet. Equine dental technicians were discussed in Chapter 9 and, additionally, physiotherapy, acupuncture and various complementary treatments can play an important role in helping an injured or off-form horse. Take care in these respects because, whilst there are many genuine qualified practitioners, there are also some charlatans out there with very little training, minimal qualifications and no veterinary approval to back up their claims. Before consulting people offering such treatments, always check with your vet first, as it is important to ensure you have a correct veterinary diagnosis right from the start.

## WHEN TO CALL THE VET

IT IS IMPORTANT to have clear and accurate communication between yourself and your vet. It is always better to ring your vet for advice rather than treat your horse yourself and make things difficult for both horse and vet at a later stage. If or when you have a major emergency, if the vet knows you and where and how you keep your horses, he or she will be in a better position to respond promptly. Even though vets are required to provide a 24-hour emergency service, the same vet who you disturb at night is likely to be required to work the following day, so try to avoid unnecessary night-time calls. Vets usually work in relatively small private practices with only a limited number of experienced individuals sharing the equine on-call duties. It is frustrating for the vet to be contacted late at night about a horse who would have benefited from being seen the previous morning, so give the vet as much notice that you can. Clearly, this does not apply to an unforeseeable emergency, such as if a horse suffers a major injury or suddenly comes down with colic; however, many minor equine problems can be scheduled to fit more reasonably into a working day. On the other hand there are some problems, in particular apparently minor injuries, which some owners dismiss as unimportant

*Sick horses may require large quantities of intravenous fluids.*

initially, but which would also benefit from urgent veterinary attention. It is, of course, impossible to describe every situation or set hard-and-fast rules, but the key point is that, if you are able to recognize at an early stage conditions that have the *potential* to become emergencies, your horse can have more rapid and effective veterinary care. Of course, in between the real emergencies and minor problems you may be confronted by conditions that can cause concern and uncertainty over whether a visit from the vet is justified. If in doubt, the simple answer is call your vet for help or advice. Keeping a watchful eye on your horse and discussing any concerns at an early stage will mean less worry and expense for you and fewer emergency calls for your vet.

## WHAT BASIC CONDITIONS CONSTITUTE AN EMERGENCY?

If your horse has the misfortune to suffer any of these conditions, you should make an emergency call and consult your vet.

- A broken limb.
- Lameness of a severity that means the horse cannot bear weight on the affected limb.
- A horse who is recumbent and unable to stand.
- Choke, where coupled with obvious distress.
- Colic pain that is violent and/or continuous.
- Continuous bleeding from mouth, nostrils, rectum, vagina, penis or wound.
- Wounds that require stitching: i.e. if the edges pull apart, the wound is less than 12 hrs old and is clean. Older, dirty wounds may not be repairable by stitching but may still need to be seen by a vet.
- Diarrhoea that is continuous and/or painful.
- Difficulties at foaling.
- Punctured or ulcerated eye.
- Severe sudden onset laminitis.
- Sudden onset of disorientation and incoordination.

## EMERGENCY PLANNING

Forward planning can make dealing with emergencies much less stressful. Everyone should have an adequately stocked first aid kit and essential telephone numbers to hand. Store your vet's number in your mobile phone to save time, and have a list of all emergency contact numbers on a board at the stable yard and keep a copy of your insurance documents to hand.

To avoid panic in a crisis:

- Know how to contact your vet in an emergency.
- Know where to obtain horse transport in a hurry.
- Keep a well-stocked first aid kit available.

# THE FIRST AID KIT

This can be simple or elaborate, but at least some of the following are worth having:

- List of key phone numbers – vet, doctor, insurers – paper and pen and a copy of any relevant equine insurance policy.

- Torch, ideally a small pen torch and a larger torch ( plus spare batteries).
- Thermometer.
- Curved stainless steel scissors.
- Small pair of tweezers or forceps.
- Clean bucket or big bowl.
- Antiseptic wound cleaner, e.g. povidone-iodine (Pevidine) or chlorhexidine (Hibiscrub).
- Surgical spirit.
- Petroleum jelly, e.g. Vaseline.
- Wound gel, e.g. Dermagel, Intrasite gel, Nugel or Vetalintex.
- Dressings and bandages including:
  - *Roll of cotton wool.*    *Gamgee and scissors large enough to cut it.*
  - *Ready-to-use poultice, e.g. Animalintex.*
  - *Non-stick sterile dressing squares to go over wounds, e.g.Rondopad or Melonin.*
- A selection of good clean bandages, to include:
  - *Cotton stretch bandages, e.g. K band.*    *Adhesive bandages, e.g. Elastoplast.*
  - *Self-adhesive bandages, e.g. Vetrap.*    *Zinc oxide tape or electric insulating tape.*
  - *Exercise bandages.*    *Stable bandages.*
- Extras:
  - *Shoe removing kit.*    *Pliers and wire cutters.*    *Spare hoofpick.*
  - *Salt.*    *Sterile bag of saline to flush wounds.*
  - *Moist baby wipes to clean wounds.*
  - *Sterile antiseptic impregnated nail brushes to clean wounds, e.g. E-Zscrub.*
  - *Proprietary ice wrap or cooling bandage.*    *Clean towels.*
  - *Baler twine and some rope.*
  - *A rope halter that adjusts to fit different sized horses and ponies.*

- Medications: to be discussed with your own vet and prescribed as necessary. Ask your vet to advise on the best options for your individual situation. Avoid giving any treatment that has been prescribed for one horse to another without first consulting your vet.

It helps to have a plan to enable you to cope in a crisis, as inevitably you will need to care for the ill or injured horse until assistance arrives. Recommendations include:

*1. Stay calm:* a sensible approach will reassure the horse and benefit all concerned. Equine veterinary nurses are taught to make a rapid assessment and formulate an action plan, as below:
- **S**  *Scan* – to rapidly evaluate the people, horse, and the environment.
- **I**  *Identify* – the relevant problems and predict the most likely results.
- **P**  *Prioritize* – decide where the immediate needs lie.
- **P**  *Plan* – what action is to be taken and by whom.
- **E**  *Execute* – the plan.
- **R**  *Reassess* – repeat and continue until the horse and the people involved are stabilized.

The more urgent the situation, the less evaluation and the more action required immediately.

*2. Safety:* a distressed horse can behave in an unpredictable manner, so always ensure everyone's safety. Never put yourself in danger, as the situation will only be made worse if you are hurt as well as your horse! If you are first on the scene, secure the horse, ideally by putting on a headcollar (which is a good reason for always carrying one in your car) and try to reassure the horse, then stop and think and summon help.

*3. Contact help:* if practical, seek help before doing anything drastic.

*4. Consult your vet:*
- Always say when you ring if you think you have a possible emergency. Have all the information ready regarding the horse's name and location and the owner's details, together with your phone numbers so you can be rung back. Then try your best to keep the line free, so that the vet can ring you straight back.
- The best person to talk to the vet is the person who knows most about the horse's present condition. Vets are trained to ask the necessary questions, but you need to be aware of what is going on to give them helpful answers.
- Most medical and surgical conditions are more likely to have a successful outcome if they are caught early and treated before any disease process has really taken hold. Furthermore, if a horse is seriously ill or injured, it may be necessary to transport him to a clinic where better facilities are available for management. It is always going to be better to travel early, whilst the horse is still fit to do so. No one will complain if a horse is better by the time he arrives. Certainly, if he has already been travelled to an equine hospital he is in the right place if he deteriorates. If your horse is stabled far from a specialized equine hospital facility or is completely unfit to travel, then you and your vet may have to manage more major problems at home. In general though, most serious conditions will benefit from treatment at an equine veterinary clinic which has all the facilities to cope with emergencies.

Whilst you are waiting for the vet to arrive, do what you can to comfort the horse. There are specific things you can do to help certain conditions, (see next section), however the golden rule to remember is: above all, do no harm. How much you can safely and legally do, depends on the condition with which you are coping. Use common sense, for instance, if you have a wound that is bleeding badly, you need to apply a pressure pad to staunch the blood flow rather than waiting for the vet to arrive and do it for you. Most lame or injured horses are best brought in from the field; however if a horse has a possibly broken leg, it is obviously unreasonable to distress him by trying to make him walk.

## THE TEN MOST COMMON EMERGENCIES YOU MAY FACE

### WOUNDS

Wounds are the most common emergency. Effective first aid helps to ensure successful healing. First aid should aim to:

- Prevent further injury.
- Control blood loss.
- Minimize contamination.
- Clean the wound and reduce the risk of infection.

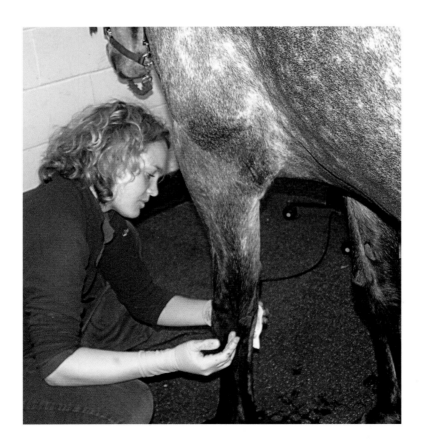

*It is important to cover a wound to protect it.*

It is important to remember that a small amount of bleeding will look colossal when it is your favourite horse (or yourself!). Think of a spilt bottle of milk.... it looks like far more on the floor! Most bleeding can be controlled by applying a clean, dry bandage pad with moderate pressure. If you are out in the middle of nowhere, sacrifice a T-shirt or whatever else is to hand to hold over the wound. If you can tape it in place or hold it there for at least 5 minutes, it should allow blood clotting to occur. The ideal is to use a sterile, or at least clean, bandage to reduce contamination by dirt and dust. This is where dressings from a well-stocked first kit are useful!

The rules to remember with every wound are:

**1. *CLOT***: first stop the bleeding.
**2. *CHECK*** and ***CLEAN***: contamination and infection prevent wound healing and if infection penetrates vital structures such as joints or tendon sheaths, a horse may be permanently crippled. Hence it is vital to carefully check the position, depth and severity of any wound.
**3. *COVER*** the wound where possible to protect it.

Always contact your vet if:
- The horse is very lame, even if the wound itself is tiny.
- Any wound is more than 5 cm (2 in) long and has gone right through the skin, where it gapes open and may need to be stitched.
- There seems to be excessive bleeding.
- There is any suspicion of a foreign body in the wound.
- There is any suspicion that a vital structure such as a joint may be involved.
- The horse has not had an anti-tetanus vaccination.

Although the nature of wounds has not changed, improved wound management is available in the twenty-first century. Instead of the traditional approach of slapping on a poultice and then reaching for antibiotics to control complications, there is now a very sensible emphasis on careful cleaning of wounds to encourage rapid healing. Even a small cut can become badly infected, so should be washed carefully, for instance with a hose at low pressure so that it does not drive dirt deeper into the wound. Another option is to wash a wound with a saline solution, either ready-made or using 1 teaspoon of salt to a 0.6 litre (a pint) of previously boiled water.

People are often tempted to put all sorts of powders and potions on an injury. It is important to remember that raw tissues are exposed. A good guide is never to put anything on a wound that you would not put in your own eye. Often the best option is to use the new water-soluble wound gels that are now available. These can be applied safely to the area of damage to help keep a wound clean and moist. It is thought that they reduce the number of bacteria in the wound and encourage healing. They are a useful addition to any first aid kit and a safe and satisfactory answer to the question, 'How shall I cover a wound?' There are various such products on the market, including Dermagel, Intrasite gel, Nugel and Vetalintex.

These wound gels are particularly useful to help heal those small wounds that do not really need to be stitched, yet can still be an entry site for infection. If you think a wound may need to be stitched, you should consult your vet as soon as possible since a wound will heal more effectively if it is stitched whilst still fresh. (This does not mean that your vet has to attend instantly as there is a 6–8 hour optimum period for wound repair.)

Many wounds that look appalling at first inspection will repair very well given time and proper care.

### COPING WITH COLIC

Colic simply means any sort of abdominal pain and it can affect horses of all ages and types. Colic can vary from a mild bout of discomfort that resolves on its own, to something more serious that requires medical management or, most dramatically, a serious abdominal crisis requiring surgery. Most colic cases are successfully cured medically, but somewhere between 5 and 10 per cent will require emergency surgery to survive. The problem lies in knowing which colic case fits into which category as, in the early stages, the clinical signs are the same. The important thing for the horse owner is to recognize as soon as possible that the horse has colic that requires veterinary attention. Colic is best controlled if treatment is started early on and any colic that requires surgical intervention has a much better chance of success if surgery is undertaken *as soon as possible*. The case every vet dreads is the morning call to the horse found with colic first thing who may have been in agony all night. Regular checks on the horses under your care will allow early detection of any problems.

#### SIGNS TO LOOK FOR

The signs of colic vary, but studies have shown that, of horses with colic:

- 44% roll
- 43% paw continuously or intermittently
- 29% lie down for long periods
- 21% get up and down
- 14% look repeatedly at their flank
- 13% curl their upper lip
- 10% back into a corner
- 7% kick at their abdomen
- 4% stand in a stretched position as if trying to pass urine
- 1% fail to pass droppings for longer than 24 hours.

In severe cases of colic, the affected horse can roll violently and may throw himself on the ground alarmingly in response to the pain. In such cases it is obvious that the vet should be called straight away.

It is sensible to contact your vet if even mild colic signs persist for more than half an hour because of the potential for colic cases to worsen unpredictably.

WHAT TO DO

- If a horse with colic is violent, it is essential to ensure you are not injured. If you can, try to calm the horse; many will panic with the pain – getting him up and walking him may help in the short term. If the horse is determined to go down, make sure he has a big enough box with a deep bed, where he is less likely to get cast. Ensure he cannot injure himself on fittings such as mangers or buckets, or turn him out in the arena or a field where he cannot damage himself. Although it is not ideal, rolling is unlikely to make colic worse. By the time a horse rolls, his intestines may already be twisted and it's nature's way of attempting to relieve the problem.

- It is wrong to try to walk a horse with colic for hours as that will only exhaust the horse and will not cure severe pain. Walking should only be a stopgap measure, whilst waiting for the vet.

- Remove all feed from the horse's reach.

- Colic drenches are rarely beneficial and should not be given without consulting your vet.

- Have clean water, soap and towel ready for the vet's arrival.

- If the colic is severe, the horse may need to be transported to an equine hospital for observation and treatment, so make sure you have transport available if there is a possibility that it might be needed.

*Good nursing and intensive care are needed after colic surgery. This horse is being walked out wearing a belly band.*

The crucial thing with treating colic is catching it early. Painkillers work better if given before the pain is very severe. In the small number of cases needing surgery, the chances of success are much greater if an operation is carried out as soon as possible. Nowadays, if a horse with colic has surgery, there should be at least a 75% chance of survival, provided that you can reach an equine hospital rapidly and there are the facilities and veterinary expertise available to provide the intensive aftercare that is required, as well as the surgical skills to perform the surgery. The chances of success also vary on the type of surgery that has to be performed; where lengthy sections of bowel have to be removed, the risks are greater than if a small area of gut just needs to be untwisted and returned to its rightful place. Clearly, the condition of the horse at the start of colic surgery is another deciding factor; the horse who is toxic and has been ill for a day is likely to fare worse than one who is bright and has only been in pain for a short time. There are many other factors to consider and important veterinary research is being done to help maximize success rates of colic surgery.

There is also the question of what defines success. Many horses will be able to return to full work, whilst others will have lengthy, complicated recoveries. The costs of such surgery are high, both financially and emotionally, and it is worth deciding in advance whether you would submit your horse to colic surgery and ensuring that those involved in caring for your horse know of your intentions, just in case it ever becomes necessary.

## LAMENESS

Lameness may require urgent treatment. Some people will wait days before calling a vet for a horse who is hopping lame, whilst others will consider the slightest degree of lameness to be a dire emergency. In general, if a horse is standing on only three legs and cannot walk, you should contact your vet straight away. If a horse can walk on the lame leg, but prefers to rest it, the condition is less critical, but it would still be best for the horse to be seen by a vet the same day. When a horse has suddenly become noticeably lame, for instance overnight or with a wound, then it is sensible to contact your vet the same day. It is harder to know when a gradually worsening lameness becomes a serious problem. Certainly, if it does not respond to a few days rest or cannot be resolved by your farrier checking the foot, then it is time to call the vet.

### How to identify which leg a horse is lame on

It will be obvious when a horse is very lame, i.e. he cannot stand on one leg. However, subtle lameness is much harder to appreciate. If you are unsure whether your horse is lame, it is best to ask someone else to trot the horse away from you and then back towards you on the end of a lead rope, with the horse's head held loosely so that you can watch it move. A horse who is lame in front will lift his head up as the lame leg hits the ground. The head nods down as the sound leg hits the ground.

Hind limb lameness can be harder to discern, but it is easier to see as a horse trot away from you. The hip on the painful, lame side appears to rise and fall more obviously as the horse tries

**The sound horse**

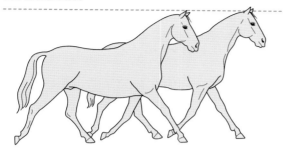

*How to tell when a horse is lame on a front leg.*

A sound horse shows an even head carriage

**The lame horse**

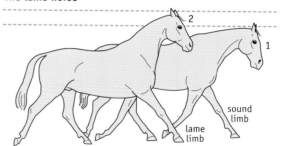

The lame horse nods as the sound front leg falls (1) and raises his head as the lame limb meets the ground (2).

to avoid taking weight on that leg. With hind limb lameness there is not likely to be a nodding of the head unless the lameness is severe. In these cases, the horse will attempt to shift his weight forwards and will lower his head at trot when the lame limb contacts the ground. For example, if the horse is very lame on his left hind, he may lower his head as the left hind contacts the ground. *Since the horse moves his limbs in diagonal pairs at trot, if he is viewed only from the front, this could easily be mistaken for a left forelimb lameness.*

If a foot problem is present, a stronger than normal *digital pulse* may be felt where the artery runs over the fetlock on the affected foot. This happens because of the change in blood flow to the foot and it will be more obvious on the affected foot. Compare the different feet. If there is an abscess or some other foot problem developing, that may cause a more pronounced pulse to be present in the affected foot. If you find a pounding digital pulse in more than one foot the most likely cause is laminitis. Unless one hoof is *considerably* hotter than all the others this is not always an accurate indication of the site of pain; it may just be the case that the one foot has been in the sun or out of a draught, and so appears warmer.

FOOT PAIN

This is the commonest cause of equine lameness. The most frequent cause is pus in the foot, which is properly called a sub-solar abscess. This is particularly common in wet weather, when moisture, dirt and bacteria track up through tiny cracks in the hoof. Infection then develops rapidly with a build-up of pus within the confines of the hoof, which is extremely painful for the horse. In the early stages of infection there may be only a slight lameness, which can progress to a horse who is so sore that he will not put the foot to the ground, i.e. he is literally hopping lame. Other signs include:

- Pointing the toe (see photograph below).
- Increased heat in the foot, i.e. the affected hoof may feel hotter than the others.
- Increased pulse to the foot.
- Pain and discomfort.
- Swelling up the leg, so this may be mistaken for a tendon injury.
- Pus discharging from the coronary band. If the abscess is not drained, it will burst out from the coronary band.

If you suspect that your horse has pus in the foot, you should contact your vet or your farrier to attend to the horse as soon as possible. The cure is to drain the abscess and this will often involve removing the shoe. Once the abscess has been located and the pus drained out, the horse will immediately feel very much better.

First aid treatment includes putting on a poultice to encourage the abscess to drain. This will soften the hard horn, making the job of paring with a hoof knife easier. Unless an abscess is about to burst there, you should avoid poulticing around the coronary band because, first, a hot poultice could burn the skin and, second, it is best to encourage the infection to drain downwards rather

*A lame horse*
*pointing his toe.*

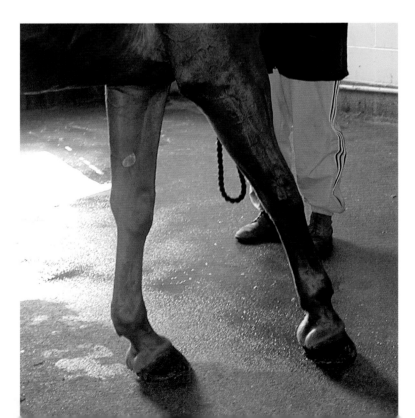

than burst open at the coronary band.

The whole foot should be cleaned, which may help show up the problem area, pus or foot puncture. Sometimes soaking the foot in a tub of warm water with a little table salt or Epsom salts will help the horse and clean the foot. The vet or farrier will advise you on how to clean the actual area of the abscess. It may need to be flushed with hydrogen peroxide or an antiseptic to eliminate the infection. It is then important that it is kept protected with a suitable dressing until it has healed sufficiently to prevent further dirt entering the area of damage.

A horse with pus in the foot is best kept stabled, particularly when the foot is bandaged.

SUDDEN SEVERE LAMENESS

Eight out of ten lameness problems originate in the foot; the ninth is also likely to be in the foot but you just cannot find it, and only the tenth will be somewhere else on the leg altogether. Everyone dreads a broken bone, but remember that most lameness is caused by something in the foot rather than a fracture.

> **KEY POINT**
>
> Always ensure that tetanus vaccinations are up to date.

A broken leg can occur in many different situations and should be suspected when:

- A horse is suddenly seen to be non-weight-bearing lame, i.e. he cannot use the leg at all.
- A loud crack is heard prior to the onset of lameness.
- The limb is totally unstable and may bend at an unusual angle.
- The horse is in extreme pain.

If you think your horse has broken his leg:

- Contact your vet immediately, requesting immediate emergency attention. Ensure that the vet knows the potential seriousness of the situation.
- Whilst you are waiting for help, you should:
  * Try to cover the injured horse with any coat or rug as he will be shocked and feel cold.
  * Keep the horse quiet. If a horse is found like this in the field, do not attempt to move him. Put a headcollar on and hold him still, so that he does not try to walk on the injured limb. It is movement which is the most distressing as the horse realizes he cannot use the leg. Offering food is often a good way of calming the horse: hay and a bucket of feed can act like an emergency painkiller in many such cases.
  * To save time when the vet arrives, try to organize transport in advance, so that everything is ready if the horse has to be moved. Horses with a leg injury may find it easier to walk up a gentle trailer ramp than a steeper one into a horsebox. Racecourses and other equine facilities have special horse ambulances for just this purpose. If a horse with a broken leg is to be travelled, the way in which this is done can make an enormous difference to the final outcome. A good supporting splint and an easy journey with a good driver can help reduce the chance of further destabilizing the broken bones.

Regrettably, many fractures in the horse are untreatable, particularly those where there is an open wound with the bone visible through the skin. In these cases the tissue damage and infection will be overwhelming. The majority of broken long bones of the upper limbs will also be impossible to repair. Other lower limb fractures are potentially repairable, but you and your horse will be facing a long and costly course of surgical treatment. In many cases it is kindest if the horse can be euthanased as soon as possible. If you are not the owner, try to contact them, so that they are available to discuss the situation with the vet.

*Many suspected fractures turn out to be relatively easily repairable bone chips rather than complete fractures, or other causes of sudden severe lameness such as pus in the foot or a locking patella.* So do not despair, obtain immediate veterinary help and an accurate diagnosis as soon as possible.

LOCKING STIFLES

The equine mechanism for sleeping standing up involves the patella or kneecap catching over the end of the thigh bone. Normally, horses can unlock or free their patella, but occasionally one catches and locks, hence the name.

The sudden, severe lameness caused by a locking stifle can be confused with a broken leg or pus in the foot. The condition is properly known as 'upward fixation of the patella'. It mostly occurs in the following groups of horses:

1.  Young, immature animals who are not in regular work.
2.  Horses who have been taken out of training and confined to a stable, often as a result of illness or injury.
3.  Some breeds, particularly small ponies such as Shetlands, are prone to locking stifles.

Signs of a locking stifle are:

● A sudden severe lameness, never during exercise, but during box rest or at the start of movement. It is usually seen as the horse walks out of the stable.
● The affected hind leg will point backwards and appear unable to bend fully. The animal may hop forward, dragging the toe along the ground, with a slightly bent fetlock.
● The leg may appear stuck at an odd angle, hence the possible confusion with a fracture.
● The stifle may click back to normal after a few strides, or the condition may persist for longer. Usually it is intermittent, with affected horses moving relatively normally and then the stifle occasionally gets caught up for a few strides.

To help distinguish between a locked stifle and a suspected limb fracture, check that the leg is stuck backward rather than hanging at an odd angle. The animal with a locked stifle is unlikely to be distressed, whereas a fracture is obviously painful. As mentioned, the patella will frequently free itself after a few strides. If not, it is often possible to make it shift by:

- Making the animal move forward suddenly.
- Backing the horse up.
- Manipulating the stifle.

Immature, unfit or poorly muscled animals will frequently grow out of this tendency as they become older and stronger. Most are improved by increasing fitness, regular exercise and good foot care. If it keeps happening, consult the vet, as surgery is sometimes a possibility. Also discuss special shoes with the vet and farrier. Individuals vary, but often slightly raising the heels, shortening the toes and lowering the medial wall a little more than the lateral can help.

**FOREIGN BODIES**

A nail stuck in a horse's foot is a common emergency. The majority of these wounds are superficial and respond well to treatment, but a deep puncture wound can permanently cripple a horse. If you find a nail in your horse's foot, it is crucial to note:

- Where the nail penetrated the foot.
- The angle at which it went in.
- How deep it went in, i.e. the length of nail within the foot.

In theory it is sensible to leave foreign bodies where they have become wedged, until you have help to remove them. A nail in the foot is generally an exception to this theory since, if a horse is bearing weight on the limb, he may push the nail in further. However, always take care in removing any foreign body to ensure it that does not break off as it is removed and, ideally, if a nail has been removed, mark the point where it went in. If the horse is so lame he is not bearing weight on the limb, leave the nail where it is and contact your vet urgently!

It is important to consider where and how far the nail went. The deeper a nail goes the more dangerous it is, particularly if it happens to pierce the middle third of the foot (see diagram p.214). This is the real danger zone. If a nail or anything else has pierced the middle of the foot deeply, call your vet immediately. This is because several vital structures are located in the middle of the foot. These include:

1. The navicular bone and associated structures.
2. The deep digital flexor tendon and its sheath.
3. The coffin joint.

Wounds that penetrate deep into the toe of a horse's foot may infect or break the pedal bone. Wounds in the heel tend to produce infection in the area of the puncture, but are rarely life-threatening. A superficial puncture may be treated by scrubbing the site with antiseptic, then applying a clean dressing or poultice.

If a dirty foreign body such as a nail reaches any of the vital structures within the foot, aggressive treatment is needed to eliminate infection. Poulticing is unlikely to be sufficient.

Punctures to the foot can be misleading in that they can look so much better when the nail is removed that treatment may be delayed until it is too late. In these cases pain is not always a clear indicator that something serious is wrong. With a nail puncture that goes more than 2 cm (⅘ in) into the foot do not delay before contacting your vet.

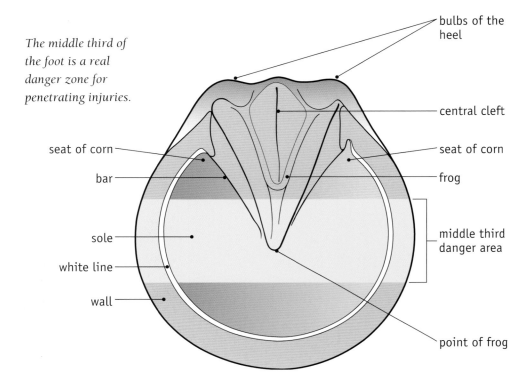

*The middle third of the foot is a real danger zone for penetrating injuries.*

## LAMINITIS

Laminitis is an agonizing condition affecting the feet and is, unfortunately, a common emergency. The chances of recovery are maximized if treatment is started early.

Laminitis can occur in two forms:

*ACUTE LAMINITIS* needs *prompt, early and effective* treatment in the early stages of the condition, when the horse or pony is uncomfortable and showing lameness but major changes have not yet happened within the foot. Unfortunately, severe changes can occur within hours.

*CHRONIC LAMINITIS* occurs when the pedal bone has rotated or sunk. These cases are not necessarily such an immediate emergency, but a vet should be contacted if the horse or pony is in pain.

How to recognize laminitis

In severe cases of laminitis, the feet are so painful that the horse or pony simply will not move, or may not even want to stand. This is obviously urgent and a vet needs to be called immediately. Signs to look for are:

- Reluctance to move.
- A tendency to stand with the legs stretched forward and leaning backward to shift the weight off the front feet.
- Milder cases will be uncertain which foot to stand on, so they constantly shift their weight because whichever foot they stand on hurts.
- Hooves that may feel hot, but this not a reliable sign as the hooves can be hot for other reasons, such as pus in the foot or simply in a horse who has been standing in the sun.
- Feet that are painful in response to pressure to the sole.
- Severe cases spend a lot of time lying down.
- Horse may tremble and look stressed and anxious.
- The intense pain associated with severe laminitis means that the pulse and respiratory rates rise. Frequently, a prominent pulse is obvious where the digital artery runs over the fetlock. This digital pulse (which is where the blood flows going to the foot) will be pounding on all four feet in a severe case.

*A shoe for a laminitic horse, with resin to support the foot.*

*MILD CHRONIC LAMINITIS* is less obvious and can be confused with other sorts of lameness. Clues to look for are:

- The animal who is said to 'feel his feet' and so may be lame on and off, especially on rough ground or when turning.
- The animal who is often footsore or lame after having his feet trimmed.
- Funny-shaped feet: Rings in the hoof wall or foot wider at the heel than at the toe, which produces a foot with long toes. Also common clues are dropped soles with wider than normal white lines and flat feet.
- Pus in the foot is common because of the weak horn growth in the diseased hoof.
- Visible red bruising within the hoof, particularly when the farrier trims the feet.
- This form is commonest in fat ponies, but any horse who is overweight is at increased risk!

WHAT TO DO
- Contact the vet: severe cases will need painkillers and other treatment urgently.
Mild chronic cases will need a planned campaign of action involving both the vet and the farrier.
- If laminitis is suspected, never force the horse or pony to walk, which was the old-fashioned treatment. Allow him to lie down and rest his feet.
- Standing in cold water, or hosing, will provide some relief to the sore feet, but this is only a temporary help as it reduces the weakened foot's blood supply. Current thinking is that warm-water hosing or applying warm water compresses around the lower limbs (e.g. warm, wet towels) is better.
- Stable on deep, non-edible bedding such as shavings, paper or sand that will mould to the feet and help to support them.
- It is possible to tape frog supports on to the feet to help. There are now several types of tape-on frog support available, ranging from purpose-designed pads or rubber wedges to home-made bandage supports. Your vet can advise on the most appropriate support.
- Prevention is far better than first aid for laminitis. In the overweight or overfed animal, a carefully controlled diet, increased exercise and good regular farriery are the obvious, but not easy answers. If the laminitis developed as a result of another condition such as Cushing's disease, that also needs proper management.

**CHOKE**
This occurs when a horse gets some food stuck in his oesophagus (gullet). One moment the horse is well and the next he is coughing and spluttering, with saliva and food drooling from the mouth and nostrils. This has the appearance of a dire emergency, but is usually less serious than it seems and the majority of cases will clear themselves before your vet arrives. First aid treatments include:

- Stop the horse from eating or drinking anything further. It is best to put the horse in a box with no hay or water and non-edible bedding, then contact your vet for advice. By the time you have done so, the obstruction will frequently have cleared.
- Keep the horse quiet, with the head low to allow saliva to drain.
- If the obstruction does not shift within an hour or two, you may need your vet's help.

WHAT YOUR VET WILL DO

This depends on how long the choke has been going on and how uncomfortable the horse is. The majority simply need injections to relax them and allow the obstruction to pass.

If the problem persists, the vet may use more aggressive treatments to move the blockage. Sometimes a stomach tube is passed and fluid gently pumped through to soften and shift the blockage. Giving the horse large amounts of fluids as an intravenous drip can help, as horses can become dehydrated through continually dribbling saliva and being unable to drink because of the blockage. On rare occasions a general anaesthetic and a surgical procedure may be needed to dislodge the blockage.

WHAT YOU SHOULD DO AFTERWARDS

Offer only water for the 12 hours immediately after an obstruction has cleared and then soft food for the next 12 hours because of residual pain in the gullet and the increased chance of a repeat obstruction. With a mild choke that cleared within 10 minutes, it is possible to allow the horse to nibble a bit of grass in a couple of hours to check that he is back to normal.

Many horses develop choke because they are greedy eaters who bolt their food. If this is the case, it is important to slow down the horse's eating, e.g. by putting a round stone or salt lick in the manger so the horse has to nibble around it, and using a haynet with small holes so that it takes longer to eat. Classically, horses are said to choke on unsoaked sugar beet. If this feed is used, it must be well soaked before it is given to any horse. Also, the unsoaked sugar beet must be kept somewhere safe where it cannot be accessed by any hungry horses or ponies.

In all cases of choke, get the horse's teeth checked to ensure he is chewing his food properly. With repeated choke cases, soaking the hay and moistening feeds can help reduce the risk.

**BREATHING PROBLEMS**

As mentioned earlier, the normal respiratory rate for a horse at rest is between 8 to 14 breaths per minute and the best way to measure this is either to hold a hand close to the horse's nostrils to feel each breath, or count flank movements as the horse breathes in and out. On a cold day you will be able to see the breath each time the horse exhales.

The respiratory rate increases with exercise, pain and high temperatures, as well as with respiratory disease itself. To help determine whether disease is present, it is worth noting that a horse usually has around three heart beats to every one breath; this ratio stays about the same with exercise, but not with disease. Thus any significant deviation from the normal ratio should be taken seriously. A horse with a severe breathing problem will have only one heart beat for three breaths, or even worse. When horses have difficulty breathing they flare their nostrils and the whole of their flanks will heave up and down with the extra respiratory effort, hence the name 'heaves' for severe stable coughs.

## IMMEDIATE ACTION

If the horse is gasping and really breathless and does not improve rapidly; is coughing continuously as if there is something stuck in the throat or airway; has recently suffered an injury to the chest or has a new loud snoring / roaring sound all the time, then contact your vet straight away, particularly if the condition has come on suddenly.

Whilst waiting for help, you could:

1. Move the horse to a dust-free, open, airy space, e.g. a paddock and keep him quiet and under close observation. Obviously any exercise is liable to make breathlessness worse, so do not make the animal move unnecessarily.
2. Check the horse's temperature to see if there is a fever. This is unlikely but, if there is, it suggests an infection and again you should tell your vet.

In the UK, most equine breathing problems are associated with a dust allergy, and are only occasionally caused by other conditions, such as pneumonia. People with asthma are allergic to certain things, which make them breathless and wheezy. Similarly, horses develop recurrent airway obstruction (RAO), which was previously called COPD (chronic obstructive pulmonary disease). This is also known as 'broken wind', 'heaves' or a 'stable cough'. These diseases develop as a result of an allergic response to organic dusts, particularly hay and straw dust and the fungal spores therein. If a sensitized horse is exposed to a lot of these allergens, he will start to wheeze, cough and have difficulty breathing.

## WHAT YOUR VET WILL DO

This depends on the suspected cause. Medicines can be prescribed that will effectively control many breathing problems, although they may only help temporarily rather than provide a cure. If there is an obstruction in the airway the vet may perform a tracheostomy, i.e. insert a tube into the airway to allow the horse to breathe. Your vet may recommend passing an endoscope to examine the inside of the airways and lungs to make a diagnosis. (An endoscope enables the vet to do this effectively.)

## AZOTURIA

Also known as 'set-fast', 'tying-up' or, most properly, equine rhabdomyolysis syndrome (ERS), this is a disturbance of muscle function, best compared to muscle cramp, which can happen suddenly when a horse is being exercised.

## SIGNS TO LOOK FOR

● The horse seems unwilling to go forward, may take short steps, and feel unsteady or stiff on his hind legs.

- The muscles of the hindquarters feel hot and hard.
- In some severe cases the horse seizes up and cannot move.
- Horses can even collapse and be unable to stand and so the condition can be confused with colic or laminitis.
- The horse may appear distressed and uncomfortable.

Basically, the muscles hurt and this alarms the horse. There will be a raised pulse and a slight increase in temperature. There may be frequent attempts to urinate, but the muscle pain may prevent the horse from adopting the normal stance to stale. In cases with severe muscle damage, the urine may be a red-brown to dark chocolate colour.

WHAT TO DO
- If you had bad cramp, you would not want to move so, in these circumstances, you must stop and let the horse rest.
- Put rugs or coats over the horse's back to keep it warm.
- Try to encourage the horse to drink, if possible. Fluids will help flush out the kidneys and reduce the problems associated with muscle breakdown. At the same time, it is sensible to watch that the horse is urinating properly and that the urine is a normal colour. Hay and a wet mash should be offered to encourage fluid input. Bran is not an ideal regular feed to recommend, but can be useful immediately after an attack. The very fact of giving the horse a haynet and feed may help to reduce his anxiety.
- If at or near to home, the horse should be put in a stable and offered water. A thick, dry bed should be provided in case the horse wants to lie down. If he does go down, let him do so and do not force him to stand up again.
- If away from home, try to arrange transport home for the horse rather than riding or walking back. A horsebox is best, as it is less effort for a horse to stand in, compared to a trailer in which he will have to brace himself more, thus using his already sore muscles.
- In the worst and very rare cases, when the horse cannot move and may not be able to stand, contact your vet immediately, requesting emergency attention.

Once a horse has had an episode of azoturia, you should discuss future management with your vet. Blood tests to measure raised levels of muscle enzymes may be necessary to confirm the diagnosis and to monitor progress.


**SKIN CONDITIONS**
The most common skin conditions are ringworm and urticaria.

RINGWORM
Ringworm is a fungal infection of the skin. It cannot be classified as an emergency, but an outbreak of ringworm can be very disruptive and costly in terms of lost days of work.

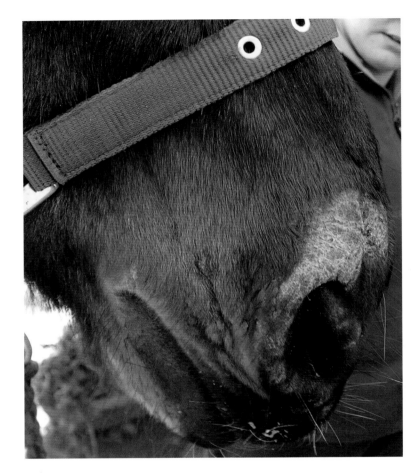

*Ringworm: although not an emergency, it is infectious both to other horses and people.*

Competition schedules, training programmes and other planned activities are interrupted, plus there is the problem that it can infect people as well as horses.

The fungal spores that cause ringworm can survive for a long time in the environment e.g. in stables, horseboxes and on wooden fences. They can also live on tack, grooming kit, rugs and clippers. Horses become infected through small abrasions in the skin. The fungus colonizes the superficial layers of the skin, the hair follicles and the hair shafts. This causes the hair to break off resulting in unsightly stubble which, despite the name, is not always ring-shaped.

The incubation period is usually between 4 and 14 days, but can be longer. The condition can spread rapidly from horse to horse, so whole yards can be infected. Young horses are particularly susceptible, especially when kept close together in damp winter conditions.

SIGNS OF RINGWORM

- Ringworm can occur anywhere on the body but usually affects regions abraded by tack e.g. the head, neck, girth and saddle regions.

- The lesions are very variable in appearance. In the early stages, tufts of hair may stand up from the rest of the coat. Affected areas vary from a couple of millimetres in size up to 4–5 cm (2 in). They are often round but can be any shape.
- The tufts of hair then fall out, leaving an area of grey, scaly skin. The patches may enlarge as the fungus spreads outwards from the edge of the lesion.
- Some horses react to the fungal toxins and their skin becomes inflamed. A crust of exudate forms under the hair tuft. However, the lesions are not generally itchy, unless secondary bacterial infection occurs.

### What to do

Even if not treated, the condition is self-limiting; most horses recover in 4–12 weeks. However, prompt treatment can reduce the severity and duration of the disease. There are new treatments available, so it is advisable to ask your vet what is the best approach in your particular circumstances. Good hygiene reduces contamination of the environment and the risk of spread to other horses (or humans). Human handlers of infected horses should wear disposable gloves and take hygiene precautions as advised by the vet. Grooming kit and tack of infected horses should not be used on other animals.

### Urticaria

Urticaria is also called 'nettle rash' or 'hives'. It is the result of an allergic reaction to something that the horse has been in direct contact with, or inhaled. It can be very hard to determine the precise cause. Possibilities include pollens, insect bites, insect repellents or other topical treatments such as shampoos or medicines, which have been given to your horse. The other possibility is something the horse has eaten, including medication or feed supplements. It will be something that he has been previously exposed to and become sensitive to, so that his body reacts to it, rather than a totally new substance.

Although urticaria rarely causes emergencies, the allergic reaction can be dramatic, with raised patches all over the skin. In this case you will see lumps of all different sizes appearing rapidly under your horse's skin, rather like what you would see on yourself if you had the misfortune to fall into a patch of nettles. These skin lumps develop rapidly and will often disappear within a few hours. They start as small bumps, which spread together into larger, doughy, areas of swelling. Sometimes the whole head will appear swollen and frequently there is concern that the swelling around the nostrils and airway will restrict breathing. In reality the chance of this happening is slim, but a severely affected horse with this sort of allergic reaction looks uncomfortable. Despite the alarming appearance, most cases get better rapidly, often with minimal treatment.

### What to do

You should call the vet if:

- The horse is distressed or the breathing is laboured.
- The eyelids and muzzle are very swollen.
- There is no improvement after 24 hours.

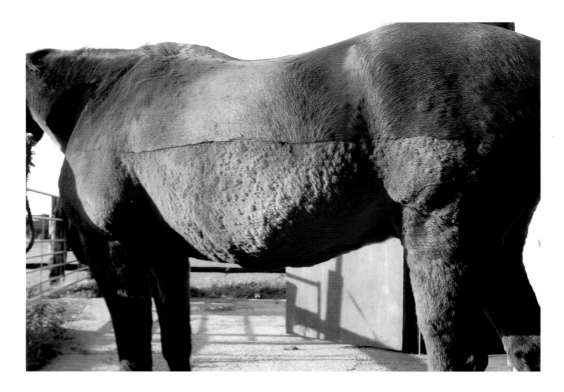

*This horse is covered in skin lumps typical of urticaria.*

A large number of cases will clear up without treatment and never recur. If it does happen more than once, you should consult your vet in case there is a risk of a more serious underlying allergy. Sometimes the skin lumps will persist and then efforts can be made to eliminate the cause or treat the condition, usually with corticosteroids.

Occasionally a horse will fall or roll into nettles. This can be very uncomfortable, particularly in a thin-skinned Thoroughbred type of horse and the horse will be very distressed by it. If it were not for the nettle rash and often the circumstantial evidence of squashed nettles nearby, it would be easy to think it was something much more serious. The horse may look very lame, weak and wobbly or repeatedly turn round to look at his flank as if he had colic. The condition should settle down rapidly, but if it does persist, contact your vet.

### EYE CONDITIONS

If your horse is keeping an eye partially or completely closed, it means it hurts. Infections, inflammation or foreign bodies in the eye will cause this, and also reddening of the membranes around the eye and an obvious discharge from the eye itself. Eye ulcers are the commonest condition affecting the horse's eye.

If there is any cause for concern regarding an eye condition, contact your vet. A painful eye should never be ignored. It is not worth taking risks with eyes, as they are irreplaceable and conditions can deteriorate very rapidly.

WHAT TO DO

- First aid for eyes includes wiping away any discharge and keeping flies away from the eye. Application of petroleum jelly to the face around the eye may reduce scalding of the skin from tear overflow or discharge.
- Never try to force the eyelids open if the eye is shut. It can damage the eye further. It is far better to allow your vet to do this, using appropriate painkillers to help the horse.
- If there is something sticking out of the eyeball, never pull it out, as it may be a part of the inside of the eye itself, plugging a wound that has perforated the front of the eye. Gently bathe around the eye if you can do so without causing discomfort. Water that has been boiled then cooled is best in an emergency. If an irritant chemical is splashed into the eye, then flushing the eye with clean water may be justified. If in doubt, consult your vet before using anything in the eye, which may irritate it further.
- The irritation and discomfort from an eye problem will often tempt a horse to rub his eye, making things worse. Any sensible way of preventing this happening is a very useful first aid measure. One of the best ways of preventing a horse from rubbing his eye is to use a pair of blinkers to protect the eye. In an emergency you could stay with a horse to prevent him from rubbing whilst professional help is sought. If the horse is well-behaved, an ice pack (frozen peas would do!) in between layers of soft, clean cloth held against the eye for 5 minutes may help to soothe it.
- Many horses with eye problems are sensitive to light. They may feel better if placed in a quiet, dust-free, fly-free dark stable.
- Feeding hay on the floor will help reduce dust irritating an already sore eye.
- Any eyelid wound involving the eyelid margin should be repaired by your vet to avoid later complications. If repaired properly, these wounds usually heal very well. If they are left to heal on their own, you can get serious scarring and damage to the eye itself.

Whatever the actual eye problem, the same basic approach applies as first aid.

In addition to the common conditions that have been mentioned in this chapter, there are many other illnesses and injuries that can affect your horse, which would need a whole book to describe. A useful up-to-date source of further information is *The Veterinary Care of the Horse* – see Suggested Reading for details.

## EUTHANASIA

Euthanasia is a difficult subject to consider, but it is part of responsible horse ownership. When the time comes it is important to be able to provide a humane and painless death for your horse. Having any animal put down is a distressing experience and there are several choices to be made, so it is a good idea to plan ahead in order to avoid rushed decisions under difficult circumstances. If you have any questions or worries, discuss them with your vet, who will be accustomed to helping with such sad situations.

## HOW IS IT CARRIED OUT?

There are two methods of euthanasia commonly used:

### LETHAL INJECTION

The horse is given an overdose of anaesthetic-type drugs by intravenous injection. A sedative may be given first. The horse loses consciousness and slowly collapses, with death occurring shortly afterwards. If this method of euthanasia is used then the options for disposal are limited, as the carcass will have to be either buried or cremated.

### SHOOTING

This method of euthanasia results in instant death of the horse. Again, a sedative may be given first. The muzzle of the gun is placed on the horse's forehead. When the gun is fired, the horse will collapse down instantly as the legs buckle, and blood may pour from the nose. With this method there can be involuntary twitches of the horse's legs and occasional gasps for a short period after the horse is dead, which is normal. Not all vets carry a gun, so this may not always be an option.

## HOW TO DISPOSE OF THE CARCASS?

The information given here is specific to the UK: regulations may vary in other countries. The options for disposal of the carcass in Britain are limited and depend on the method of euthanasia and the health of the horse immediately prior to death.

### CREMATION

This option is costly, but is available regardless of the method of euthanasia. If your horse is cremated you can choose to pay for an individual cremation and have the ashes returned to you for burial. The ashes may be returned in a special casket if requested, either as a small amount of token ashes or as a separate individual cremation. The precise arrangements vary in different parts of the country.

### HUNT KENNELS/DISPOSAL TO THE ZOO

Provided that the horse was not put down by lethal injection, or was not suffering from a disease making the carcass unsuitable for consumption, many hunts will use the carcass as food for the hounds; alternatively, some equine carcasses may be taken to the zoo.

### BURIAL

You need to check with your local Trading Standards Office whether this is permitted in your area. The European Union Regulations do not allow burial of pet horses as they consider the horse to be a food animal. At the time of writing, DEFRA does allow burial of pet horses at the discretion of the local authority. Each case is considered on an individual basis.

## SHOULD I BE THERE?

Rest assured that everyone concerned will want your horse's last minutes to be peaceful. The people involved are professionals who care about animals and are used to dealing with this sensitive task. If you are able to be calm during the procedure, then your presence is likely to be reassuring for your horse. If you are visibly distressed, then it may be better to ask a trusted friend to do this for you. Your vet may require you or someone on your behalf to sign a consent form. In a yard of several horses it is obviously essential that someone is present who knows which horse is to be put down.

## NOTIFICATION OF THE INSURANCE COMPANY

If the horse is insured for loss of use and a claim is going to be made, the insurance company must be notified in advance of euthanasia. With the exception of an emergency situation, the permission of the insurers is needed otherwise the claim may be invalidated.

If a horse is destroyed on humane grounds, this action must meet certain criteria to satisfy the requirements of a mortality insurance policy. The British Equine Veterinary Association guidelines state that euthanasia should be carried out if *'the insured horse sustains an injury or manifests an illness or disease that is so severe as to warrant immediate destruction to relieve incurable and excessive pain and that no other options of treatment are available to that horse at that time'*. In such cases, the insurers should be notified as soon as possible. They will require a veterinary certificate confirming the identity of the horse and the reason for euthanasia, and may also ask for a post-mortem to be carried out.

# 11.
# TRAVELLING

TRAVELLING HORSES SAFELY is an important skill. Even if you don't want to compete, there will be times when you need or want to transport your horse or pony – perhaps to take part in training clinics or lessons, or to enable him to be seen at a veterinary hospital, or even simply to ride in different surroundings. If you do compete, getting him to the venue in a comfortable and relaxed state is an essential part of your preparations and can have a marked effect on his performance.

Too many owners give too little thought to travelling their horses. At best, this may leave you with problems to solve, such as reluctance to load and/or arriving at your destination with a stressed horse. At worst, you could be putting lives at risk, including your own and those of other road users.

Even if your horse loads beautifully and is a seasoned traveller, are you sure that when you get behind the wheel of your horsebox or towing vehicle you're not actually breaking the law. For example, if you passed a British driving test after 1997, you also need to take a towing test before you can legally tow a trailer.

If you passed a British test *before* 1 January 1997, there is legally nothing to stop you hitching up a trailer, loading your horse and driving off into the sunset. Similarly, you will probably be entitled to drive a horsebox up to 7.5 tonnes and again, you could simply load up and go. To do so would be naive and dangerous – yet sadly, many people think that because they can drive a car, they can automatically drive a much larger vehicle or tow a trailer, not realizing that there are different skills to learn. In addition, regulations concerning what you are allowed to drive, vehicle maintenance and use and the transport of animals vary considerably around the world and must be checked locally.

*If travelled considerately, most horses soon become relaxed about the whole business.*

Before buying your own transport, try to have some lessons with a professional, specialist instructor. It's often best not to rely on family and friends even if they are experienced, competent drivers: they won't necessarily have the same teaching skills and so may not explain things that they take for granted. Even worse, they may not recognize their own mistakes or bad habits. Many lorry driving schools offer lessons to private as well as commercial drivers and there are also instructors who specialize in teaching towing skills.

Here are some things to remember that will make you a better and safer driver:

● Read the latest edition of the *Highway Code*. If you have been driving for several years, the chances are that it is some time since you read it and there will be a lot of new information.

● Make sure that you know your vehicle's size, whether you have a horsebox or tow a trailer. You need to know this not only for negotiating bridges, but for situations where height and width restrictions are in force, such as car parks and roadworks. It's a good idea to note your horsebox or towing outfit's dimensions on a small card and fix it somewhere in the vehicle where you can check these details at a glance.

● Be aware that speed limits for lorries and tow cars are lower than for cars on their own outside urban areas.

● Practise driving your horsebox or towing your trailer without a horse on board to gain some initial confidence. You may then want to add a dummy load, such as bales of hay, to add weight. Note, however, that a 'dead weight' behaves differently from a live one. Your horse *may* stand like a rock, but chances are that he will shift his weight. Some horses tend to doze off on long, straight stretches, so if you're coming off a motorway or dual carriageway, slow down gradually and in plenty of time.

*When cornering, remember that the back of a large vehicle corners tighter than the front and a trailer turns in closer than the towcar.*

- Be extra observant. All drivers need to be observant, but the importance of this when transporting horses cannot be stressed too highly. Look well ahead so that you can slow down in plenty of time for bends, approaches to roundabouts and so on.
- Don't assume that because you are observant, are other road users are too. Some have no idea that drivers of larger vehicles or towing outfits need extra room to manoeuvre. There have been reports of accidents where pedestrians and other drivers have claimed that they saw a car but didn't notice that it was towing a trailer.
- Be prepared for other drivers pulling out in front of you – especially when you are entering a roundabout, even when you have right of way – or overtaking and cutting back in front of you without allowing a safe distance.
- Gear changes should be smooth and made in the right place, at the right time. Slow down and change gear before reaching a bend; changing gear in the middle of a bend makes your vehicle less stable. This will help you to drive through a bend with maximum control, rather than coasting through it dangerously.
- Your vehicle's steering will feel different from that of a smaller car. Hold the wheel with your hands positioned at 'ten to two' or 'quarter to three' on a clock face, whichever feels more comfortable and secure. Don't grip the wheel tightly, or you won't feel what the steering is doing and will probably overcompensate.
- When cornering, remember that the back of a large vehicle corners tighter than the front and a trailer turns in closer than the towcar.
- Never go anywhere without a mobile phone, in which is stored numbers for your home, yard and vet as well as your own ICE (in case of emergency) numbers.

*On the approach to roundabouts, get into the correct lane in plenty of time.*

**WAYS TO GO**

MOST HORSE OWNERS eventually want their own transport, so that they have the freedom of going where they want, when they want to. We can all dream of owning a brand new luxury horsebox with all mod cons, but financial reality means that the choice is inevitably between a second-hand box and a trailer and tow car. If you can afford it, a horsebox is obviously desirable. But if the choice comes down to a geriatric horsebox and a well-maintained, safe towing vehicle and trailer, remember that horsebox repairs, maintenance and testing and specialist breakdown cover can be horrendously expensive.

You will also be taxing and insuring a horsebox even if it sits on the drive most days of the year, whereas a trailer should have much lower maintenance costs and carries no road tax. The downside of opting for a trailer is that it probably wouldn't give as much protection in an accident and if you don't already own a suitable tow car, you will need to buy one; obviously you can use it for normal transport, but it may not be as economical to run as a smaller, more modest vehicle.

Whatever you buy, get expert advice. Choose your expert carefully: there have been instances of car sales personnel assuring potential customers that a certain model will tow a horse trailer quite easily, not realizing that when you put a sizeable horse on board you are adding another 500–600 kg (1,100–1,320 lb).

## TRAILERS

Because good second-hand trailers made by reputable manufacturers hold their value, the difference in price between a new and second-hand one might not be as much as you think and a new one might be within your budget. However, if you do buy second-hand, make sure you or your adviser knows how to check it thoroughly, covering the floor, ramp, brakes, lights, tyres and hitching mechanism. Warning bells should ring if, for instance, the seller isn't prepared to lift the matting so you can see what's underneath, or if there are obvious signs that the trailer hasn't been looked after. If there is still a pile of dung in there from the last time it was used, beat a retreat: if the seller can't be bothered to clean it out, what else hasn't he or she bothered to do?

Single horse trailers are rarely seen in the UK and are not as stable as wider two-horse trailers. Even if you intend to transport just one horse, a two-horse trailer will give him a more comfortable and safer ride. Modern designs have rear and side ramps, which makes for easier unloading; trailers which unload to the rear only may still be available, particularly second-hand, but a horse is more likely to slip if asked to back down a ramp than if he can walk off forwards.

If you travel your horse alone, either take out the centre partition and use a full-width breast bar to allow him the whole width of the vehicle – using tie ropes on each side – or stand him on the offside, so he is near the centre of the road rather than the kerb. When travelling two horses, put the heavier one on the offside.

### Maintenance mistakes

Because horse trailers are mechanically simple compared to a car or horsebox, a lot of owners ignore the fact that they need regular maintenance and servicing. Ignore this and you put everyone on the road at risk; for instance, if wheel bearings seize, the wheel locks up, sending the trailer to the side and perhaps even leading to it tip over. Britain currently has no equivalent of the car MoT test for trailers, but it is still an offence to use one that is unsafe. Some routine checks can be done at home but for a full service you're usually better taking the trailer to your local dealer.

## HORSEBOXES

When you buy a horsebox, you are buying two products at the same time: the chassis and the body. Few people can afford to buy both brand new and will either buy a used horsebox or find a horsebox builder who will build the horse's accommodation on to a used chassis. The second option gives you the chance of deciding exactly how you want your horsebox laid out in terms of travelling positions and facilities, but you may find a ready-built horsebox that satisfies all your needs. Put your horse's needs first: it's better to give him more room and have restricted accommodation for people than to cramp his space so you can have luxurious living room.

Most experts advise that, if you want to have a horsebox built, the best way is to find a reputable horsebox builder who is prepared to source a chassis that works well with their designs and fits in with your budget. Make sure you know *how* they are going to find it and discuss the age and mileage that your budget allows and what guarantees you will get. The emphasis must be on a *reputable* builder; as there have been several well-publicised cases of horse owners handing over – and losing – large sums of money to companies that have gone under without completing the ordered vehicle. Some owners were reported to have paid deposits without obtaining written agreements, so make sure everything is above board and on paper.

Make sure that your horsebox has an adequate payload, as if you overload it you will be both illegal and unsafe. All vehicles have a gross weight which the manufacturer declares. This comprises the kerb weight (the weight of the vehicle ready to be driven) and the payload, which is everything you will put on board – horses, people, tack, water and so on. Some 3.5 tonne 'two-horse' boxes in particular come very close to the limit when everything is on board. Again, there have also been cases of manufacturers building horseboxes to individual specifications that would be illegal as soon as a horse was put on board.

## STANDING ROOM ONLY

Research suggests that horses should travel best if they face backwards, as they naturally carry more weight on their forehand and facing backwards allows them to cope better when the vehicle brakes. It would be dangerous to try this in a trailer designed to take the horses facing forwards, though there are indications that we may eventually see more trailers designed to this specification.

A horsebox may allow more leeway in the way horses are positioned, and of course if you have one built to your own specifications you can choose the stalling arrangement. Experiments where horses have been travelled loose have suggested that many prefer to take a diagonal position, so herring-bone stalls may be worth considering. Different horses have different preferences, so if you are buying a horsebox and intend to keep your horse for a long time, try to take him for test journeys in different vehicles to see if he seems to prefer a particular standing position.

A horsebox or trailer is a stable on wheels and, as such, you should pay the same attention to the environment it provides. Ventilation outlets are essential to keep a free flow of air moving through; use rugs if necessary to keep your horse warm and protected from draughts rather than shutting windows and vents. Clean out the vehicle immediately after every outing – though be considerate at competition venues; it isn't fair to muck out straight on to someone's land or car park.

### Healthy travelling

Never start a journey if you know or suspect your horse is unwell. An abnormally high temperature means it is unsafe to go anywhere except to your vet!

If you are setting off particularly early or making a long journey, you may want to give your horse a small net of soaked hay or haylage and take another for the trip home. *Don't* fasten a spare net to the back or roof of your vehicle – it will be covered with dirt thrown up from the road and subjected to vehicle fumes.

### HIGH-TECH HELP

Advances in technology, as well as simple, effective and relatively cheap ideas, have helped make travelling horses easier and safer. Things to consider include:

- In 2002, anti-lock braking systems (ABS) became compulsory in Britain on all new horseboxes. If you are buying a second-hand horsebox or having a body built on to a chassis, it is worth stretching your budget if necessary to buy a chassis with ABS fitted. It has to be factory fitted, so you can't buy an old chassis without ABS and have it added.
- Air-sprung suspension systems on horseboxes give a smoother ride, but are obviously more expensive than conventional metal springs.
- Large horseboxes often have powered ramps, but you must also be able to lower them by hand in an emergency.
- Closed-circuit TV enables you to check on your horse as you are travelling.
- Satellite navigation systems are useful for horseboxes and tow cars. Portable systems can now be bought cheaply and there are websites from which you can download the locations of low bridges. However, they are not foolproof: for instance, some may not recognize the difference between unmade tracks and proper roads.
- Coupling mirrors which attach to the front of the trailer make it far easier to hitch up alone.
- Blade stabilizers, which have a blade or bar between brackets on the car and the trailer's A-frame, help to reduce any see-saw movement.

### SECURITY MEASURES

Horsebox and trailer theft is big business, so anything that protects your transport is a good investment. Certain measures will be mandatory for insurance, so check your policy – and don't forget common sense. An amazing number of people leave their vehicles unattended at a show with ramps down and equipment in plain view and insurance companies report that some owners think it is perfectly reasonable to leave their horseboxes with the keys in the ignition whilst they go off competing or hunting. Ideally, park your horsebox or trailer where it can be seen from your or your yard owner's house when not in use.

Make sure you have all chassis numbers and make and model details written down and keep all documentation, including receipts. If you are offered a vehicle on which an attempt has been made to erase or alter a chassis number, don't buy it and do tell the police, because it could well be stolen. Use your postcode: paint it somewhere inside your trailer or horsebox body where it won't easily be found, but will help you or a police officer identify the vehicle if necessary.

Ignore people who tell you that it's not worth taking security measures because determined thieves will find a way round them. Horsebox and trailer thieves, like burglars, go for the easiest pickings and anything that will make stealing your vehicle more difficult or time-consuming is worth having.

Some thieves have nerves of steel, so don't assume that your horsebox or towing outfit is safe just because it is parked where there are plenty of people around. There have been cases of riders going off to compete and returning to find that thieves have unhitched a trailer, hitched it up to their own vehicle and driven it off the showground. Security devices only work when they are in place – so, for instance, think about fitting your trailer's wheel clamp before you go and walk that cross-country course.

SPECIFIC SECURITY MEASURES FOR HORSEBOXES

If you are having a horsebox built, or buying one from a specialist dealer, you should be given advice on how to protect it. Vehicle alarms can be fitted either when your horsebox is built, or afterwards. If, for some reason, this is impossible, disconnect the battery when your horsebox is parked up, or have a battery isolator switch fitted. *Do not disconnect the battery on a vehicle with an alarm or tracking device fitted.*

Tracking devices which send out a signal if a horsebox is stolen may seem relatively expensive, but can prevent a lot of hassle and financial loss. You should also find that your insurance company will give you a discount on your premium if one is fitted.

All doors should have locks and you need somewhere safe to leave documents and valuables when the vehicle is unattended. A vehicle safe is ideal and gives more security than a locking cupboard. External tack lockers are safe and convenient and cut down on the need for internal storage space.

SPECIFIC SECURITY MEASURES FOR TRAILERS

Security devices for trailers are not as sophisticated as those for horseboxes, as trailers do not have batteries to power tracking systems and alarms. However, you can still fit an alarm that runs off its own battery.

Wheel clamps are mandatory in most insurance policies. Choose one that is difficult to remove even when the tyre is let down and has substantial locks that are difficult to knock off or drill out. Fit your clamp to a back wheel, not a front one, so thieves can't hook the hitch over the back of a pick-up truck and move it somewhere isolated where they can remove the clamp without being seen.

Rooftop postcodes are a simple but effective measure. These are large, adhesive letters and numbers that can be seen from above – so if your trailer is stolen, it can be identified from a police car parked on a bridge, or from a police helicopter.

## SAFETY KITS

Keep everyone safe whilst travelling – horses and humans – by kitting out vehicles correctly. Fire extinguishers are as important in horseboxes and tow cars as in any other vehicle and it's important that everyone likely to travel in the vehicle (including helpers) knows how to use them. In general, the best type for a vehicle is a dry powder extinguisher. This can be used on most types of fire with the exception of fat fires. All vehicle fires are frightening and those involving animals as well as people can seem even more so.

Fire brigades usually have officers with special responsibility for fire prevention, so ask them for advice if there's anything you're not sure of. If you belong to a Riding Club or a branch of the Pony Club, why not ask your local fire prevention officer to come and give a talk?

Every vehicle should have a basic tool kit. Cars and small horseboxes should already have a wheel brace and jack, though not all are suitable for use with trailers. Special wedge-shaped trailer jacks make changing a wheel easier; pull the trailer forward so that the undamaged wheel on the same side as the damaged one goes on to the wedge jack, which in turn lifts the damaged one off the road. Changing a wheel on a larger horsebox is a job for a specialist breakdown company because of the equipment needed.

Your basic tool kit should include:

Double-ended screwdriver with a flat head at one end and a cross head at the other
Set of ring spanners
Pliers
Set of vehicle fuses

Torch with alkaline batteries (rechargables run down when not in use)
Penknife
Roll of insulating tape
Warning triangle
At least one high-visibility vest

Carry first aid kits for horses and humans and make sure you can tell immediately which one is which. Items should be packed in hard cases and always stored in the same place, so that you can find them immediately in an emergency.

The British Red Cross Society suggests that a driver's first aid kit should contain:

A bottle of distilled water
Adhesive dressings
Large, small and medium sterile dressings
Crepe and gauze roll bandages in various sizes
Roll of surgical tape

Triangular bandages
Cotton wool
Foil blanket ('survival' blanket)
Tweezers, scissors and safety pins
Surgical gloves

A travelling first aid kit for horses should contain:

A range of dressings, such as non-stick dressings; stretchy conforming bandages; surgical or insulating tape to secure bandages; Animalintex poultice; cool bandages which damp down inflammation when wet
Large roll of cotton wool

Hydrogel to protect wounds, sold under brand names such as Vetalintex and Derma Gel
Antiseptic wipes
Antiseptic such as Hibiscrub or Pevadine
Card with details of yard and vet's phone numbers as back-up to those stored on your mobile phone

| **TRAVELLING GEAR** | IT'S COMMON PRACTICE in the UK to use protective gear when travelling a horse to safeguard him from injury, in particular to his limbs. The exceptions are mares with foals at foot and some unshod youngstock, the reasoning being that, in addition to unshod horses being less likely to damage themselves, very young animals may |

react badly to wearing leg protection, particularly if it slips.

However, if you are travelling a youngster regularly, perhaps because he is being shown in hand, there seems no reason why 2- and 3-year-olds with some experience of the world cannot learn to accept leg protection – in fact, travelling and the preparations that go with it are something that should be introduced with care and consideration to any inexperienced horse, no matter what his age. It's unfair and unrealistic to take a horse out of the field and expect him to wear unfamiliar equipment, walk up a ramp and be driven off, yet it often happens.

So what does a well-dressed horse wear on the road? From top to toe, the basics are a leather headcollar, suitable rug, leg protection and a tail bandage and/or tail guard. Optional extras include a poll guard and perhaps a tail wrap or other means of keeping the long tail hairs clean.

A leather headcollar isn't just smarter than a synthetic one – it's safer. If, despite all precautions, your horse gets hooked up on something in the vehicle, a leather headcollar will break. A nylon one might not and even the standard and recommended practice of using a breakable twine loop between

*A pony equipped for travelling in summer, wearing a cotton summer sheet, travel boots, tail bandage and leather headcollar.*

the rope and the tying-up ring might not be enough to prevent injury. If you prefer, you can use a quick-release, rubber- or plastic-covered chain instead of a twine loop. Fasten the quick-release clip to the tying-up ring rather than the headcollar, as this makes it easier to reach in an emergency.

### TACK AND TRAVELLING

Traditionally, horses being taken to a hunt meet were travelled fully tacked up so that their riders could unload them and get straight on. Most riders would now agree that this particular tradition isn't the best practice, as it's all too easy for a horse to catch his bit rings inside the vehicle and injure his mouth, or to damage his saddle. Whilst you might want to put a bridle on to give more control when loading your horse and put it over his headcollar when unloading, don't leave it on in the horsebox or trailer.

Always take your horse's bridle and a spare headcollar and lead rope on every journey. If something breaks, you'll have a replacement and if you have to unload on to a road in an emergency, it's far safer to use a bridle.

If your horse is tall or tends to throw up his head, use a poll guard to protect this area. Designs range from simple foam pads to shaped, padded caps with ear holes. Check that the holes are big enough and if necessary, enlarge them. If your horse's ears are pinched, he will be uncomfortable and will be even more likely to throw his head around.

Choose your travelling rug according to weather conditions when you set off and take extras to cover other scenarios. For instance, a cotton summer sheet or lightweight cooler might be great for protecting your horse from draughts, but you may need a warmer rug if the temperatures drop. Some riders like to use a magnetic therapy rug before a competition, or before a schooling session at home, as magnotherapy is believed to increase the blood flow and help with warming up – but most vets and chartered physiotherapists believe it is better not to use them when actually travelling, as the horse may break out in patchy sweat.

If your horse is inexperienced or moves around a lot when travelling, there is a risk that he will bang his hips and/or shoulders. There are now rugs with built-in padding over these areas for extra protection. However, also check that he isn't losing his balance because his driver isn't giving him a smooth enough journey.

Leg protection is a choice between travelling boots, or bandages over padding. Boots are quicker to put on and remove and there are some well-shaped designs that protect the legs from knees and hocks downwards. However, unless you find boots with the perfect dimensions for your horse's legs, they may slip. Bandages may therefore be the more secure option, but if you choose to use them, remember that it takes practice to put on any kind of bandage correctly – and the best way of learning is to get a demonstration from someone like a veterinary nurse or a professional groom.

Knee and hock boots give extra protection to joints, but can sometimes cause rather than prevent problems. Keeping them secure usually means fastening the top straps tightly, which applies pressure and can restrict joint movement.

Another possible problem to be aware of is that some horses have the knack of treading on their own feet whilst travelling and may injure the coronet area or pull off shoes. To try to prevent this, travel your horse with overreach boots; if necessary, fit them front and back. They are just as effective as traditional coronet boots, and more practical.

## BANDAGING ESSENTIALS

- Always apply leg bandages over padding to avoid pressure.
- Start by making sure that your bandages are rolled the correct way.
- Always bandage from front to back to prevent pressure on the flexor tendons.
- If you use bandages with tape fastenings, tie them on the outside, not at the front or back where they could put pressure on tendon and bone.
- Each turn of the bandage should overlap the bottom third of the previous one.
- The bandage should not be so tight that you can't slip your finger between it and the horse's leg, but not so loose that it slips down.

Tail bandages are used to prevent the horse rubbing the dock hairs in transit, but they won't provide much protection. If your horse leans back against the ramp or trailer breeching bar, use a padded tail guard or a piece of foam rubber sandwiched between two tail bandages. To keep long tail hairs clean, use a tailwrap or tailbag, available from most saddlers – or, to save money, cut the foot off an old stocking or leg from a pair of tights, pull it over the long tail hairs, stretch it up to the dock and bandage as before.

## LOADING LOGIC

IF A HORSE associates travelling with a comfortable journey and perhaps an enjoyable time out, you shouldn't have problems loading him. But if he's had one or more bad experiences or you confuse him during the loading process, you could have problems. There are lots of ways to make loading less stressful, as detailed below, but if you get serious problems, call in a professional. Many trainers who are particularly skilled in groundwork have great success in solving loading problems, but pick someone whose reputation and results match his or her skills in self-promotion.

Always allow plenty of time for your journey and build in a good leeway for traffic hold-ups and other problems. If you're in a hurry, you'll be tense and your horse will pick up on it. Get everything ready beforehand so that it's simply a case of putting on your horse's travelling gear and getting him on board: park the horsebox or trailer so that the ramp can be let down on to level ground and the interior is light and inviting.

If necessary, use a pressure halter or a bridle when loading to give extra control. A bridle can be put on over the horse's travelling headcollar, but this would interfere with the action of a pressure headcollar and you will need to swap this for a normal headcollar when the horse is on board and partitions, bars and ramps are in place. Wear a hard hat, gloves and suitable footwear and lead your horse up to the ramp so that he approaches it for five or six strides on a straight line.

Walk confidently, looking ahead – not at your horse – and in most cases, he will walk on with equal confidence. If he wants to 'test' the ramp with a front foot, let him; he's trying to find out if it's secure. An inexperienced horse will gain confidence if an experienced, confident one is loaded ahead of him and travelled with him, at least for his first few journeys.

Is he worried because the ramp is steep, something which applies particularly to horseboxes? If so, practise loading into a trailer; a trailer can also be made more inviting by letting down the front ramp so he can see daylight all the way through. You may find a hesitant horse is happy to follow a helper who walks calmly up the trailer ramp without looking back at him. Another useful strategy is to feed your horse from a container placed on the bottom of the ramp. Over a few days, gradually move the container up the ramp so he steps on the ramp and eventually walks in.

Unload with the same care and calmness as when your horse went on board – make sure no one is standing at or near the bottom of the ramp in case he suddenly decides to make an enthusiastic exit.

- Don't hit a horse who refuses to load. It won't do any good but will make the situation worse.
- Don't allow anyone to blindfold him.
- Don't allow anyone to throw pebbles at him/ spray or throw water at him/push a broom at his back end. These are all methods that may be suggested and may result in your horse loading once – but they are equally likely to result in serious injury to horses or people and will certainly not make him likely to load next time.

## BREAKDOWNS

ANY BREAKDOWN or road accident is traumatic and one involving animals can be even more so, even when there is no injury involved. Specialist breakdown cover will help prevent a problem becoming a nightmare – don't fall into the trap of assuming that ordinary car breakdown cover will be enough, as standard breakdown organizations will not cover vehicles over 3.5 tonnes or be prepared to recover a trailer with horses on board.

Further information about how to proceed in the event of a problem in transit can be found in *The Glovebox Guide to Transporting Horses* (see Suggested Reading).

## GOING THE DISTANCE

THE WORLD HAS got smaller, for horses as well as people. Nowadays, racehorses and competition animals cross the globe regularly, and horse owners who head off for a new life in a new country often take their animals with them. Depending on your destination, the main part of your horse's journey will be by land, sea or air.

Even journeys in the UK that are longer than eight hours are subject to restrictions and regulations so if intending to make such a journey you must check with DEFRA to see if any paperwork is required.

### ON THE ROAD

Jackie Potts, head groom to event rider William Fox-Pitt, regularly travels abroad with her charges. Her advice for those intending to transport their own horses long distances is:

- Ventilation is vital. Don't be so worried about draughts that you cut down on ventilation. Jackie uses special net covers so that windows can be left open.
- Keep your horse hydrated by offering wet hay or haylage. Jackie puts hay in mangers so the horse isn't putting his head up, which helps with drainage through the sinuses.

- Every 4 hours, stop at a safe, suitable place and take the horse off the box for 20 minutes. Let him walk around and pick grass; again, putting his head down helps the drainage.
- The biggest health risk relating to long journeys is shipping fever, linked to respiratory problems from travelling. Know your horse's normal temperature beforehand, then take it 8 hours into the journey and when he has arrived and settled. If it is higher than it should be, keep taking it and get veterinary advice if necessary.

## NEW HOME, NEW COUNTRY

Some people move themselves and their families for practical reasons, usually because they or their partner takes a new job, but many fall in love with a country they have visited on holiday. As so many of the reality TV programmes show, living somewhere for real isn't always as idyllic as spending a few weeks there without pressures.

Different countries may have different methods of keeping horses and even buying your horse's favourite feed might not be easy. Don't assume that you'll find a major equestrian tradition in a new country: for instance, Greece's eventing star Heidi Antikatzidis was the first person to represent her country at Olympic level in the 2000 Games. This means that skills horse owners in some countries take for granted, such as specialist vets and farriers, may be in short supply – or non-existent – in other areas.

## EXPERT QUOTE

*'It might sound obvious, but you need to check out your new home in terms of what being a horse owner will be like before you actually move there. Once you leave the UK, you leave behind things like livery yards and hacking. Most horses are kept on special competition yards and everything is competition orientated. If you're used to the freedom of English riding, the pure riding for pleasure aspect, it can be a bit of a culture shock.'*

ANNA BERGEN, WHO MOVED TO GERMANY WITH HUSBAND AND HORSE

Anna's horse had needed specialist treatment that was not available in Germany and in the end, her friends all paid for a qualified physiotherapist to go over and treat her horse. This story had a happy ending – but it could have been very different had he needed colic surgery.

## PAPERWORK AND PRACTICALITIES

Regulations for exporting horses change all the time, so don't try to do it yourself – find a reliable shipping agent who will advise you on current paperwork specifications and veterinary tests. An equine passport is not a permit to travel, but a basic ID document.

Importing countries are not bothered whether or not your horse is sound, but are very concerned about whether he may bring in any diseases. Requirements in this respect vary between destinations and change all the time, which is why it's easier and quicker to go through a professional agent, but for long-haul destinations you may be looking at checks for equine infectious anaemia (Coggin's test), equine viral arteritis (EVA) and contagious equine metritis (CEM) amongst others; horses also need current 'flu vaccinations.

If you're heading for destinations such as Australia or New Zealand, your horse will have to go into quarantine for 2–3 weeks at *each end* of the journey. This is where you really need the professionals – international transporters and agents have dedicated quarantine yards where they will take care of everything, including, if necessary, clipping your horse so that he does not arrive in a different hemisphere and climate with his winter coat.

*Check insurance: your transporter should have mortality cover for the journey, or you can arrange it through your own insurance company or broker.*

## FLYING FACTS

Flying horses has become almost routine, especially in the racing world. But whether you're transporting a mega-money stallion or the family Shetland, he will go through the same procedure and get the same care. However, while horses can be flown out from all major airports in the UK, note that they can only be landed at destination airports geared to deal with them.

Horses being flown are loaded in containers that are put on to the aircraft by scissor lifts. These rise slowly and horses are rarely worried by either the loading or the actual flight. All international transporters employ specialist flying grooms, who usually look after the horses during quarantine periods as well as on the flight – so have got to know them by departure time. Owners sometimes hope to fly out with their horses, but this is usually impractical because of insurance. And with very long flights it really is best to leave it to the professionals, who will monitor and look after your horse from start to finish.

*All international transporters employ specialist flying grooms – flying with your own horse will usually be impractical because of insurance.*

# 12. PROGRESS AND COMPETITION

**R**IGHT FROM THE START, it's important to have lessons with someone you can trust, who will encourage you and help you make the most of the partnership with your horse. It doesn't matter what label you put on him or her – there is no difference between a teacher, an instructor or a trainer – but you do need to feel that you are on the same wavelength. If you've been having lessons at a riding school before buying your horse, you may want to continue with the same teacher, but this may not be possible.

If you need to find a freelance teacher, one of the best ways is through your local Riding Club or branch of the Pony Club. Most organize tuition for members and you will probably be able to benefit from private and group lessons; talk to people who are already taking them and go and watch a couple where riders are working at a similar level to you. Do you understand what the teacher is saying? Do horses and riders seem happy and enjoying the work? Do you like the teacher's approach? A good teacher will always encourage you to push your boundaries to an appropriate extent, because otherwise you don't progress – but would you get on with this person's manner and attitude?

The right teacher will be able to assess you and your horse and help you work out where you want your relationship to go. This is an area where you may surprise yourself. There is absolutely nothing wrong with owning a horse simply for the pleasure of looking after and riding him and if you don't get this satisfaction, you shouldn't own him at all. But improving your riding and his

*Keep life interesting with fun experiences for you and your horse,*
*such as going for a beach ride.*

*Make sure you have regular lessons with a good trainer to help build the partnership with your horse.*

schooling will also improve your communication and make hacking and other non-competitive activities more enjoyable.

Hopefully, you'll build up a long-term relationship with a teacher, but you should also make the most of other opportunities. For instance, clubs and equestrian centres often organize clinics where successful riders pass on schooling techniques and useful exercises. Learning to take what is useful from these sessions and deciding what perhaps wouldn't work for you is all part of becoming an independent, thinking rider.

## HAVE A GO!

Keep life interesting for you and your horse by trying new things. For instance:

- Go for a beach ride. Get together with a friend or two and enjoy a ride on a local beach with suitable going. Check with your local authority to see if there are any restrictions, particularly in summer. It's vital to check tide times before setting out.
- Sign up for a sponsored ride and you'll often get the chance to ride on land that is normally not available. Many are organized to raise funds for charity, so you can help a good cause at the same time.
- If you live in a country where it is a tradition, go hunting. British riders can contact their local hunt through the Masters of Foxhounds Association (see Useful Addresses) and find out if they run newcomers' days, where experienced riders will act as escorts and explain what's happening.
- Have a lesson on a dressage schoolmaster. Being able to feel a horse who is truly working on the bit or who can perform more advanced movements when given the correct aids will raise your game and inspire you to work with your own horse.
- Go Western. We all know how important weight aids are, but try a lesson or two on a trained horse with a good instructor and you'll be inspired. You might even get hooked.

*Most hunts will run newcomers' days where experienced members of the field will act as escorts.*

## THE ROAD TO COMPETITION

A GOOD TEACHER is essential if you want to compete, so that you enjoy it and learn how to set yourself up for success – not just in terms of winning prizes, but in making progress. For professional riders, competing is inevitably a job – both as an end in itself and, perhaps, as a shop window for horses they produce and sell.

Amateur riders usually look on competitions as an enjoyable challenge, though there is no reason why an amateur rider can't have standards as high as a professional and even beat them at their own game. But to be a winner, you have to look beyond the rosettes: think of competing not as a trophy collecting exercise, but as a chance to widen your and your horse's boundaries and as a yardstick of how your training is progressing.

Of course, you don't have to compete to enjoy different activities with your horse and make progress with his schooling and your riding. Some riders avoid competing because they say they don't enjoy it – usually because of nervousness or because they don't have a 'competitive instinct'. But turn that mindset around and you might find that competing is more rewarding than you imagined: the right preparation will, in itself, produce results and give you a sense of achievement. Approach a competition purely in terms of building on a previous performance rather than beating other riders and you could find that you enjoy it. You may also find that you start to achieve results that are a pleasurable surprise.

## EXPERT QUOTE

*'As an amateur, you have to make sure everything is doubly perfect to get your foot in the door.'*

NIKI HALL, WINNER OF THE SMALL HACK CLASS AT THE HORSE OF THE YEAR SHOW
WHEN HOLDING AMATEUR STATUS

### WHAT'S FOR YOU?

Riders new to competing will find a huge variety of options open to them and there is no reason why you can't have a go at most things. One of the commonest mistakes riders make is to try to specialize too early: this applies to children as well as adults. A well-rounded education and experience of different activities will give you and your horse or pony a solid grounding that will hold you in good stead if you eventually decide to concentrate on one area of equestrian sport. For instance, being able to keep a horse balanced and in rhythm on the flat and being able to lengthen or shorten his stride will translate into a better performance round a course of fences, and the coordination required to jump will help you be more effective on the flat.

*Amateur riders can compete at the highest level – and beat the professionals. Niki Hall on the small hack, Take Silk won at top level whilst still holding amateur status.*

ABOVE *Dressage competitions at Preliminary or Novice level are within the scope of most partnerships.* LEFT *Show jumping is one of the most popular disciplines, with competitions for all levels of horses and riders.*

One of the best ways to enjoy your horse or pony – and to benefit from training opportunities and the chance to make new friends – is to join a local Riding Club or branch of the Pony Club. This will allow you to take part in well-organized competitions in all disciplines without necessarily spending a fortune. Having said that, you will still need to work hard at preparation and to ensure that you and your horse are turned out correctly and safely.

The best-known competitive disciplines are dressage, show jumping, hunter trials, one-day events, showing and endurance riding. To begin with, you'll probably want to compete at unaffiliated (local) level, then perhaps progress to affiliated competitions run under the auspices of ruling bodies such as British Dressage, the British Show Jumping Association and the British Show Horse Association (or equivalent bodies in other countries). You'll usually find that unaffiliated competitions follow the relevant discipline's rule book; for instance, when you compete in a Preliminary level dressage test you will be riding under British Dressage rules unless the organizers state otherwise. This means that you need to buy or borrow a current rule book and make sure you're aware of regulations on, for instance, permitted tack and clothing.

Many show organizers do all they can to encourage novice competitors and those with young or inexperienced horses. For instance, you may find local venues including walk and trot dressage tests in their schedules, without any movements performed in canter. Similarly, you'll find show jumping classes starting at about 0.5 m (1 ft 8 in). If you're aiming at endurance, you can start off with pleasure rides of 13 km (8 miles) upwards, whilst showing opportunities range from standard categories to those for absolute novices. All these provide a lot of fun in their own right as well as providing the first stepping stones in competing.

Other competitive areas include side-saddle equitation, Western riding and TREC. The last of these originated in France and has only recently become established in the UK. It tests the all-round ability of horse and rider and is divided into three phases: orienteering, control of paces and a short cross-country section including dismounted challenges. Riders accumulate points throughout the event, so if you don't want to complete part of a challenge – for instance, if you don't want to jump a particular obstacle – you won't be eliminated but will simply lose points.

## BLAZING TRAILS

You need to make sure that whatever discipline you want to try, you are competing in safe surroundings with, for instance, a show jumping course built on correct distances. One way of doing this is through the Trailblazers dressage and show jumping series for senior and junior riders. There are four levels of competition in each discipline: Preliminary, Novice and Elementary dressage classes and 0.75, 0.85, 0.95 and 1.05 m (2ft 6 in, 2 ft 9 in, 3 ft and 3 ft 3 in) show jumping courses. The series is divided into first and second rounds, held at centres throughout the UK, with a national final. To qualify for the second round in dressage, combinations must achieve a first round score of 58 per cent or more and to go through to a second show jumping round, you need to jump a double clear.

### BE PREPARED

Competition success begins with the preparations you make at home; it's often said that rosettes are won nine-tenths at home and one tenth in the ring. This means making sure that your horse is fit for the job you intend to do, that his teeth, feet and tack are in good condition, that his vaccination schedule is correct and that he and you are confident in your work.

### STUDS

Many riders like to use studs in their horses' shoes to give better grip when galloping and jumping, though opinions vary on how and when they should be used. If you think they might help, talk to your farrier and, if necessary, your instructor. Your farrier will need to know in advance in order to make sure that your horse's next set of shoes has stud holes.

*Ask your farrier's advice if you think your horse needs studs for better grip.*

Choose studs according to the going and always use the smallest size possible. Pointed studs are designed for harder going and square ones for softer ground. Don't assume that studs can make atrocious ground acceptable: there may still be times when you get to a show or event and find the going isn't suitable. It's better to pull out, even at the expense of making a journey for nothing and losing entry fees, than to risk your horse. What does losing a day matter compared to the consequences of your horse suffering a tendon injury?

There are varying opinions on whether it's better to use one or two studs in each shoe. Most top riders use two on each hind shoe and one or two on each front shoe, depending on the ground and the horse's way of going. Don't confuse screw-in studs with road studs or nails designed to give greater security on road surfaces. Screw-in studs should never be used on the road, because they will cause imbalance and may lead to injury.

For safety's sake, never load and travel horses with studs in. It's bad enough if a horse treads on your toe with studs fitted, but if he kicks out, he can injure himself and the people around him. Be careful when fitting studs and wear a hard hat. Every time you use them, clear the thread with a screw tap and tighten them with the screw tap's built-in spanner. In between uses, clean impacted dirt and grit from stud holes with a horseshoe nail and plug the holes with cotton wool plugs soaked in hoof oil or WD40.

## RECONNOITRING AND CHOOSING CLASSES

It's a good idea to go to shows to reconnoitre before you start competing – both so that you can watch what happens and, if necessary, ride an inexperienced horse round so he can get used to the atmosphere without being put under pressure. Offer to act as groom at a show for an experienced friend; volunteer as a writer for a dressage judge; spend a day as a fence judge at a local hunter trials or one-day event. This will give you an insight into what's involved.

Simply spectating can also be useful, as you can see how successful competitors warm up their horses, how they cope when things don't go quite according to plan and what the difference is between an adequate performance and a good one. Never miss a chance to see top riders working behind the scenes. There are some wonderful free lessons available in collecting rings.

Experienced riders who are bringing on inexperienced horses will take them to low-level competitions as part of their education, not worrying if they throw a buck down the centre line of the dressage arena or spook at a scary filler in the show jumping ring. But if your horse is more experienced than you are, don't try to start off competing at a level you're unsure of. It's always best to compete at a level below the work you are coping with at home, when possible: if you're jumping 0.85 m (2 ft 9 in) courses at home, enter for a 0.75 m (2 ft 6 in) class until you are confident enough to move up.

Be honest; if you know your horse is over-qualified for a class but feel you don't have the experience to compete at the next stage, enter *hors concours*. This means that you compete alongside all the other combinations, but will not be awarded a prize if you end up in the placings. However, the experience and confidence it will give you is worth far more than a rosette and you won't be guilty of 'pot-hunting', taking an easy or unfair option purely to try to win.

You can usually work out a rough estimate of what time your class will start, but allow plenty of time for loading, the actual journey, finding the location of the ring where you are due to compete (and its collecting ring) and visiting the secretary's base to collect your competitor's number. Ring stewards will be able to tell you whether or not classes are running to time and you can then decide when you need to start warming up; the more you get to know your horse, the easier it will be to work out how much time this will take.

*You can learn a lot from watching the way top riders warm up at competitions. Here, William Fox-Pitt prepares for the show jumping phase of Burghley Horse Trials.*

## COMPETITION TIPS

- Local showing classes are a great introduction to competing even if your real aim is, say, to show jump. You'll have all the experience of preparation and travelling and will gain experience of riding in a competition atmosphere. And with a huge variety of classes, from traditional showing classes to those for family ponies and Riding Club horses, there's something for everyone.
- Read schedules and rule books thoroughly. There's nothing worse than being eliminated in a dressage test because you're using an 'illegal' bit or noseband – or jumping a clear round and finding out too late that in this particular class you should have immediately gone on to a jump-off course.
- Always make sure that you and your horse are well turned out. Not only is it a compliment to organizers, judges and helpers, it puts you in the right frame of mind.
- If something goes wrong, don't panic. It's only a glitch, not a disaster – if you can work out why you had that fence down, or executed that dressage movement badly, you'll be able to work on it at home. There's always another day and another show.
- Even if you think you have been unfairly judged, keep smiling. Judges have personal opinions and by opting to ride in front of them, you agree to accept them.


## A QUESTION OF NERVES

Everyone gets nervous – or at least feels their adrenalin pumping – before a competition. When that gives you a heightened awareness and sharpens your focus, you can benefit from it; when nervousness take over and affects your enjoyment and your performance, you may be tempted to decide that competing isn't for you.

Rather than passing up on a lot of fun and enjoyment, give yourself a chance to replace negative nerves with positive ones. You aren't alone, as even top event rider Pippa Funnell has had to learn how to develop a new mental approach to competition. You're in good company and you can do it.

First, as mentioned earlier, make sure that your preparations leave nothing to chance. Ensure that everyone who helps you, from your trainer to whoever acts as groom, is positive. You'll be thinking positively and you'll need to feel that everyone around you is doing the same: you'll walk that show jumping course thinking, 'This is easier than we're coping with at home' and don't need a voice adding, 'I don't think he'll like that filler'.

Analyse *why* you feel nervous. Is it because you're frightened of making a mistake or looking stupid, or are you worried that you're overfacing yourself or your horse? Remember that everyone makes mistakes, even top riders at top competitions. Think back to times when you've watched a show jumping class or dressage test and someone has had a run-out or a stop, got the wrong canter strike-off or forgotten which movement to perform next. Did you laugh at them and think how stupid they were? Of course you didn't – you felt sorry for them, then forgot about it.

Horses are sensitive to their riders' feelings, so try some mental and physical techniques to break the vicious circle. Just the way you breathe can make a huge difference; in fact, make sure you aren't holding your breath. A lot of riders either do this or take shallow breaths, with resulting tension. Focus on taking slow, deep breaths and breathe from your diaphragm; Pilates (see Chapter 8) is excellent in this respect.

Before you get on your horse, tense and relax groups of muscles in turn. Start with the muscles in your feet, then work upwards through calves, buttocks, abdomen, shoulders, arms and hands. Raise your shoulders as high as you can, then drop them down and repeat as many times as you like.

You could also try a mounted technique that's a favourite with American riders; if your horse is settled and you can find a quiet warming-up area, put your reins in one hand, hold the other in the air and walk a few quiet circles. Do this with alternate hands to stretch the spine and loosen taut shoulders.

## THE MENTAL APPROACH

Beating nervousness is very much a case of mind over matter and sports psychology has become increasingly important for top-class athletes in all sports. One approach you can borrow from them is to make a 'mental video'. If, for instance, you're planning to ride a dressage test, keep rehearsing it in your mind and visualize it going exactly as you want it to. Imagine entering the arena feeling calm and confident, with your horse light, balanced and forward, then ride through the test. Absorb what each movement feels like and picture how it looks to a spectator.

Although you may not realize it, you've probably been doing this exercise already, but in a negative form. How many times have you thought: 'We're bound to lose balance here', or 'We're going to have that fence down' – and then done just that?

### HOT COMPETITION

Any competition, however low-key, puts your horse under greater stress than working him at home. Stress need not necessarily be bad – a lot of horses seem to enjoy going to different places – but it does mean that you need to be meticulous in looking after your horse's welfare. For instance, don't use him as a grandstand and sit on him for hours whilst you chat to friends and watch classes other than your own, and don't leave him standing on your vehicle with minimal ventilation.

Climate change means that horses and riders now face the double whammy of heat and humidity more often – and in traditionally temperate as well as hot climates. Research into how to combat this problem started in the run-up to the 1996 Atlanta Olympics; this and later work has taught us how correct management can minimize risks. The most important thing is to keep horses hydrated, both at home and competition.

*'A horse doing a 100-mile ride may have lost 30 kg in weight, equivalent to 30 litres of water. The horse may have sweated 10 litres per hour in warm conditions, so will have lost a total of 100 litres, but replaced 70 litres by drinking to end up at the finish only 30 litres down. Most will have drunk the 70 litres – about five ordinary buckets – on their way round. If they didn't, they probably wouldn't get past the halfway vetting'.*

DR DAVID MARLIN

Management practices vary amongst disciplines. For instance, racehorse trainers often limit water intake before a race because of its weight. However, endurance horses need to drink during a ride and in general, horses should be allowed to drink at any time.

An old cliché says that you can take your horse to water, but can't necessarily make him drink. This becomes a particular problem when horses are reluctant to drink when away from home, though there are also horses who do not drink enough when stabled. Try these techniques:

- At home, place water buckets away from the door. Research has shown that some horses will not drink when their water supply is near a door or window, perhaps because they feel vulnerable when their heads are down near an opening. It's also worth placing them up off the floor, or using a corner manger as a water container, as studies have shown that some horses prefer drinking from a higher level.
- Take containers of your own water from home. This is good practice anyway, in case it's difficult to find a water source. If you can't take enough water to last whilst you are away, mix home water with local supplies.
- Add apple juice or peppermint cordial to drinking water if your horse is reluctant to drink, as this makes it more palatable.
- After a short journey, offer water as soon as you arrive and at regular intervals throughout the day.
- On a long journey, stop and offer water en route. Some competition grooms travelling their charges in large horseboxes like to fit corner mangers containing water, so horses can drink at will. This is an excellent practice, if you can manage it.
- Remember that a horse who is working hard may need electrolytes (see Chapter 5).

*When cooling down a hot horse, alternate between short periods of washing and short periods of walking.*

### WORKING UP A SWEAT

Sweating is good for a horse in that it helps to keep him cool, but excessive or prolonged periods of sweating will cause dehydration. Horses sweat in a number of situations – for instance, if they are upset or excited, when working hard for relatively short periods or when travelling. Nervous or excited horses may sweat more than relaxed ones in the same situations and unfit horses will sweat more when doing the same work as a fit horse. The lessons here are self-explanatory!

Horses may also sweat more than normal if there is a hot day in spring after a period of cold weather and horses are not used to it. This is because they haven't become acclimatized to it; we know that acclimatization is vital for racehorses and performance horses being prepared for competition in another climate, but it's easy to forget that heat stress can also be a problem at home. The following strategies will help you protect your horse and yourself – remember that a weakened horse is more likely to makes mistakes when jumping and travelling at speed.

● Make sure your vehicle is properly ventilated, as explained earlier. Remember that you won't get the same airflow when it's parked as when it's moving, so take extra care to open vents and lower ramps.
● Look for areas of shade on the showground.
● Physiologically, your horse will not need as much time to warm up on a warm day as on a cold one.
● When you've finished a period of concerted effort – for instance, after a cross-country round – don't come to a sudden stop and keep your horse standing. Walk him round.
● If he's sweating, wash him off. Don't concentrate on cooling the front end of the horse and forget the back end, where most of the heat comes through. Alternate between short periods of washing and short periods of walking. Cooling with water is a great help to a hot horse; it used to be thought that using cold water caused muscle damage and 'tying up', but research has proved otherwise.
● If you feel you must use grease on an event horse's legs – a technique which some riders believe minimizes accident risks by helping the horse 'slide over' fixed fences – keep it to a minimum. Don't smother his legs and half his chest, as he can't sweat through it.

## GOING HOME

When you've finished competing, cool down your horse and check him over for any tiny knocks or scrapes. If his legs are muddy, clean them off with plain water so you don't miss anything and make sure he's relaxed and comfortable before setting off for home. Think about whether he needs a different rug: is he tired, in which case he'll probably feel cooler, or has the temperature dropped?

Once home, check him over again and, depending on the time and his lifestyle, turn him out so he can have a roll and graze, or give him his normal hay or haylage. Feed him as normal, ignoring the old advice to give him a bran mash. He's expended energy and needs to take it in – and as has already been covered in Chapter 5, sudden changes to a horse's diet should be avoided.

Before you go home to a hot bath and a large glass of something, clean out your horsebox or trailer and remember to set any alarms or security devices. Wash off any mud and obvious dirt from your tack and (if you have the time and energy) clean it thoroughly. If not, do it the next day.

Next day, check your horse over first thing in the morning. Feel for heat and swelling in his limbs and for any signs of soreness or stiffness. Get someone to walk and trot him up in hand so you can see how he moves and, if there is any sign of lameness, get expert (and if necessary), veterinary advice. Let him enjoy his day in the field, as walking and grazing will relax tired muscles.

## EXPERT TIP

*"Keep a competition diary. Write down everything from how long your journey took to the state of the rings and any comments the judges made. Make notes on how you could improve your performance next time, because it's the little things that make a difference.'*

LYNN RUSSELL

The more time you spend with your horse, the more you'll get to know his – and your – strengths and weaknesses. Many people are lucky enough to find a horse who progresses with them and even turns out to have hidden talents. However, it's a fact of life that in some cases, owners get to the stage where they want to go on to bigger things and are faced with the prospect of selling a horse so that they can buy another. In the case of children's ponies, this happens all too literally; if there isn't a smaller brother or sister waiting to take on an outgrown pony, you need to find him another home.

When you need to sell or, perhaps, loan a horse or pony, behave as you wanted sellers to behave towards you when you were on the other side of the fence. There is nothing wrong with trying to get the best price as well as the best home for your horse, but be honest. When you look back at what he's done for you, it's the least you can do for him and another vital part of being a responsible, caring horse owner.

# USEFUL ADDRESSES

ASSOCIATION OF BRITISH RIDING SCHOOLS:
Queen's Chambers, 38–40 Queen Street,
Penzance, Cornwall TR18 4BH.
Tel: 01736 369440.
Website: www.abrs-info.org

BLUE CROSS EQUINE CENTRE: Shilton Road,
Burford, Oxon OX18 4PF. Tel: 01993 822651.
Website: www.bluecross.org.uk

BRITISH ASSOCIATION OF EQUINE DENTAL
TECHNICIANS: cannot answer telephone queries
from owners but website includes a list of
qualified members.
Website: www.equinedentistry.org.uk

BRITISH DRESSAGE: National Agricultural Centre,
Stoneleigh Park, Kenilworth, Warks CV8 2RJ.
Tel: 024 7669 8830.
Website: www.britishdressage.co.uk

BRITISH EQUINE VETERINARY ASSOCIATION:
cannot answer individual queries from owners
but website contains general advice on horse
health.
Website: www.beva.org.uk

BRITISH EVENTING: National Agricultural Centre,
Stoneleigh Park, Kenilworth, Warks CV8 2RH.
Tel: 024 7669 8856.
Website: www.britisheventing.com

BRITISH HORSE SOCIETY: Stoneleigh Deer Park,
Kenilworth, Warks CV8 2XZ.
Tel: 08701 202244.
Website: www.bhs.org.uk

BRITISH SHOW JUMPING ASSOCIATION:
National Agricultural Centre, Stoneleigh Park,
Kenilworth, Warks CV8 2RJ.
Tel: 024 7669 8800.
Website: www.bsja.co.uk

ENDURANCE GB: National Agricultural Centre,
Stoneleigh Park, Kenilworth, Warks CV8 2RP.
Tel: 024 7669 8863.
Website: www.endurancegb.co.uk

FARRIERS REGISTRATION COUNCIL: Sefton House,
Adam Court, Newark Road, Peterborough PE1 5PP.
Tel: 01733 319911.
Website: www.farrier-reg.gov.uk

INTERNATIONAL LEAGUE FOR THE PROTECTION OF
HORSES: Anne Colvin House, Snetterton,
Norfolk NR16 2LR.
Website: www.ilph.org

ROYAL COLLEGE OF VETERINARY SURGEONS:
Belgravia House, 62–64 Horseferry Rd, London
SW1P 2AF.
Tel: 020 7222 2004.
Website: www.rcvs.org.uk

SOCIETY OF MASTER SADDLERS: Green Lane Farm,
Stonham, Stowmarket, Suffolk P14 5DS.
Tel: 01449 711642.
Website: www.mastersaddlers.co.uk

# SUGGESTED READING

Bishop, Ruth, *The Horse Nutrition Bible* (David and Charles, 2003).

Coumbe, Karen, *First Aid For Horses* (J.A. Allen, 2000).

Devereux, Sue, *The Veterinary Care of the Horse* (J.A. Allen, 2006).

Henderson, Carolyn, *Getting Horses Fit* (J.A. Allen, 2006).

Henderson, John, *The Glovebox Guide To Transporting Horses* (J.A. Allen, 2005).

MacLeod, Clare, *The Truth About Feeding Your Horse* (J.A. Allen, 2007).

Marks, Kelly, *Perfect Manners* (Ebury Press, 2002).

Oliver, Robert and Langrish, Bob, *A Photographic Guide To Conformation* (J.A. Allen, 2002).

# INDEX

Note: Page numbers in *italic* refer to illustrations

## PICTURE CREDITS

All pictures © *Horse & Hound* except photos p2, p25, p48, p50, p53, p57, p97, p102, p114, p120, p128, p162, p262-3 © John Henderson and p170, p173, p179, p182, p183, p185, p186, p187, p193, p196, p198, p200, p204, p207, p210, p215, p220, p222 © Karen Coumbe.

Illustrations p188, p209 and p214 by Rodney Paull.